D0088348

# The Seven Sources
# of Pleasure in Life

# The Seven Sources of Pleasure in Life

## Making Way for the Upside in the Midst of Modern Demands

Luciano L'Abate

 PRAEGER

AN IMPRINT OF ABC-CLIO, LLC
Santa Barbara, California • Denver, Colorado • Oxford, England

**Library of Congress Cataloging-in-Publication Data**

L'Abate, Luciano, 1928–
   The seven sources of pleasure in life : making way for the upside in the midst of modern demands / Luciano L'Abate.
       p. cm.
   Includes bibliographical references and index.
   ISBN: 978–0–313–39579–6 (hard copy : alk. paper) — ISBN 978–0–313–39580–2 (ebook)
1.  Pleasure.  I. Title.
BF515.L33   2011
646.7—dc22                2011001727

ISBN: 978–0–313–39579–6
EISBN: 978–0–313–39580–2

15  14  13  12  11     1 2 3 4 5

This book is also available on the World Wide Web as an eBook.
Visit www.abc-clio.com for details.

Praeger
An Imprint of ABC-CLIO, LLC

ABC-CLIO, LLC
130 Cremona Drive, P.O. Box 1911
Santa Barbara, California 93116-1911

This book is printed on acid-free paper ∞

Manufactured in the United States of America

### Pleasures Inherent in Living

Early daybreak arises in pure delight with
                Mandarin oranges and
                Juicy horizons
never without their own arts.
Joy is earth's food for the spirit,
obviously nature's music.
                Flute, fiddle and
                Pennywhistle.
You blow on antique whistles while
meandering to enjoy your hobbies,
even the lighthearted harp.
Newborn satisfactions arise
to bestow novel creations with color-palette relationships:
                Primary colors on earthen, red clay
                trees of aboriginal life.
                They were doused in fertile soil
                by you like your forefathers.
Even scholars
now examine the effects of joyful
jests upon health and wellness.
Only bright observers recognize
youthful palettes
made naturally by each morning's sunrays so
eager to warm human hearts, even blending with light rainfall.
New days burst out with creative content
triumphant and sunbathed in ecstasy. I perceive
                rainbows of seven colors;
                the seventh color is golden daybreak.

By Dr. Laura Gail Sweeney from the New Dadaist Collage Poetry
Chapbook (http://poetryartandstories.blogspot.com/)

# Contents

*Foreword by Edward W. L. Smith*                                      ix

*Preface*                                                             xi

*Acknowledgments*                                                     xvii

Introduction: The Elements and Meanings of Pleasure and
Displeasure                                                           1

1   Arts and Creativity: Observing, Studying, Watching, and
    Producing                                                        25

2   Avocations: Doing Whatever You Like When You Want To             65

3   Being, Doing, and Having: The Triangle of Life                   73

4   Food: For Survival and for Enjoyment                             93

5   Music Does Not Need to Be Loud to Be Enjoyable                   135

6   Play Is Just as Important as Work                                149

7   The Body: Sensuality, Sensibility, Sexuality, and Sex            161

Conclusion: Moderation, Self-Control, and Self-Monitoring           183

*Notes*                                                              205

*Index*                                                              227

# Foreword

In 1911, speaking through *The Devil's Dictionary*, Ambrose Bierce[1] defined *pleasure* as "the least hateful form of dejection." Such was the ilk of humor that earned him the sobriquet "Bitter Bierce." But behind the humor, dark as it may be, lies evidence of the sometimes ambivalent and uneasy approach to *pleasure* that has been taken by many writers, including psychologists. In *Limbo*, author Aldous Huxley expressed this uneasiness in the following way: "I can sympathize with people's pains, but not with their pleasures. There is something curiously boring about somebody else's happiness."[2] (Dear reader, the pleasure of a wry smile would be most appropriate at this point.)

During much of the development of modern-cum-contemporary psychology, hedonic experiences were shunned in favor of anger, depression, fear, grief, and the like. Psychoanalytic theory, which dominated psychiatry and clinical psychology in the 1940s and 1950s, probably added to this bias by Freud's setting the *pleasure principle* and the *reality principle* in opposition, or least this is the way most of his readers have interpreted his theory.

> According to Freud . . . the psyche is initially actuated solely by the pleasure or pleasure-pain principle, which leads it to avoid pain or unpleasure aroused by increases in instinctual tension and to do so by hallucinating . . . the satisfaction necessary to reduce the tension. Only later, after the ego has developed, is the pleasure principle modified by the reality principle, which leads the individual to replace hallucinatory wish-fulfillment [*sic*] by adaptive behaviour [*sic*].[3]

In this theoretical discourse we find, then, "pleasure" associated with "hallucinatory wish-fulfillment," and "reality" with "ego" and "adaptive behaviour." Given that this pleasure is based on a hallucination, it is ersatz and surely inferior to the real thing. This maladjustment bias, if we can call it that, was challenged by the blossoming Humanistic and Transpersonal psychologies of the 1960s and 1970s and more recently by emerging Positive Psychology.

In keeping with this present trend of expanding psychological work into the realm of healthy living, Dr. L'Abate has in this volume explored the elusive yet vitally important experience of pleasure. Empirical evidence is the thread that has run throughout his work over the years, and this book is no exception. Dr. L'Abate demands evidence and backs his assertions with such. Importantly, he has successfully navigated between the Scylla and the Charybdis of dry pedantry and jejune self-help promises. That is, while remaining true to the careful scholarship that his readers have come to expect, he has tempered his writing with humor and personal anecdotes. In addition, he offers practical exercises that, if entered into conscientiously, will surely lead to increased self-understanding and a workable plan for infusing one's life with a greater measure of pleasure. The pleasure of reading this book may in itself be the start.

Edward W. L. Smith, Ph.D., ABPP
Emeritus Professor of Psychology
Georgia Southern University

# Preface

After coediting one volume about homework assignments in psycho-therapy and prevention,[1] editing one volume on low-cost approaches to promote physical and mental health,[2] co-writing a volume on self-help,[3] completing a whole volume on play,[4] and another one on hurt feelings, all by myself,[5] I concluded that there was not sufficient atten-tion given to pleasures. Functionality, contentment, and satisfaction in life are related to the ratio of pleasures over displeasures, or of joys over hurts. Having covered the waterfront of ways to deal with hurt feelings,[6] I wanted to balance this negative topic with as many pleas-urable positives as possible, hence the writing of this volume.

I am aware of the secondary sources about Positive Emotions, such as Happiness, Subjective Well-Being, and Positivity. However, I wanted to review in primary references the relationship between the seven sources of pleasures in physical and mental health, wellness, and well-being. Given this information, I wanted to pass it on to adult readers who may enjoy knowing more about the positive effects of these seven sources of pleasures on their lives, and how they can improve their own lives by using these sources more creatively and positively.

A seemingly competing source[7] consists of the pleasure of hearing oneself and others recite (on a CD) poems from all walks of life. This seems a rather limited (if not narcissistic) source of pleasure to me, but it may be great pleasure to those who speak and hear it. *De gusti-bus non disputandum est*. We cannot argue about personal tastes, as the Romans used to say.

With all the pressures of these days—to Be, to Do, and to Have—sometimes we just lose sight of, and time for, the true joys of life. Many of us might be hard-pressed to even identify many, or any, such sources of pleasure. Witness the dramatic rises of late in depression, anger issues, stress-related disorders, burnout, and the like. Additionally, note the reduction of playtime experienced with an increase of work hours for adults, and even for our children in schools where recess and gym may be a thing of the past.[8]

We might have lost sight of the "upside" of life and its pleasures, but in these pages I needed to bring these back into focus, for us, for our physical as well as our mental health. I tried to turn the spotlight on those factors we know that bring us smiles, laughter, emotional and spiritual rewards, fine memories, and even improve our overall health. For those who might see these strengthening, powerful moments as less vital "guilty" pleasures that are self-indulgent, I've also tried to explain how appreciating and nurturing these pleasures not only benefits the pleasure-seeker but also family, friends, and others in each of our small worlds.

As I reviewed the literature on pleasant and pleasurable activities in all the foregoing references, I saw that there was little if anything about the everyday sources of pleasure that come from our daily experiences. Another way to reframe this issue is to show how pleasurable some activities are, can, could, should, must, or ought to be. If the two goals of life are survival and enjoyment, then this book focuses on enjoyment. One could even argue that survival without enjoyment would be a sadly limited goal. The goal of this volume, therefore, is to increase sensitivity for how to convert and transform everyday, taken-for-granted survival sources and resources into pleasures. And that transformation begins when we STOP to savor, think, observe, and plan accordingly.

The *purpose of this manuscript, therefore, is to look at the scientific bases of the relationship of each of the seven sources of pleasures by cross-indexing each pleasure with evidence in primary references about its association with health, well-being, and wellness.* This will be another way to become more specific and concrete than has been achieved in the movement called "positive psychology."

## PLAN OF THE BOOK

### Introduction

Here I define the nature of pleasures and displeasures and I review critically the three seemingly separate but much overlapping fields of happiness, subjective well-being, and positivity. Comparing these three fields with sources of pleasure, I compare and specify how sources of pleasure are different from happiness, well-being, and positivity.

## Chapter 1

Art consists of pleasures to create and enjoy visual, auditory, kinesthetic, and sensory productions, from writing poetry, fiction, and nonfiction, to produce photographs, paintings, sculpture, interior design/decoration, and other crafts, such as textiles or even pottery. Color is crucial in all these sources of pleasure.

## Chapter 2

Avocations (hobbies), from bird watching to volunteering at a soup kitchen, research shows, help increase health and prolong our lives, including collecting.

## Chapter 3

Being means just enjoying solitude or the company of loved ones, without any demands for performance, perfection, production, or problem-solving. This includes lone meditation and reflection on the pleasure of doing nothing, or as Italians say, *"Dolce far niente"*: Being able to fully feel and enjoy the moment. Love is included here but love is not enough. To survive and to enjoy we need intimacy to Be, Do, and Have someone and something.

## Chapter 4

Food: The list of cookbooks published in the United States is nearly endless. Food is an especially prominent and growing pleasure, especially with the influx of immigrants since World War II bringing their novel additions to the menu. We even have an entire channel on television dedicated to food! But here we talk, too, of what happens when pleasure becomes out-of-control—as in the obesity epidemic. Given the amount of information on this source from a variety of sources, I decided that I could not really contribute anything original about this source except to review all the many entrepreneurs (using a positive term, but really quacks, scammers, and charlatans) who sell their promises of better health and longer life through the mail using fancy brochures and expensive advertising to lure naive and needy readers to buy their wares: foods, herbs, supplements, and vitamins.

## Chapter 5

Music of all kinds, from *American Idol* tunes to Vivaldi greats: What is it about these sounds that can change our mood, perhaps even change our present for the better, within seconds? Why do some of us draw pleasure from the classics, while others feel good listening to popular lyrics or loud rap? We all enjoy the many and growing ways to seek this multivariate source of pleasure, from concert halls, to mega-stereo systems, to ear-filling iPods.

## Chapter 6

Play can be a board game, dance, exercise, sport, or other action taken without intention of any final product—just for the action itself. Research shows the strong link between play, wellness, and health.

## Chapter 7

The Body: sensation, sensibility, sensuality, and sex. From nonsexual holding, hugging, huddling, and cuddling with loved ones to the most intimate moments of two partners during sex and orgasm, all the senses of body, mind, and spirit find pleasure in this togetherness. Included here are also 10 surprising health benefits of sex. Sex is also the source of many entrepreneurs (charlatans, quacks, and scammers) who sell lotions and mixtures to improve erections and size of the male organ. A perhaps incomplete list of these fraudulent manufacturers is included in this chapter.

## Conclusion

*Moderation*, *self-control*, and *self-monitoring* mean avoiding making an addiction out of a source of pleasure. Synonymous are terms such as *savoring*, *tuning in*, and *increasing* healthy pleasures, that is, self-monitoring to become fully aware of our sources of pleasure, and ways to increase awareness and sensitivity to a particular pleasure.

## Readership

In this manuscript I have attempted to use minimal technical jargon. I have lightened my usually pedantic and professorial style by including personal anecdotes, jokes, and, unfortunately for some readers, some maybe awful but amusing puns. I could not help myself. I love to make them up. I hope I will be forgiven for these puns. Given this uncharacteristic style, I hope that readers will be mature adults who can introduce and use some concrete and relevant information to add spice and variety to their perhaps too humdrum lives.

Luciano L'Abate
Atlanta, GA

# Acknowledgments

This book is dedicated to women acquisition editors who understood and supported my proposals over my five-decade publishing career. They evaluated my proposals and gave me the pleasure of receiving a book contract. Listed in order of seniority since I have worked with them, and frequency of publications, the first is Sharon Panulla at Springer-Science, who has covered my work over decades since my first book was published with Grune and Stratton in 1964 and who gave me the pleasure of receiving my 50th book contract. These 50 pleasures offset all the inevitable rejections I received over the years for work I submitted for publication. I forgot the rejections, but I kept the book contracts in a fire-proof box.

Second is Debora Carvalko with ABC-CLIO, who specializes in adding suitable subtitles to my original title and suggesting ways and means by which I can enhance the readability of my work. Third is Maya Columbus at Nova Publishing Company, who took to my work without hesitation or misgivings. Fourth is Simina Calin at Cambridge University Press, who did not hesitate to obtain a second opinion from an anonymous reader when the first one was not very helpful. I am sure that Bess L'Abate, who has been my constant and unwavering support throughout this process, will not mind or object if I were to tell these women that "I could not have done my work without you!"

Introduction

# The Elements and Meanings of Pleasure and Displeasure

In a warp-speed world where modern demands and stress seem unyielding, where is the pleasure? And who would have time for it, anyway? Why look at all kinds of pleasures—where we find them, why they appeal to us, and what good they do us in terms of mental and physical health—body, mind, and soul? Let us count the reasons. Including the most recent research on the scientific basis for benefits of pleasure-seeking, this book explains how to increase our sensitivity to everyday moments or opportunities that could bring pleasures into our focus, our awareness, then fully experience and appreciate them within our wills, whims, and the wonders of our bodies. The basic conflict and choices of our lives is to approach sources of pleasure and avoid the same sources that can also provide displeasures. Sources are composed of resources. Resources are comprised of objective and subjective advantages—and disadvantages. No, one cannot look at the advantages without including disadvantages as well. But do let us look.

## WHAT IS A PLEASURE?

What we know about pleasure on sensory, physical, psychological, and cultural levels all joins in the conclusion that—bottom line—sources of pleasure are not an utterly nonproductive use of time, because what they bring us is invaluable—better health and well-being. This book will help readers identify and understand personal predilections regarding their sources of pleasure: how to increase sensitivity to them and the increasing ways society and technology are developing new means to fit pleasures into ever-busy lifestyles, where we can easily become "too busy to stop and smell the roses."

It seems obvious this book itself should be brighter, more pleasurable than most scientific treatises, so I write here in a more personable way than ever before, with numbers in the text for references and chapter notes at the end. I simplify scientific information as much as possible for an adult audience, students and professionals in the mental health disciplines. Furthermore, I include selected anecdotes and jokes relevant to each chapter.[1, 2]

If our two major goals in life are indeed *survival* and *enjoyment,* then the purpose of this volume is to help readers learn more about both. However, it needs to be clear from the outset that the list of so-called sources of pleasures included in this volume should be understood as *sources* of pleasure, not as pleasures in and of themselves. These *sources* can provide pleasure, as well as displeasure, to one extent or another. A source can be used for enjoyment and pleasure as well as displeasure and self-destruction, slowly or speedily. The choice is ours.

The APA Dictionary of Psychology defines a pleasure as "the emotion or sensation induced by the enjoyment or anticipation of what is felt or viewed as good or desirable." Here, however, one will need to differentiate between *giving* pleasure and *receiving* pleasure, whether there is reciprocity in the exchange—whether such an exchange is reciprocal but not in kind—for example, producing a composition and selling it versus buying it, or a reciprocal exchange in lovemaking. Pleasures, therefore, represent *exchanges* that occur between us and selected aspects of our immediate and close environment, whether people, objects, or intangibles. We choose who and what gives us pleasure and who and what we give pleasure to. However, this process of exchange can only occur reciprocally. If one gives pleasure all the time and does not receive pleasure in return, then it is questionable whether this exchange will last very long.

## DEFINITIONS OF PLEASURES

This section covers most definitions given by a representative sample of notable psychologists who were also asked to give at least two concrete examples of pleasures they experienced in their lives. Eventually, we will have to refer to sensory bases for pleasures, that is: "Pleasures are embodied in our memories to offset the influences of negative and painful experiences in our lives. Strangely enough, a great many of our pleasures are forgotten while many of us keep inside a great many hurts."[3]

Professor Philip R. Zimbardo (personal communication, December 12, 2009), of Stanford University, a former president of the American Psychological Association and world-renown psychologist, offers this simple but profound definition: "Pleasure is the joy we feel when life gives us a special treat that elevates our existence beyond survival to a new level of engagement, however transient."

Another colleague and friend, clinical psychologist Edward W. Smight, former director of clinical training at Georgia Southern University, Statesboro, comments on the definition of pleasure (personal communication, December 13, 2009):

> Although the affective component is the core aspect, pleasure is an experience wherein affect, cognition, and conation converge and interplay. We feel pleasure, we re-"cognize" the situation that brings it about, and we normally are inclined toward those actions that we know to lead to it. (To be inclined toward actions that bring the opposite of pleasure would most likely suggest abnormality-cum-pathology to most observers.) I recall that in a letter to his fiancé, Martha Bernays, Freud drew the distinction between those who act in order to seek pleasure and those who act in order to avoid unpleasure. Interestingly, he included Martha and himself in the latter category. . . . I am wondering if the seven pleasures are related to the seven deadly sins, the latter being the pleasures perverted through excessive indulgence or misunderstandings of context.

More about this last point later.

And another colleague, neighbor Doug Slavin, Ph.D., writes (personal communication, December 14, 2009):

> I would define "pleasure" as an enduring emotional state that is triggered by some event that is important in a person's life.

This emotion is more than just a temporary, brief pleasant feeling one might get from eating something delicious or watching a good movie. It is a positive feeling that endures over time and can be invoked when recalling the situation. It is a feeling of delight and joy that the psychologist Abraham Maslow called "a peak emotional experience." For me, I can recall the feeling of delight and pleasure I had when my children were born and they were first presented to me. There is something profound in that experience for most people since it is linked so powerfully to our biology, and/or evolutionary history.

On the flip side, the delightful feeling of pleasure can occur when we invest a lot of energy and time in a difficult activity or feel worry and tension and we successfully complete the task or resolve the worry. When I completed my graduate work in psychology at Northwestern University and received my Ph.D., I grinned with pleasure then and can do the same now as I recall it. When I was worried about my mother's health, she was 90 at the time and was at risk for possibly losing her leg to a circulatory problem, and the surgery was avoided and she went on to live a comfortable life to age 94, I was immensely relieved and my pleasure at her recovery and the avoidance of difficulty and pain for her was a pure a pleasure as one can experience.

A retired professional woman who does not want her name used (she's shy on this subject) also suggested that *novelty* is another pleasure of life. "One pleasure that I experienced was the birth of my son and daughter. Another was having a very intimate interaction with my husband on the island of Crete in a lovely cabin with a fire burning in the fireplace."

Accomplishment was also suggested as another pleasure from various sources.

However, neither novelty nor accomplishment fall within the requirements to define a pleasure listed below, as explained by Bernardo Carducci, professor of psychology at University of Indiana, Southwest (personal communication, December 15, 2009):

> To me, pleasure is a sense of positive affect resulting from the anticipation or actual gratification of a need or desire. I include the notion of anticipation because sometimes the act of anticipating the pleasure is more enjoyable than the sense of pleasure obtained from the actual experience. I would also like to make the distinction between active and passive pleasure. Active

pleasure is the pleasure one receives from taking action to achieve pleasure. For example, actively initiating contact with a romantic partner that I know will result in obtaining sexual pleasure. Passive pleasure is the pleasure one receives based on the actions of others we care about letting us know that they are experiencing pleasure. For example, I experience passive pleasure when my daughter calls me to talk about something good that has happened to her, as when she called recently to talk about the wonderful time she and her husband had on their vacation. . . . And I hope we find that my response to this query gives me as much pleasure as I received from doing this favor for my most cherished friend.

And from Karin Jordan, professor and chair, Department of Counseling, University of Akron (personal communication, December 9, 2009): "Pleasure is a feeling of extreme gratification, aroused by the expectation or the enjoyment of something good, something satisfying, or something desirable. It is intimately connected to contentment or happiness and central to human motivation. Example 1. It was a pleasure to watch the graceful movements of the dancers. Example 2. It was a pleasure being in Mary's company."

The insight from Mary Costa (personal communication, December 16, 2009): "As to the 7 Pleasures of life: Chocolate, most Italian food, grandchildren, humor, a well designed car (preferably Italian), anything by Vivaldi, a good book. Did I miss anything? Or were we thinking different pleasures (Sex, Money, Power, Love, etc., etc.)."

These and other definitions helped clarify which criteria have been used to select these seven sources of pleasures over others. For instance, the difference between happiness and pleasure can be found in the dimensions that define any behavior, and that is (1) *duration*, a concrete pleasure is obtained from specific sources considered in this volume, while happiness is a much more abstract, ephemeral, and variable state that is available to a wide range of persons and intimate relationships; (2) *frequency*, how often one can obtain pleasure, which may occur many times a day, but happiness is much more difficult to obtain on the basis of this criterion because there is a limited to personal and intimate relationships one can encounter every day, and experiencing happiness all the time would represent an unrealistic and impossible state of pick ecstasy that would seem fake if present all the time; (3) *rate*, when a pleasure occurs between intervals of no pleasure, at what kinds of intervals does a pleasure take place, every minute, every day, every month, every year, etc.; (4) *intensity*, how strong or how weak is the pleasure experienced, from weak, momentary, and temporary to consistently strong and powerful; (5) *nature*, what is the nature of the pleasure, being concretely physical versus being completely abstract, moving from physical versus the metaphysical, that is, going beyond the five senses and moving in the world of evanescent, difficult-to-describe sensitivities that include delicate and difficult-to-define feelings above and beyond the strictly physical, such as esthetic and spiritual pleasures. Nature involves also (6) *direction*, how we want to orient ourselves in regard to whatever source of pleasure we are engaged in.

## DISPLEASURES: THE DOWNSIDE OF PLEASURE

Displeasure is what brings us pain and unhappiness. These important historical comments were given by Edward W. Smith (personal communication, December 14, 2009) in response to my comment about Dante's list of seven deadly sins.

Dante did not identify the 7 deadly sins, as such. His list was much longer and more elaborate. Chaucer, however, did write of them in his "Canterbury Tales" of about 1386, specifically in "The Parson's Tale." Therein, he named them and gave their remedies, as follows:

| "Sin" | "Remedy" |
| --- | --- |
| Pride | Humility or true knowledge |
| Envy | Love God, neighbor, and enemy |
| Anger | Patience |
| Accidie or Sloth | Fortitude |
| Avarice | Mercy or "pity largely taken" |
| Gluttony | Abstinence, Temperance, Sobriety |
| Lechery | Chastity and Continence |

Chaucer wrote of Envy that "it is the worst of sins as it sets itself against all other virtues and goodness." "A Catechism of Christian Doctrine for General Use" of 1866 listed the sins as follows, naming them the "seven capital sins." "Pride, covetousness, lust, anger, gluttony, envy and sloth are the seven capital sins."

I took this material from some old notes, it would be advised to check the original sources for accuracy.

A more recent reframing of those deadly sins[4] related to cerebral (brain) and physiological (body) factors is as follows: Lust, Gluttony, Sloth, Pride, Greed, Envy, and Wrath. Take your pick. I know I am a glutton and Dante Alighieri in his *Devine Comedy* put gluttons in the lowest rung of hell, close to thieves and assassins. Woe unto me!

Many of us take these seven sources of pleasure for granted, not stopping to appreciate their full impact on all of us. In one way or another, we all do have a (secret?) pleasure that, unfortunately, often becomes an obsession and, worse, an addiction. This is why the seven sources of pleasure are presented in alphabetical order because only individuals can rank-order them according to personal preferences in different ways from others.

## CRITERIA FOR SELECTION

What does it take to be selected as a source of pleasure? In contrast to the vast literature on happiness, well-being, and positivity, which could be considered as a temporary state due a variety of factors reviewed below, sources of pleasure and displeasure can be selected according to a variety of criteria.

1. The source must occur in everyday life according to its easily identifiable nature.
2. The source must be long-lasting, if not other, in memory and not occasional or temporary, such as happiness or euphoria.
3. The source must be *available to everyone*, regardless of culture, gender, age, skin color, sexual orientation, ethnic group, or religious affiliation. It is universal.
4. The source must be concrete enough to be seen and heard, ingested, touched, photographed, and recorded. It produces a visible product, including a smile or laughter, or even tears of joy and happiness.
5. The source must be controllable, to be regulated at will by whoever uses that source and its resources. That means that there are highs and lows in the particular product available to everybody; it can be regulated as one wishes for its good or for its bad.
6. The source must have definite links to health and well-being on the basis of visible evidence, not wishful thinking, fantasies, or idiosyncratic whims or wills, that is, specific to an individual's desires.
7. The source must be used to benefit and not, in its excesses, harm an individual. There are excesses or extremes reachable in each

pleasure, too much or too little, such as anorexia nervosa and bulimia in eating on one extreme and obesity at the other extreme, as in addictions or obsessions. If a pleasure is achieved at somebody else's cost, including the self, it is no longer a pleasure, it's abuse.

Each of these points will be discussed in its various implications throughout this volume. After hearing, seeing, or buying a pleasure-giving product, at what level does that enjoyment occur? Is the source of pleasure produced actively versus enjoying it passively? Furthermore, what is the difference between happiness and pleasures? Happiness is a momentary pleasure that may even reach euphoria sometimes but is nonspecific to any source, while sources of pleasures are specific and concrete in one way or another. They can be recorded, photographed, and videotaped.

## WHY ONLY SEVEN SOURCES OF PLEASURES?

This introduction reiterates what has been said earlier, that is, there are three overall categories of pleasures that meet the seven criteria for choosing one pleasure over another.

1. Pleasure in producing something actively
2. Pleasure in enjoying passively a person or product, including doing nothing but listening or observing
3. Pleasure in sharing something with someone we love

What is the difference between a source and a resource? The former is whatever gives us pleasure and displeasure. The latter is the outcome of a source, available to us if and when we need it. For instance, sensuality as a resource in our body is composed of senses. Each sense can be used or not used as a resource. Some senses have different advantages from other senses. The more sources and resources we rely on in a balanced, sensible, and realistic way to meet our everyday demands, the better off we are. If and when we rely just on one source and within a source just on one resource, at the expense of other sources and resources, we are in trouble. Here is where being jack-of-all-trades and master of none may be helpful, provided we sample appropriately whatever sources and resources are available to us according to our age and stage of life, considering also their advantages and disadvantages.

## DIFFERENCES BETWEEN SOURCES OF PLEASURE AND HAPPINESS

Happiness is psychology's most recent and popular hobbyhorse. Whether it is a passing fad and fashion remains to be seen. Psychology as a science has experienced a great many theoretical paradigms, interesting theories, and exciting models that have attempted to represent the ultimate answer to understand and solve humanity's problems. Indeed, it remains to be seen whether happiness is another "orphan" notion, appearing suddenly from nowhere without any connection to known psychological paradigms, theories, and models, except for finding its reason d'être within the domain of another possible fad and fashion, positive psychology.[5] This movement emphasizes that the glass is half full as a reaction to the assumed traditional emphasis on the glass being half empty.

However, positive psychology is a movement but is not in and itself a theory or a model, and even less a paradigm.[6] Its followers, with few exceptions,[7, 8, 9, 10, 11, 12] repeat the same, do-it-yourself, self-report, paper-and-pencil procedures to learn how to become happy through self-rating scales, measures, exercises, and homework assignments that allow readers to "pursue" happiness according to the mission statement of our own Constitution.[13, 14]

Whether these approaches were helpful to readers of these self-help books is still unknown, or at least I tried to find out but could not find evidence of how much and how many people these books helped achieve happiness. And, if participants indeed achieved happiness, how long did it last? As you can see, I am somewhat dubious of approaches that do not allow us to evaluate any intervention where there is no continuous interactive feedback between a participant and an interested and informed helper, professional or semi-professional.[15]

Researchers have shown that about 40 percent of our happiness is accounted for by intentional activity whereas 50 percent is explained by genetics and 10 percent by circumstances.[16] Consequently, efforts to improve happiness might best be focused in the domain of *intentional, willful and self-directed activity.*[17] Such activity is nested in the "sustainable happiness model" proposed by Lyubomirsky. Sheldon and Schkade,[18] for instance, stated that happiness is in part within our ability to manage our lives, and, in this case, our pleasures. Pleasures, therefore, it's worth repeating, are within the realm of willful and self-directed activities.

As you see thus far, quite a few psychologists have entered in the now-fashionable happiness wagon in the last decade. Among the many who are cited here, I shall cite two major contributors to this topic.

## Michael W. Fordyce

Earlier work[19, 20] supports the premise that individuals can sustain levels of happiness through volitional behavior and intentional activity—such as composing letters of gratitude. For instance, writing three letters of gratitude over time would enhance important qualities of subjective well-being in the writer, such as happiness, life satisfaction, and gratitude. Fordyce,[21] a pioneer in the study of happiness, developed a self-study program to increase felt personal happiness and life satisfaction based on then current literature of happiness. He hypothesized that normal community college students (total $N =$ 338) could become happier if they could modify their behaviors and attitudes to approximate more closely the characteristics of happier people. In a first study, two of three pilot programs produced statistically significant happiness boosts compared to a placebo control. From these pilot programs Fordyce then designed a single program that combined the best aspects of the pilot programs. In the second study, an experimental group receiving this combined program showed significant boosts in happiness compared to a placebo control. In a third study, the combined program was presented to participants on a take-it-or-leave-it basis—those applying it showing significant boosts in happiness compared to those who did not. These studies suggested that the resulting self-study program may be helpful to individuals wishing to increase the emotional satisfaction they derive from living.

On a subsequent date,[22] Fordyce reported new studies (226 adults in a community college participated) that were continuations of Studies 1, 2, and 3 reported in the previous paragraph. These studies, however, used a self-study training program to increase happiness that centered on 14 fundamentals, including keeping busy, spending more time socializing, developing positive thinking, and working on a healthy personality. Measures of happiness included the Depression Adjective Check Lists and Happiness Measures. In Study 4, the complete program demonstrated significant happiness increases over a control group receiving summary instruction in the program. In Study 5, the complete program showed slight superiority over a control group receiving almost half the information. In Study 6, the full program was compared to groups receiving partial instruction from the program in their pre-determined areas of "happiness weakness" and to a control receiving "placebo expectations" of greater happiness. All treatment groups demonstrated significant gains in happiness compared to controls, though no difference between the treatments was apparent. Study 7 involved a 9–28 month follow-up of the program's effects on 69 past participants, with the vast majority of anonymous respondents reporting continued happiness increases. The collected findings indicate that the program had a long-lasting effect on happiness for most participants and that this effect was due to the content of the information.

Lyubomirsky, Sheldon, and Schkade[23] followed up on Fordyce's early pioneering work by arguing that the pursuit of happiness is an important goal for many people. However, surprisingly little scientific research has focused on the question of how happiness can be increased and then sustained, probably because of pessimism engendered by the concepts of genetic determinism and hedonic adaptation. Nevertheless, emerging sources of optimism exist regarding the possibility of permanent increases in happiness. Drawing on the past well-being literature, these authors proposed that a person's chronic happiness level is governed by three major factors: (1) a genetically determined set point for happiness; (2) happiness-relevant circumstantial factors, and (3) happiness-relevant activities and practices. Adaptation and dynamic processes show why the activity category offers the best opportunities for sustainably increasing happiness. Following this model, these authors included two preliminary happiness-increasing interventions.

In a follow-up to the original three-factor "sustainable happiness model" introduced above, Sheldon and Lyubomirsky[24] reviewed all the research about subjective well-being (SWB), rather than happiness, about the demographic/circumstantial, temperament/personality, and intentional/experiential correlates of SWB. On the basis of this information, these authors introduced the sustainable happiness model, which suggests that changing one's goals and activities in life is the best route to sustainable new SWB. However, the goals and activities must (1) be of certain positive types; (2) fit one's personality and needs; (3) be practiced diligently and successfully; (4) be varied in their timing and enactment; and (4) provide a continued stream of fresh positive experiences. After reviewing research supporting their model, new research suggests that happiness intervention effects are not just placebo effects and can last a long time.

## Daniel T. Gilbert

[H]appiness is a subjective experience that is difficult to describe
to ourselves and to others, thus evaluating people's claims about
their own happiness is an exceptionally thorny business.[25]

More recently, Daniel T. Gilbert at Harvard University has contributed as much research on happiness as some of the scholars cited in
this chapter.[26] If you find some of his research too technical, blame
me for not making it simpler and more readable. I promise that if
you pass through it, I shall try to write more enjoyably. Gilbert suggested that people initially take their subjective experience of an object
as an accurate reflection of the object's properties, and only subsequently, occasionally, and effortfully consider the possibility that
their experience was influenced by extraneous factors. Two studies
demonstrated that this is true even when extraneous factors are the
person's own disposition. Dispositionally happy and unhappy participants were falsely told that they had been subliminally primed with
words that might have influenced their moods, and were then asked
to identify those words. Dispositionally happy participants were more
likely than dispositionally unhappy participants to conclude that they
had been primed with positive words, but only when they made these
judgments under time pressure. These results indicate the need to correct human judgment.[27]

Although we tend to think of unhappiness as something that happens to us when we do not get what we want, much unhappiness
has less to do with not getting what we want, and more to do with
not wanting what we like. When wanting and liking are uncoordi-
nated in this way one can say that a person has *miswanted*. How is it
possible to get what we want and yet not like what we get? At least
three problems bedevil attempts to want well: imagining the wrong
event, using the wrong theory, and misinterpreting feelings. There
are at least two flaws in a naive analysis of **happiness**: (1) Human
wants are, like any other prediction, susceptible to error. (2) Even if
we could predict how much we would like an event when it happened, we might still be unable to predict how that event would affect
us in the long run.[28]

The durability bias, the tendency to overpredict the duration of
affective reactions to future events, may be due in part to focalism,
whereby people focus too much on the event in question and not
enough on the consequences of other future events. If so, asking

people to think about other future activities should reduce the durability bias. College football fans, for instance, were less likely to overpredict how long the outcome of a football game would influence their *happiness* if they first thought about how much time they would spend on other future activities. Alternative explanations were ruled out and found evidence for a distraction interpretation, that people who think about future events moderate their forecasts because they believe that these events will reduce thinking about the focal event. There are implications of focalism for other literatures, such as the planning fallacy, that is, planning without considering all possible alternative.[29]

Do people learn from experience that emotional reactions to events are often short-lived? It depends on whether the events are positive or negative. People who received positive or negative feedback on a test were not as happy or unhappy as they would have predicted. People in the positive feedback condition did not learn from this experience when making predictions about their reactions to future positive events. People in the negative feedback condition moderated their predictions about their reactions to future negative events, but this may not have been a result of learning. Rather, participants denigrated the test as a way of making themselves feel better and, when predicting future reactions, brought to mind this reconstrual of the test and inferred that doing poorly on it again would not make them very unhappy. Experience with a negative event (but not with a positive event) may improve the accuracy of one's affective forecasts, but the extent to which people learn from their affective forecasting errors may be limited.[30]

People prefer to make changeable decisions rather than unchangeable decisions because they do not realize that they may be more satisfied with the latter. Photography students believed that having the opportunity to change their minds about which prints to keep would not influence their liking of the prints. However, those who had the opportunity to change their minds liked their prints less than those who did not. Although the opportunity to change their minds impaired the post-decisional processes that normally promote satisfaction, most participants wanted to have that opportunity. These results demonstrate that errors in affective forecasting can lead people to behave in ways that do not optimize their *happiness* and well-being.[31]

Why do people believe that future events will have greater emotional impact than they actually do? Our ability to imagine the future, remember the past, and foresee the transformations that events, including happiness, will undergo as we interrogate and explain them is limited. Therefore our ability to predict our own emotional reactions to future events is limited as well. This conclusion applies also to the pursuit of *happiness*.[32]

People tend to overestimate the emotional consequences of future life events, exhibiting an impact bias. The impact bias was replicated in a real-life context in which undergraduates were randomly assigned to dormitories (or "houses"). Participants appeared to focus on the wrong factors when imagining their future happiness in the houses. They placed far greater weight on highly variable physical features than on less variable social features in predicting their future happiness in each house, despite accurately recognizing that social features were more important than physical features when asked explicitly about the determinants of happiness. This discrepancy emerged in part because participants exhibited an isolation effect, focusing too much on factors that distinguished between houses and not enough on factors that varied only slightly, such as social features.[33]

People often overestimate the impact future events will have on their happiness. People may also show a retrospective impact bias, overestimating the impact of past events on their happiness, explaining why they do not learn from experience and correct their forecasts. Such a bias for positive events was found; e.g., supporters of George W. Bush overestimated how happy they had been when the U.S. presidential election was determined. For negative events, people's recall was related to how much they were still rationalizing the outcome. Gore supporters rationalized the election by changing their views of the candidates. Four months later their positive view of Gore had returned, and they overestimated how unhappy they had been. In a second study, poor performers on a test rationalized their performance by downplaying the test's validity. Two weeks later they continued to rationalize and recalled accurately that they had not been very upset by their performance.[34]

The hedonic benefit of a gain, that is, pleasure (e.g., receiving $100), may be increased by segregating it into smaller units that are distributed over time (e.g., receiving $50 on each of two days). However, if these units are too small (e.g., receiving one penny on each of 10,000 days), they may fall beneath the person's pleasure limits and have no hedonic benefit at all. Do people know where their limits lie? For instance, participants in various studies predicted that the hedonic benefit of a large gain would be increased by segregating it into smaller units, and they were right; but participants also predicted that the hedonic benefit of a small gain would be increased by segregating it into smaller units, and they were wrong. Segregation of small gains decreased rather than increased hedonic benefit. These experiments suggest that people may underestimate the value of the hedonic limit and thus may over-segregate small gains.[35]

If one is interested in reading a thoughtful but humorously written yet scholarly, if not philosophical, source that summarized most of the research reported above, Gilbert's book[36] will be appreciated.

## DIFFERENCES BETWEEN SOURCES OF PLEASURE AND SUBJECTIVE WELL-BEING

While happiness might be a temporary state of being, with limitations considered in the previous section, subjective well-being (SWB), that is, "feeling good," on the other hand, is more like an attitude, how we view ourselves and our lives: half full or half empty, positively or negatively.[37] SWB is another topic that has captured the imagination of many psychologists, and especially Ed Diener at the University of Illinois at Urbana-Champaign.[38] His pioneer work stimulated a whole range of studies by researchers all over the United States[39, 40] and the world. Since feelings of positive pleasure and negative displeasure may be separate from each other, representing two different dimensions and processes, what is relevant to well-being may be the ratio between the two dimensions, that is, frequency of positive compared to negative experiences and states in a person's life over time.[41] We shall see this ratio repeated in other references used in this chapter.

What determines SWB? First of all, what kind of personality are we? If we are extraverted, that is, sociable and easily approachable, if we like to be with people and enjoy being with loved ones and friends rather than a solitary grouch, the more likely we will be able to experience SWB. Here is where SWB intersects with happiness because "Happy people (in case it was not made clear in the previous section), are more social, altruistic, active, like themselves and others more, have strong bodies and immune systems, and have better conflict resolution skills than unhappy people."[42, 43] Furthermore, happy people may be more creative than unhappy ones.

SWB is also related to (1) income; (2) individualism, whether a culture is oriented toward individuals, such as American culture, or collectivism, whether a culture is oriented toward the collective group;

(3) human rights and societal equality.[44] SWB may include contentment with one's state and stage of life, including tranquility.[45]

Elsewhere[46] I have indicated how individuals who keep hurt feelings inside themselves and are unable or unwilling to express and share them with loved ones or with professional helpers are more likely unable to experience SWB. Individuals who are depressed, chronically anxious, and in continuous conflict within themselves and with others will very likely not be able to experience SWB.

However, in a strange turn-around that equates all that has been written and researched on SWB and happiness, as two separate fields of inquiry,[47] finally acknowledged the overlap between the two conditions to the point of being synonymous conditions, or two sides of the same coin. The major contribution this father-son pair made in this book relates to our happiness being built over our *psychological wealth*,

> which extends beyond material riches and beyond popular concepts like emotional intelligence and social capital. Psychological wealth is your true total net worth, and includes your attitudes toward life, social support, spiritual development, material resources, health, and the activities in which you engage (p. 3) ... is the experience of well-being and a high quality of life ... is the experience that our life is excellent—that we are living in a rewarding engaged, meaningful, and enjoyable way (p. 6).

This definition means that viewing our glass as half full does not deny the reality of its being also half empty. It is a matter of which half we choose.[48] The thesis of this pair and the evidence they cite support the position that happy people function better, not only financially but primarily socially, at home and at work. Money does not buy happiness but it helps provided we also include a religious spirituality. However, happiness is relative to culture. There are extremely deprived (seemingly to us) individuals in some cultures that are apparently satisfied with what they have, which is very little according to our consumerist standards.

As an approach to achieve even greater happiness,[49] three resources are recommend: (1) paying *Attention* to what is going on inside and outside ourselves; (2) *Interpretation* that consists of how we perceive and give meaning to internal and external events; and (3) *Memory*, how we keep track of past and present events, depending on their pleasurable and non-pleasurable nature. At the end of the book there is a Well-Being Balance Sheet that allows participants to discover how they fit and measure how they fit inside happiness.

As much as I respect both father and son as worthy colleagues and researchers, I could not get away from their overall preachy, advice-giving style throughout their book. I happen to believe that few people follow free advice because they are not usually motivated to take it. We must be in the depths of a negative life spiral to admit needing help, and even then, it is difficult for some people to ask for help. Happy people by definition are able to take and benefit by feedback given in the right way, but if they are happy would they need advice? If I want a sermon I will go to a house of worship. If I want to change and become happier than I am, I better rely on professional help, even and especially if it is expensive. Free advice freely given is usually freely denied or rejected.

Therefore, being and becoming happy depends on motivation to change, and I question whether reading a book and following standard operating procedures based on self-report, paper-and-pencil questionnaires and measures will produce significant change, especially in troubled individuals. College sophomores, who constitute the major bulk of research on SWB, are young and enthusiastic participants. Let's try to produce happiness in those people who need it the most, more than just young and enthusiastic college sophomores: the hurting and the troubled ones.[50]

## DIFFERENCES BETWEEN SOURCES OF PLEASURE AND POSITIVITY

Enter Barbara L. Fredrickson, Ph.D., Kenan Distinguished Professor of Psychology at University of North Carolina at Chapel Hill. Her schtick is *positivity*[51] and she does not like the term *happiness*: "You may have noticed that the term *happiness* [italics hers] is not in my top ten [terms she uses to define positivity]. I avoid this term because I feel it's murky and overused (p. 37)." Instead Dr. Fredrickson defines positivity according to 10 different "forms" consisting of joy, gratitude, serenity, interest, hope, pride, amusement, inspiration, awe, and love. In case you have missed the nature of these forms, they cover essentially a whole range of what have been called positive feelings and emotions.

Among the many advantages of positivity are (1) broadening of one's mind; (2) creating an upward constructive spiral within you; (3) allowing to relate more intimately with those we love and who love us; and (4) connecting to something larger than us. Furthermore, positivity increases once we start using it and gets better with time, making life more enjoyable, opening our hearts and mind to live our lives on a solid foundation, building psychological strength, social connections, physical health, and resilience, that is, the ability to bounce back after experiencing adversities and losses.

On the basis of a detailed case study of Nina, a woman who was described as being at the bottom of positivity, Dr. Fredrickson showed how attending a free mindfulness workshop given at her place of work, and following its guidelines, changed her life from an unhappy introvert to a relatively happy extrovert. From this example, the author built a ratio of how many positives overcame negatives. Positives may vary and range from 0 to at least a dozen, but for her purposes Dr. Fredrickson set an upper limit of 6 with negatives being a constant: one. Nina, then, from a 1 to 1 ratio, the lowest possible score, moved up and raised to a 6 to 1 ratio. Hence, from this ratio what we need to do is decrease negativity and increase positivity. If you follow the instructions, rating scales, and measures given in the book, as given in most self-help books cited in this chapter, participants should be able to achieve a modicum of positivity.

What are the guidelines to achieve positivity? Here they are:

1. Be open to experiencing new events in your life
2. Create higher-quality connections with people and activities
3. Cultivate kindness
4. Develop distractions to get away from unpleasant feelings
5. Dispute negative thinking
6. Find nearby nature in trees, water, and the sky, i. e., stop to smell the roses
7. Learn and apply your strengths
8. Meditate mindfully, allowing to accept what is going on within you without value judgments as to its goodness or badness
9. Meditate on loving-kindness
10. Ritualize gratitude
11. Savor positivity
12. Visualize your future

In sum, these guidelines should allow participants to change from languishing to flourishing because positivity feels good, broadens minds, builds resources, fuels resilience, raise the positivity ratio up to at least 3 to 1, and people can raise their positivity ratios.

I am envious of this contribution on two counts. First, Prof. Fredrickson backs her conclusions and recommendations with a vast and reliable amount of creative and innovative research. Hers is no fantasy or pie-in-the sky invention. As she freely admits, she is a "junkie" to quantification and to empirical evidence, worthy of a real scientist. Second, her writing style is what I would like to achieve but which I will never obtain, full of personal anecdotes, painful as well as pleasurable, and easy-to-understand examples. Serious and important results from research seem easy to read and understand by her uncanny ability to convert them from technical to easy-to-comprehend explanations.

But I do have concerned reactions to this worthy contribution that do not in any way detract from its value. I hope these reactions will be helpful rather than hurtful. One criticism I have about the feelings and emotions defining positivity relies on my arguments[52] that giving a positive versus negative value or valence to feelings is a misleading and inaccurate value judgment. Feelings in and of themselves cannot be defined as positive or negative. They indeed can be defined as pleasurable and unpleasurable, but whether they are helpful or unhelpful relies on how these inward feelings are expressed outwardly as emotions. Furthermore, feelings on the receiving, internal side of experiencing are different in their processing from emotions expressed outwardly. Feelings are internal and emotions are external. Feelings need to be elicited to be evaluated and measured, whereas emotions are freely visible and measurable.

For instance, historically and still up to the present time, most emotion researchers and theorists have lumped together as negative emotions (rather than feelings) anger, fear, and sadness. However, these three basic feelings have distinctly separate developmental trajectories. Anger usually leads to acting out, criminality, and even murder. Fear leads to severe psychological illness, and sadness leads to depression and even suicide.[53] Here is where the list composing positivity mixes together inward feelings (joy, serenity, hope, pride, and inspiration) as well as emotions, how feelings are expressed outwardly in relationship to internal or external events (gratitude, interest, amusement, awe, and love). This criticism does not detract from the overall effect that both feelings and emotions exert in how we behave. Another way to reframe this criticism is to wonder whether these terms mix and confuse levels of discourse and interpretation, feelings on one hand and emotions on the other. They are two different and separate processes, intake in feelings and outtake in emotions, respectively.

Furthermore, I do not want to steal Prof. Fredrickson's thunder nor in any way decrease the importance of her excellent work, but more than 35 years ago[54] I advocated reframing the negativity of many patients I saw professionally into positive terms. This process of positive reframing culminated in an extremely successful book about paradoxical psychotherapy written with one of my best doctoral students[55] that was translated in five or six different countries. This positive reframing approach was recently updated within the context of Jesus's paradoxical Sermon on the Mountain.[56] The same reframing has been used in some interactive practice exercises or workbooks, especially depression, among others.[57]

Positive reframing is a process I have followed since then: We can call a half glass of water either empty or full. Which one will we choose? For instance, whenever my wife and I had an argument or we got mad at each other, I forced myself to do three positive acts, such as vacuuming the house, throwing out the garbage and trash, and emptying the dishwasher. Instead of using a generic term such as *negativity*, I prefer to use the term *hurts* or *hurt feelings*, which I defined operationally[58] just as Prof. Fredrickson did with the 10 nouns she used for positivity.[59]

However, using her 10 forms of positivity, I suggest that to teach about positivity to large audiences, it is possible to create an interactive workbook composed of practice exercises. Whether these exercises would be interactive between participants and professional feedback depends on the nature of the audience and its goals. This workbook could be easily composed by asking participants to define each term rather than assuming that participants understand them. To accomplish this first practice exercise, I would also recommend the use of a dictionary to help participants really think more clearly about each term and lead them to reflect and enlarge what I consider awareness of self and of context.[60]

After defining each term, then participants could be asked to give two examples for each term. Once this exercise is completed, participants could be asked to rank-order the 10 terms according to how important they are to them from the most to the least important. From a nomothetic task of definition and examples done equally by every participant, by rank-ordering the terms we enter into what we psychologists call an idiographic task that individualizes the sequence of importance for each participant. It would be difficult for different participants to come up with the same rank-order. At the end of this exercise, participants are asked to explain why they rank-ordered the items the way they did. A second practice exercise would use a standard format that asks participants to write in detail about the origin, duration, frequency, rate, intensity, and interactive meaning about one term at a time administered sequentially according to the rank-order given initially (L'Abate, 2011).[61]

Furthermore, I find the 3 to 1 ratio of positive to negative feelings and emotions suggested by Dr. Fredrickson rather restrictive conceptually and empirically. She applied the same value of one to everybody in negativity while she accounted for individual differences with an upper limit for positivity up to 6. This ratio, normally and normatively 3 to 1, however, does not take into account the great variability in personality functioning and dysfunctioning, especially on the negativity, i.e., hurt feelings, side. While Prof. Fredrickson kept negativity as a constant, that is, one and positivity as a variable from 1 to 6, instead I have used both joys and hurts as variables. Some of us collect inevitable hurts more than others and fewer joys than others. Consequently, the denominator in this ratio, hurts, can vary as much as joys in positive feelings, emotions, and events, as explained in greater detail below.

Using John Gottman's[62] ratio of five hurts to arrive at his conclusion about one of the most painful experiences in life, that is, divorce, and more specifically, using an arithmetical model of human interactions[63, 64] classified according to six degrees along a dimension of superior functionality to severe dysfunctionality, we obtain six types of arithmetical interactions: (1) *multiplicative* interactions mean that in addition to superior functioning at home, work, and leisure, there is a distinct volunteer leadership contributed to charitable and social institutions; (2) *additive* interactions means adequate functioning within one's family, home, work, and leisure but no significant contributions outside of those settings, following well but not leading; (3) *static positive* interactions means that there is borderline functioning but there is no improvement in how partners or family members get along with each other inside and outside home or work, the interactions remain the same over time; (4) *static negative* means that functioning is borderline but there are many conflicts within, between, and among family members, work, and other settings, however, interactions remain the same over time; (5) *subtractive* means that functioning is quite below normal, inadequate, deviant, and defective; and (6) *divisive* means that severe dysfunctioning does not allow living anywhere except in protective settings, such as hospitals and often jails and penitentiaries.

Given this classification in its relationship to the ratio of joys to hurts, the following ratio would result, respectively: in multiplicative interactions the ratio would be 6 to 1, in additive interactions 5 to 2, in static positive interactions 4 to 3, in static negative interactions 3 to 4, in subtractive interactions 2 to 5, and in divisive interactions (0)1 to 6.

Interestingly enough, as already summarized above but it need of repeating here, in the case of Nina described in detail by Prof. Fredrickson, as a result of a free meditation workshop offered at her place of work, Nina was transformed from a shy, unhappy if not depressed, isolated and introverted woman to a happy, reasonably satisfied, and outgoing personality. The ratio between positivity and negativity that Dr. Fredrickson assigned to her, as a result of her almost magical transformation, was 6 to 1 (p. 78). Unfortunately, she did not vary the degree of negativity and there was no theoretical or empirical background to differentiate such an assignment along a dimension of functionality-dysfunctionality. I hope that the foregoing classification of interactions presented repeatedly[65, 66, 67] might supply such a background and that, on reflection, Prof. Fredrickson may consider composing a Positivity Workbook using negativity as a variable and not as a constant.

## CONCLUSION

One does not need to be a rocket scientist, or even a psychologist, to figure out the amount of overlap among happiness, subjective well-being, and positivity. Rather than cover such generic and quite abstract terms, which have attracted many creative contributors and researchers to achieve fame and glory, I have chosen and prefer to stick humbly to concrete and specific sources of pleasure that, unfortunately, on the flip side, can also be the sources of displeasure.

We all have the same choice to make in our lives: approach and choose pleasures and avoid converting those pleasures into displeasures. Whether we call them happiness, subjective well-being, and positivity, sources of pleasure and displeasure as products and productions instead are readily specific, concretely visible, and unquestionably tangible. They can be photographed, videotaped, and recorded. This process is difficult to achieve with happiness, subjective well-being, and positivity. Now the reader can understand where I stand in comparison to my esteemed happiness, well-being, and positivity colleagues on the topic of pleasure.

## BEGINNING AND ENDING EXERCISE

The purpose of this exercise and of those at the end of every chapter is to help you *think* about what you are doing or not doing to achieve pleasure in your life.

On a blank, lined sheet of paper, draw a vertical line down the middle. On the left-hand column, using the Table of Contents at the beginning of this book, rank-order the seven sources of pleasure we need to *survive* according to how important each pleasure is for you, with No. 1 being the most important, No. 2 the next more important, until you have rank-ordered all the seven sources down to the least important. On the right-hand column, rank-order the sources of pleasure according to how much you like, want, or need to *enjoy*, from the one you enjoy the most (No. 1) to the one you enjoy the least (No. 7).

Keep this sheet for your records where you can find it easily, because once you complete the same exercise at the end of each chapter and finish reading this book, you will be asked to go over it and see whether you want to change what you wrote in it now. Hint: Try to rank-order these sources of pleasure without looking at what you wrote before you started reading it. Please give one or more reasons why you rank-ordered these sources the way you did.

As simple and trivial as this exercise given at the end of every chapter may seem, if you perform it well, it should start on a process of *reflection*. Without *reflection*, as a feedback change process, thinking about what has happened in the Past, what is happening in the Present, and what might happen in the Future, in ourselves and loved ones, the whole enterprise of getting pleasure out of life may be or become a shallow game.

# 1

# Arts and Creativity: Observing, Studying, Watching, and Producing

[T]here obviously are 2 ways (possibly more) to gain pleasure from the arts. One way is to engage in the making of art (performance). The other way is to enjoy art "voyeu-ristically," "vicariously" (as an audience).[1]

Frugality without creativity is deprivation.[2]

[I]magination needs moodling—long, inefficient, happy idling, dawdling, and puttering.[3]

The creation of something new is not accomplished by the intellect but by the play instinct acting from inner necessity. The creative mind plays with the objects it loves.[4]

Creativity can solve almost any problem. The creative act, the defeat of habit by originality, overcomes everything.[5]

To live a creative life, we must lose our fear of being wrong.[6]

Creativity represents a miraculous coming together of the uninhibited energy of the child with its apparent opposite and enemy, the sense of order imposed on the disciplined adult intelligence.[7]

Creativity is allowing yourself to make mistakes. Art is knowing which ones to keep.[8]

Creative work is play. It is free speculation using materials of one's chosen form. . . . This flashpoint of creation in the present moment is where work and play merge.[9]

Arts involve various channels of communication: (1) verbal, such as poetry; (2) visual, such as photography, films, painting; and

(3) kinesthetic, such a sculpture, pottery, and architecture. These aspects will be covered in the pleasure of actively producing something new and different and passively enjoying that something new and different. Here is where aesthetic pleasures will likely occur: the active pleasure of production and the passive pleasure of enjoying that production.

## WHAT IS ART?

Many of us draw, take pictures, write articles, novels, and poetry. All of us have plenty of ideas in a variety of topics. However, only few among us can realistically dream of becoming recognized in a particular field. An important aspect of arts, as well as many of the forthcoming sources in this volume, consists of masterpieces composed and produced by Heroines and Heroes. These individuals rise above the undifferentiated mass of other individuals to become historical icons within their own specialized field. All of us, in one way or another, even though using different media, may claim to be artists. However, how come only a few of us can dream of becoming recognized as a distinguished contributor in a particular field? The key word here is *recognition*, which represents the consensus from various authorities and judges that whatever artistic product has been created is worthy of attention, promulgation, and historical placement in its own right.

According to the 1971 edition of the *Encyclopedia Britannica*, art signifies a skill or ability to produce non-utilitarian objects and products that please one's auditory, visual, verbal, and kinesthetic senses. The function of art is to communicate a sense of beauty according to one's impulses expressed in various media, visual, plastic, and graphic. In the entry of art in the *Encyclopedia* the curious and interested readers will be able to read about principles, techniques, and history of art. Since this information is already available even online, there is no need to repeat here what is easily available to any curious reader.

An overworked statement about art is that it is produced for its own sake alone "... that the pure creation of the mind is somehow sullied by contact with the real world and that the more divorced from use knowledge is, the more noble it is. This Platonic view has long swayed artists and scientists and has helped make learning at once austere and unreal. In the case of science, it has produced the paradox of minds that create dangers deadly to humanity, yet deny all responsibility."[10]

This view that education was classically divorced from the practical reality and learned for its own sake influenced Italian education policies until later in the last century. For instance, in the eighth grade I was supposed to learn Greek to then enter the Classical Lyceum (read high school with an extra, 13th year added). That course would allow me to choose automatically any university curriculum. Arguing vehemently that I did not need to study Greek in the twentieth century, with my sainted mother (figuratively) tearing at her hair desperately, wondering what to do with her problem son, I managed to do my best to fail miserably in Greek. I refused to study it and consequently I received grades of 1 in written and 2 in oral on a scale of 1 to 10 (pass is 6 and a grade below 5 is failing). This counts as one of my proudest academic achievements in my entire educational career.

This desired outcome, however, allowed me, and close buddies who followed me, to attend a Scientific Lyceum where only Latin was taught but not Greek. That Lyceum, however, would not permit my attending any of the liberal arts curricula, including philosophy where, in those days, psychology was taught as a branch of philosophy. Consequently, I chose to attend the school of architecture even though I could not draw a straight line with a ruler before escaping to the United States as an exchange student. In this way I also avoided enrolling in the Italian Naval Academy, which I was supposed to attend according to family tradition. My younger brother Alberto went but washed out within a few weeks for a shoulder injury while playing volleyball. He is now the most violently nonviolent pacifist in all of Italy.

The irony of this story is that I ended up marrying a Greek American who helped me realize that when you marry a Greek American you marry a whole culture, including the language . . . and talk about art in Greece and Italy in the Roman times.

## WHAT IS CREATIVITY?

Lots of us paint, write poetry, play a musical instrument, and have a whole bunch of ideas popping into our heads, but how many among us can have creative ideas and be called creative? According to the American Psychological Association (APA) *Dictionary of Psychology*,[11] creativity consists of the ability to produce or develop original work, theories, techniques, or thoughts. A creative individual typically displays originality, imagination, and expressiveness. Analyses have failed to ascertain why one individual is more creative than another, but creativity does appear to be a durable trait. Creative thinking consists of special mental processes leading to a new invention, solution, or synthesis in any area. A creative solution may use preexisting objects or ideas but creates a new relationship between the elements it utilizes. Examples include new machines, social ideas, scientific theories, and artistic creations. A creative synthesis means the combination of several ideas, images, and associations into a new whole, especially when this (product) differs fundamentally from any of its components.[12, 13, 14] I could not have said this better myself!

## The Line between Imagination and Creativity

According to the same APA *Dictionary of Psychology,* imagination is the faculty to generate and produce ideas and images in the absence of direct sensory data, often by combining fragments of previous sensory experiences into new syntheses. However, how is imagination different from creativity? One could have an overactive imagination; however, if the imagination is similar or the same of many others, it does not reach the level of creativity, as defined above. For instance:

- *Many of us have imagination but only few of us are creative.*
  How does one go from coming up with an idea, no matter how interesting and even exciting, and is able to transform that idea into actuality? Not many can do this. If all the ideas we create every day in our heads were to be transformed into bona-fide artistic or scientific creations, there would not be any room on this planet for anything else. Consequently, from those only few of us who might be called creative, the criteria for creativity increase.
- *Few of us know how to transform imagination into a creation.*
  What does it take for one of us move from the idea to its creation? There are millions and millions of ideas, some good, some bad, some in between, some outlandish, some realistic, some fantastic, some down-to-earth simple, some out of this world. What is the extra quality that allows a few (very few) of us become creative? Creativity was not born in a day and did not rise out of a sudden without a specific background.

- *Few of us have the educational background and specific skills necessary to create.*

  If you happen to think that creativity arose from a vacuum and that everybody can become creative, think again. Creativity grows from a background of knowledge developed over years of education, formal and informal. In the olden days, apprenticeship was a form of education where one started to work with a well-known artist or scientist and acquired through a great deal of practice the skills necessary to create something new. Whether we call it education or practice, creativity is based on a great deal of knowledge acquired through formal and informal education. This type of education is present in science through what are called postdoctoral training. The world is too complex to guarantee that a mere Ph.D. will be sufficient to know everything there is to know about any topic. Most artistic and scientific breakthroughs rose from years of practice and experience.

  For instance, as Simonton[15] observes:

  > [I]t takes a full decade of extensive and intensive study and practice before you are ready to make major contributions to a given domains [of arts or science, n/a]. This degree of effort is not for the faint of heart. You have to be persistent, methodical, meticulous, and dedicated to acquire the knowledge and skill that underlie extraordinary achievement in most domains.

- *Few of us have contextual and personal resources necessary to create something original and unique.*

  Intelligence might be necessary but by itself is not sufficient to understand creativity. Creativity is a skill of its own that goes above and beyond, if not altogether outside intelligence. You've heard the expression "thinking outside the box"? It's a spark that is nurtured through a supportive environment, including, but not always, one's parents, family, and friends. The creative spark is nurtured by the self, being convinced about the importance of one's ideas and dogged determination to see to its end an idea that oftentimes is thought to be "crazy", impractical, or irrelevant. Consequently, what is this "spark" that transforms imagination into creation?

## Creativity as Imagination Put into Action

If that is the case, if indeed creativity is imagination put into action, what is the process whereby this outcome occurs?

- *Imagination in and of itself is not enough.*

   Imagination, just like intelligence, is not sufficient to transform an idea into a visible, palpable creation. As an Italian proverb reminds us: *"Tra dire e fare c'e' di mezzo il mare."* "Between talk and action there is a sea in the middle." Here is where individual and social factors come into being: the motivation of the individual to create something new and wonderful and the support from the immediate environment (partner, parents, progeny, and power structure). The Eiffel Tower, to use an overworked example, was not built just as an idea. It took many engineers and many politicians to support its construction, against the protestations of a few vociferous parties. Many artists in the Renaissance, painters, musicians, and sculptors would have not produced the many masterpieces created during that period without the support of powerful kings, marquises, and dukes, such as the Medici family in Florence, my hometown, for instance.

- *Action in and of itself is not enough.*

   On the other hand, there are many artisans, musicians, painters, and sculptors who create a great many objects every day. However, which one among these productions will become a veritable masterpiece? One must consider the immediate and distal context for the creation, when and where it occurred. Action in and of itself represents not only what an individual produces but what kind of nourishing supporting environment that individual has been able to enlist and recruit in support of a production. Whether a production becomes a masterpiece depends on the consensus of authorities, judges, industry, commerce, and even the common public. For instance, "at the turn of the last century, New York City was home to a remarkable flowering of architectural activity [produced by the very forces just cited above]. All across the city, immigrant craftsmen, mostly anonymous, created exuberant works of art out of terra cotta and the humble stone of tenements and row-houses—art that enabled the public and enlivened the streets in a vibrant new way."[16]

Consequently, once we understand how each component works synergistically toward a common goal, we can obtain what at first blush may seem a simplistic equation:

- *Imagination x Action = Creativity*

   This equation is composed by at least three parts necessary for the process of creativity. We have already attempted to explain directly both imagination and action work together (that is, synergistically) and indirectly by the x sign necessary to the multiplicative increment of one part with the other. By x is meant that extra unknown and variable parts included in the individual (skills, motivation, intelligence) but also in the variable parts necessary for the process of action leading to its completion, as involved in the surrounding supportive and cultural context, as in New York City at the beginning of the last century.

## What Is the Difference between Imagination and an Invention?

An invention is putting into practice an imagination to develop a useful gadget, a contraption or piece of machinery that did not exist heretofore. Think, for instance, about Madame Curie developing the first X-ray machines. The key word here is *useful*, a term that shows the difference between an invention and an artistic production that in and of itself has absolutely no useful purpose, except aesthetic pleasure.

Here is where creativity lies in producing something useful, mechanically and scientifically, as being different from creating something beautiful with no specifically practical purpose except an aesthetic one. The process of creativity in both invention and imagination is about the same. One needs imagination times action to create an invention as well as a work of art. However, the product is completely different as far as their usefulness is concerned. There are occasional inventions that may be pleasingly beautiful. See if you can think of one. The wheel, for instance, remains the most useful invention ever devised. It spanned an incredible number of gadgets and mechanisms leading to cars, radios, TV, etc. By the same token, the Xerox 914 was the mother of all technological inventions that gave rise to the information age, as discussed further in Chapter 3 of this volume.[17] The mother of all inventions, printing[18] just as the first printing press developed in the Middle Ages gave birth to the multiple production of unlimited copies of the same manuscript. No one, however, would call a printing press or a copy machine beautiful.

For example, according to the Atlanta *Journal-Constitution* of December 10, 2010, Paul Isbell and Sean Turnan "Reinvented the card box by breaking into the multibillion-dollar toy industry against naysayers who warned them against the dangers of entering into the toy business. By simply seeing children playing with boxes, they got the 'big idea' of making playhouses out of eco-friendly materials. As a result they turned such an idea into a million dollar business. They saw the need, they sought wise business, professional, and technical advice before opening up and forming a completely new business 'Crafty Kids Playhouses,' attractive, safe, useful (to children), and playful objects that parents could buy for their children."

## THE ROLE OF MASTERPIECES IN ARTS AND CREATIVITY

Masterpieces in any art have an important role to play in any culture. Consequently, masterpieces in any artistic field fulfill at least three functions as (1) original and unique creations; (2) enduring legacy; and (3) emblematic prototypes.

### Masterpieces Are Original and Unique Creations

What makes a masterpiece that makes it rise above and beyond the crowd of many other creations? First, masterpieces are original creations with at least two meanings, the individual who originated that particular product, and as inherently different from anything else of comparable nature and quality. They are different from previous or similar creations to the point of standing out and above any other creation in their own specific field. Second, masterpieces are unique to the point that no other production can be conceived as being equal to it. Uniqueness has also two meanings, as being the single, sole product of its kind, and being without any comparison with similar productions in the same category. Perhaps one of the most viewed works of architecture in the world is the Eiffel Tower that provoked extreme reactions in musicians such as Balzac[19] who has been said to flee screaming from its sight because of its vulgarity. The English poet William Morris, during his stay in Paris, took his meals in the Tower's restaurants so that he did not have to look at the "damn thing"![20]

### Masterpieces Endure

Because of their originality and uniqueness, masterpieces endure the test of time and conquer the world of space. They expand outside and beyond national or geographical limits and are recognized as masterpieces in different countries, even though we may have masterpieces within geographical and national confines, i. e., think of the Monna Lisa, created in Italy but housed in France

## Masterpieces as Emblematic Prototypes

What does it mean to be emblematic and prototypical? Both terms are really synonymous but indicate that certain masterpieces stand out from the commonplace to represent their own particular field, such as the Eiffel Tower in Paris or the waterfront Theater in Sydney, Australia.

Now that the role of masterpieces in arts has been considered, as a game, please try to match particular masterpieces in any of the following art categories listed below. You can use any source of information you can find, whether on the Internet, your own or your public library, family, and friends. If I were to give you this information myself, I question whether you would remember it. By actively exploring this possible match, perhaps you may be able to learn something new and even remember it. Why should I do this work for you and in the process rob you of the active experience of learning? Furthermore, owing to the overlap between two forthcoming games, while you are playing with masterpieces you are bound to find the respective Heroines and Heroes responsible for them, as listed further down below.

Architecture
Automobiles
Dance
Design (of objects)
Drawing (of people)
Fashion[21]
Food (considered in Chapter 4 of this volume)
Literature (Novels)
Movies
Music (considered in Chapter 5 of this volume)
Origami
Painting
Photography
Poetry
Pottery
Television
Theater (Plays) (for Opera see Chapter 5 of this volume)

However, you may wonder why food was included in this list. Food as art? Is this writer nuts? (Forget the pun.) Food as an art category was added because many famous chefs (listed in Chapter 4 of this volume) consider themselves artists, even if temporary, in the way they present their edible compositions and how they prepare food as a work of art. Oftentimes, chefs see their productions as consisting of an original and unique combination of ingredients that no one else ever thought to replicate. Hence, these two qualities of originality and uniqueness make food an art form, a legitimate category among other art forms.

This is especially true in Japan, where the mode of presentation is just as important as the nature or taste of the food itself. I cannot forget an incredible meal I consumed by invitation of my good friend Nobuaki Kunya, now deceased, in a lavishly luxurious (read very expensive) restaurant on top of a high-rise skyscraper in Tokyo, Japan. The whole meal, presented with ritualistic fashion by servers in local costumes, consisted of 10 courses, presumably from different regional cuisines in various parts of Japan. Food was presented ceremoniously, slowly, one course (read "morsel") at a time, with leisurely breaks in between courses, with my host emphasizing to me the importance of the artistic presentation (colors of ingredients, placement of components, shape of each place, etc.). It was an interesting, original, and unique meal in every respect. It was, therefore, a very artistically creative, visually esthetic, and gustatory tasteful experience, even though I found its portions extremely small. I was still hungry when we left. But I did not tell that to my host. The experience of that meal still remains memorable after many years.

## THE ROLE OF HEROINES AND HEROES IN THE ARTS AND CREATIVITY

Heroines and Heroes are usually called Geniuses.[22] There are different kinds of geniuses depending on which field you select. Heroine and Heroes in the arts may be different from those in the sciences and even within arts and sciences there are tremendous variations on what makes a genius. Nonetheless, certain manifestations help to create and define acknowledged geniuses, such as (1) outstanding creativity; (2) exceptional leadership in their chosen field; and (3) prodigious performance. There are evil (e.g., Hitler, Mussolini, and Stalin, among many others) and positive geniuses (such as Albert Einstein, Franklin D. Roosevelt and Dwight Eisenhower). Or there are accidental geniuses who found something completely new by chance rather than by plan, as Ian Fleming's discovery of penicillin.

Heroines and Heroes provide at least four important functions in creating arts in their specific field: (1) pioneers; (2) prototypes; (3) role models; and (4) survivors.

## Heroines and Heroes as Pioneers: Charting Unchartered Territory in Unique and Novel Ways

Here is where originality and uniqueness come into being. An artist achieves the status of a heroin or hero due to the fact that she or he was the first to produce something that had not been thought heretofore. Christopher Columbus might have been a pioneer in charting new territories but he was not an artist. He did not create America. He found it! An artist may have found a new art form or may have produced something completely new that demonstrated she or he is ahead of his or her times.

## Heroines and Heroes as Prototypes Representing Specific Art Forms

Heroines and Heroes in art stand out as representing that particular art form they used to express their creativity. Once you think of a painting, for instance, that may bring to mind Mona Lisa, including Nat King Cole's song about that painting. However, you have to remember that Leonardo da Vinci was the painter who survived as a pioneer in many other artistic and scientific endeavors (my hero!)

## Heroines and Heroes as Role Models to Emulate and to Follow

Heroines and Heroes in art sometimes create new schools of enthusiastic followers that imitate that particular art form. Think, for instance, of Dumas and the French Impressionist painters or Picasso and the revolution in abstract paintings. They may have not attended the same physical edifice implied in the term *school* but these painters claimed and proclaimed allegiance and closeness to a particular art form, thus forming a school.

## Heroines and Heroes as Survivors

Heroines and Heroes survive their time on earth and continue to be revered beyond their death. Their legacy continues to live regardless of their physical nonexistence.

As suggested in regard to masterpieces, we can play the same game with Heroines and Heroes. See if you can match specific Heroines and Heroes to one particular art category. With this double-whammy you should be able to enlarge your artistic horizons to the chagrin of your friends.

Architecture
Automobiles
Dance
Design
Drawing
Fashion[23]
Food (considered in Chapter 4 of this volume)
Literature (Novels)
Movies
Music (considered in Chapter 5 of this volume)
Origami
Painting
Photography
Poetry
Pottery
Television
Theater (plays) (for Opera see Chapter 5 of this volume)

## PAINTING AND THE HISTORY OF COLORS: EARTH PIGMENTS

Painting as well as other art forms include color, and apparently paint-ers may view scenes in a way that is similar to how the world really is: a mishmash of colors, lines, and shapes.[24] For instance, Leonardo da Vinci's *Mona Lisa*, one of the most viewed masterpieces in the world, is valued for its "vividness" that is a quality common to all great works of art.[25, 26] It is this quality of vividness, something that remains in our minds and memory, that makes us value masterpieces in the arts, and especially painting.

Therefore, color is one of the most important elements of any art form. Yet, we take it for granted and accept it without any background knowledge about its history and development. To foster an under-standing of this background, let us turn in some expanse to the writings of Binders Art blogger Ian Boccio:

Color surrounds us all the time in the natural world, the bright hues of flowers, the wings of butterflies, even the deep blue of a clear sky present us with an incredible display all the time. As humans began to develop a more complex, cooperative type of social structure that permitted more leisure time to follow pursuits that weren't survival related, visual art as we know it today began to take shape. However, the people of the stone age had no access to even the simplest manufacturing processes and everything that they created had to be made from media that was easily obtainable in the landscape around them.[27] With the help of my good friend Joe Z. Torre I am including excerpts about this fascinating topic.

It is likely that the very first pigments that were used by our artistic ancestors were black, made from the charred remnants of wood or bones (which would correspond to the modern colors carbon black and ivory black respectively), and possibly white from chalk if that were readily available in the immediate environment. Unfortunately, those materials are not particularly archival, so little or no record remains of their use.

The first colors that we can know for certain were used extensively in prehistoric times are the ones that we now call Earth Pigments. Earth Pigments are generally a variety of brownish yellows and reds that are found naturally occurring in clay throughout most of the world. The color comes from the iron content in the clay which has oxidized over time (rusted in effect) to produce a certain color based on environmental factors in the area where the clay is found.

Collecting the pigment is fairly simple, one just has to find a deposit, dig up the earth and sift out the non-ferrous material. The remainder will be an earthy pigment that can be surprisingly intense in color. The pigment would then be mixed with a binder, probably either spit or animal fat back in the stone age, which could then be painted onto a surface. Earth Pigments are among the most stable colors that we know—even today—so the appearance of the paintings created long ago would not have changed much over the years. The cave paintings at Lascaux and other Paleolithic sites are a testament to the longevity of artworks made with Earth Pigments alone and have survived for 30,000 years or more. The caves at Lascaux had to be closed to the public because the moisture brought in by all the tourists was causing a mold to grow underneath the paintings, potentially destroying them if left unchecked, but that was more a function of the weak binder than a problem with the pigments!

The most common type of naturally occurring iron oxide is the pigment we refer to as an ochre. Ochre's come in many different color ranges, but the one we still use today is called Yellow Ochre, which is a brownish yellow with a green undertone. Yellow Ochre remains, after tens of thousands of years, one of the basic colors on every painter's palette! Ochre's also come in a variety of other shades — reds, gelds and even a violet hue — but deposits of those clays are much more rare. Red Ochre was a valued and sought after pigment in ancient times, possibly because of it's symbolic association with blood, and therefore life. Powdered Red Ochre pigment has been discovered in the burial sites of the Neanderthals in Europe, suggesting some sort of spiritual connection. Red Ochre and the other non-yellow shades of ochre have, in contemporary times, been largely replaced by synthetically manufactured iron oxides, usually given the names Red Oxide, Violet Oxide, etc., since the natural pigment is not that easy to come by and the oxidization process is relatively inexpensive. Naturally occurring Yellow Ochre, however, is still common enough to be found in just about every major brand of artist's paint.

The other types of Earth Pigment that are still in use today include the Siannas and the Umbers. Raw Sienna is a pigment that derives it's name from a type of iron oxide mined for many centuries near Siena, Italy. Similar to Yellow Ochre, but with greater transparency, Raw Sienna was an important part of the color palette for all of the Renaissance Masters and obtained a great reputation because of that. The reddish brown pigment, Burnt Sienna, is created by cooking Raw Sienna in an oven to produce the red mass tone and it is also a very important color in the palette of most painters even today. The veins of clay that produced the Raw Sienna pigments in Italy have been mostly used up at this point, but natural pigments with identical qualities have been found in nearby locations such as Sardinia and even in the Appalachian Mountains of the United States! Similarly, the pigment Raw Umber, a deep brown with greenish undertones that comes from a combination of iron and manganese oxides, became famous during the Renaissance when it was mined in the Italian region of Umbria, from which it derives it's name. Raw Umber can also be heated to create a variation with a reddish undertone, known as Burnt Umber, and both of these pigments also remain a standard in the palettes of contemporary painters.

So, the next time you dip your brush in an earthy color like Yellow Ochre or Raw Umber, you can feel the connection to artists back through the Renaissance and thousands of years more into the little known world of our prehistoric ancestors who used these exact same colors to give visual form to their imaginations just as you are doing today. A thought that is both humbling and uplifting all at once!

(Courtesy of the Binders Art Blog,
http://bindersart.blogspot.com/2010/08/
subject-of-art-9-history-of-colors.html.
Used by permission.)

To this point, James McNeil Whistler, one of the early American painters, has been reported[28] to have displayed a just completed painting to Mark Twain. This famous writer looked at the painting judiciously from a variety of angles and distances while Whistler was waiting impatiently for the verdict. Finally, Twain leaned forward and making an erasing gesture with his hand, said: "I would eradicate that cloud if I were you." Whistler cried out in agony: "Careful! The painting is still wet." "That's all right," said Twain coolly: "I am wearing gloves."

## The History of Colors: The Toxic and the Fugitive

Again, blogger Boccio teaches well on this topic:

We looked at Earth Pigments, which were readily available in the ground and needed only to be dug up, sifted for purity and mixed with the binder to create a variety of reds, yellows, and browns. However, these hardly represented the full range of colors found in nature and it became an obsession for artists, and the chemists who supplied them with new paint colors, to develop new pigments that had greater intensity and could cover the varieties of blues, greens and violets that were completely missing in the Earth Pigment range. Unfortunately, the vast majority of these pigments proved to be failures over the long term because they were either terribly toxic, resulting in a variety of neurological disorders or possibly even death to many artists over the centuries from over-exposure, or they were fugitive, which is a term that is used to denote a pigment whose color fades over time when exposed to light. It was not until the mid to late 19th century, with the advent of industrial manufacturing processes, that stable, reasonably safe pigments were developed to replace the more dangerous ones.

Let's take a look at a few of the most popular ones that had been used over time and see what they were eventually replaced with in the palette of colors that we have today!

## Toxic Pigments

Of all the most toxic pigments that were used in the history of painting, the most popular was definitely lead. Although we are most familiar with lead as a dark, almost black color that was used in pencils, through various chemical processes lead could be altered to create very bright, intense hues of white, yellow and red.

Up into the 19th century these were known by the names Flake White (also the Cremnitz White which is still made by Old Holland), Chrome Yellow and Chrome Red. Lead is, extremely poisonous and can be absorbed both by ingestion and through the skin, but in it's day it was both cheap and extremely durable, so it was often the choice not only for artists but for house painting and other large scale, outdoor applications.

Although true Chrome Yellows and Reds have disappeared entirely, Flake Whites can still be found on occasion and it is still considered by some artists to be far superior to the pigment that replaced it, Titanium White. Chrome Yellow and Chrome Red have been replaced by Cadmium Yellow and Cadmium Red respectively, which are still toxic pigments but far, far less so than their lead-based predecessors.

Unfortunately, we find that lead paint is still used indiscriminately in some parts of the world with no thought to public safety. In 2009 a scandal broke in which a variety of toys manufactured in China for sale in the United States were found to be coated in lead-based paints, resulting in a massive recall to prevent children from becoming sick.

Among the other very popular pigments that turned out to be deadly are Vermilion, a very bright red-orange pigment originally derived from the mineral cinnabar, but which was synthetically produced by alchemists in Europe as early as the 12th century. An important component of Vermilion is mercury, a highly toxic chemical that can be absorbed through the skin and should be avoided at all costs. In the contemporary palette, Vermilion has been replaced by Cadmium Red Light. Another pigment that was both well-used and dangerous was Emerald Green, popularly known as Paris Green in the 19th century, which was made from copper acetoarsenite, a variety of arsenic that was also used as rat poison! The symptoms of arsenic poisoning have led some researchers to conclude that the blindness that Claude Monet experienced towards the end of his life and the neurological disorder that resulted in seizures for Vincent Van Gogh may have been caused by arsenic exposure from the Paris Green they were using in their paintings!

Fortunately for us, Emerald Green has been replaced by the infinitely safer pigments Viridian and Phthalo Green.

## Fugitive Pigments

Fugitive pigments were far more common than the toxic ones, but for most of them there is little evidence remaining except for written accounts of their use, since they have all disappeared over the years. The civilizations of Ancient Greece and Egypt were colorful places, but little remains now besides the bare stone faces that have been denuded of their fragile paint layers. The only remains that we have are in places that were found to be airtight and dark: the tombs in Egypt and some of the rooms of houses in Pompeii and Herculaneum that were buried in the eruption of Vesuvius.

From those testaments we can see that there were a great variety of colors that were used by ancient artists and that most of them were fugitive and disappeared quickly in the light. Fugitive pigments are typically those that are produced from plant and animal sources and so they lack the durability of their mineral counterparts. Carmine, for example, is a crimson red color that was manufactured by boiling thousands of cochineals, a type of scale insect, and it was the primary source of crimson for both paint and dyes for hundreds of years until it was replaced by the modern colors Alizarin Crimson and Naphthol Crimson, both of which are still moderately fugitive, but much less so than the original. Likewise Tyrian Purple, which was the royal color of the Roman Emperors, was produced by rendering down a particular species of sea snail, requiring hundreds of them to be caught and processed andresulting in a pigment that faded rapidly, but no other source for violet was readily available until industrial manufacturing produced Manganese and Cobalt Violets and in the 20th century Dioxazine Purple became the standard.

Other popular colors that have not stood the test of time include Sap Green, originally made from the juice of buckthorn berries, which has now been replaced by a mixture of modern pigments. Indian Yellow, a bright yellow-orange, was originally produced by force-feeding cattle with mango leaves and then collecting their urine, which, when dried, resulted in intensely colored crystals that could be mixed into paint. Indigo, the color used to dye blue jeans today, is actually one of the oldest dye colors, having originated in India where the indigo plant is native and quickly spreading to Ancient Mesopotamia, Babylon, Greece and Rome. The synthetic replacement for the natural and fugitive Indigo was developed around 1865, after which use of the plant dye disappeared rapidly.

Through this survey of the failed pigments of previous eras, we can see how art and technology have advanced together, bringing us the paints we use today that are both safe and long-lasting.

(Courtesy of the Binders Art Blog,
http://bindersart.blogspot.com/2010/09/
subject-of-art-11-history-of-colors.html.
Used by permission.)

Turner, a famous early American painter, had himself bound to the mast of a boat he commissioned to go into a storm so that he could feel "what a storm looks like" so that he could paint it.[29] The French painter Degas considered paining as an "absolute necessity."[30] In 1878 American-born painter James M. Whistler, already famous for his work, sued art critic John Ruskin for 500 pounds for what Whistler considered over-the-top criticism that reached the level of libel.[31] To win his case, Ruskin's lawyer had to belittle Whistler's creativity by presenting a rather abstract painting in front of the jury, asking the painter how long it took to produce such a painting. "Most of a day," replied Whistler, which produced a sardonic question from the lawyer about the jury having to believe to justify being paid 500 pounds for less of a day of work? "Not at all," replied Whistler, "I am charging for the experience of a lifetime." He won the case but was awarded just one farthing in damages.

These anecdotes illustrate how it is difficult to quantify experience and creativity. One could spit on a canvas and call it "art." How are we to know what is art and what is not art? To answer this question, for instance, a very rich man without any formal education decided that he should find a very good painting for his living room[32] by shopping in an art gallery. The art dealer showed him an entirely black painting with a while dot in the lower left-hand corner. Astonished by this sight, the intended buyer asked how could that painting represent art, by being solidly black, to which the art dealer replied that the man should understand the symbolism behind the black representing the immense and limitless vastness of space, its coldness, emptiness, and horrible depths, while the white dot would represent the soul of a naked, lonely viewer completely frightened by that blackness. Impressed by this explanation, the rich man bought the painting for a considerable amount of money, explaining its significance to whoever would visit in his home. By doing this, he became known as a deeply knowledgeable art critic. Satisfied by this outcome, the man returned to the same art gallery where this time the dealer showed him a completely white canvass with two black dots in the lower right-hand corner. Asked about the significance of this painting, the dealer explained the whiteness as representing the deity with the two dots representing sinful man and woman humbly facing their own maker. The rich man considered the painting from various angles and eventually reached a negative conclusion, because: "With two dots, it becomes too busy."

## The History of Colors: Synthetics Rule!

Boccio's writings give us great insight into this vivid history and process:

> As shown above, the search for a stable, bright and affordable blue pigment led to the discovery (or re-discovery, considering Egyptian Blue) of the process of making synthetic pigments— let's take a look at a few of the most popular!

### Cobalt Blue

Governments in 19th century Europe sometimes took a very active interest in supporting the arts. For example, in 1804 Minister Chaptal of in France appointed several chemists to do research into the creation of new, more permanent colors. One of the results of this project was the discovery that the blue pigment in Smalt—the metal known as Cobalt—could be removed from the glass it was naturally found in when roasted in a furnace with alumina, resulting in a much more intense and very stable pigment which we now know as Cobalt Blue. This bright and very pure blue became an instant hit and found its way into the skies of paintings by Maxfield Parrish, Vincent van Gogh (who described it as a "divine color") and many others. With the success of Cobalt Blue, scientists altered the formula to produce many different colors from the original metal including yellows, greens and violets.

## Viridian

The very popular and important green pigment known as Viridian was developed by the famous color-maker Pannetier in 1838. This brilliant and lightfast pigment has a bluish undertone and a very fine transparency that makes it excellent for glazing. Viridian was produced by mixing Boric Acid with Potassium Bichromate and then soaking the resulting salt crystals in water, resulting in a fiery, gem-like green color. Viridian quickly replaced most other greens because of its permanence, but also because the other most popular pigment, Emerald Green, was extremely toxic as has been detailed in the earlier section.

## Cadmium

Cadmium Yellow, a very bright, opaque and permanent pigment, was first synthesized in 1820. The process involved mixing cadmium salts with a sulfide and heating, which would result in the intense yellow hue. Cadmium was, and still is, a very rare metal, so it was fairly expensive to obtain and remains one of the most costly types of pigments even today. In 1919 the process was altered by adding selenium to the formula which resulted in a bright red-orange pigment called Cadmium Red. Variations in the amount of selenium allowed a range of colors from orange to scarlet to red to maroon, all of which are beloved and much-used in contemporary art.

These inorganic synthetic pigments became widely distributed and accepted by the middle of the 19th century in Europe and, together with the invention of pre-packaged paint tubes, contributed directly to the accessibility of art materials to a much wider group of people than at any other time in history. Today, we take for granted that we can have a wide range of colors available at relatively low cost and already pre-mixed with oil, acrylic or watercolor mediums, and it's easy to forget that it was not that long ago that none of this existed!

The artists of the time took full advantage of the new colors and it was these techno-logical innovations that allowed the color explorations of Monet, Van Gogh, Seurat, Delaunay and many others to bloom and helped to launch what we now know as the Modern Art movement.

(Courtesy of the Binders Art Blog,
http://bindersart.blogspot.com/2010/09/
subject-of-art-13-history-of-colors.html.
Used by permission).

### The Organic Revolution!

Contrary to what we may associate with this subject, this final section on color is not about food, it's about the shift in modern times towards an organic way of thinking. Most of the pigments we've looked at in previous sections were inorganic, being derived from metals and minerals. Unfortunately, mining for these inorganic pigments is a labor and/or cost intensive process, so artists, alchemists and scientists from all different time periods have always been searching for better alternatives.

The solution, however, did not come about until relatively recently, when advances in organic chemistry made it possible to create whatever colors we desired from their component parts. After that, the spectrum of color exploded into a whole new rainbow of bright, lightfast variations and completed the range of hues that we are familiar with today and that you can find in the paint aisles in any Art store.

Organic pigments have always been known and used since humans began coloring things. In our previous explorations, we have touch upon a couple: Indigo, which is derived from plants, Tyrian Purple, which comes from an insect called the cochineal, and Indian Yellow, which is derived from the urine of cows who were fed a steady diet of mango leaves. There were many others in use for thousands of years as well, most prominently the root of the madder plant, which produces a bright crimson red color (which was the red used for centuries in the uniforms of British soldiers, the Redcoats!).

Without exception these pigments derived from plant and animal sources are quite unstable, being very likely to fade over short periods of time, so, while these natural organic pigments were often used by artists, if a suitable inorganic pigment became available that filled the same niche in the color wheel then the organic one would usually be dropped right away. Natural organic colors were most popular in the textile industry as ingredients for dyes, which makes more sense because one might expect clothing not to last for more than a few years of heavy use anyway, plus they could always be re-dyed at some point if desired (which is not a particularly easy thing do do with a painting!).

The aforementioned madder root became the first natural organic pigment to be replaced by a synthetic pigment, which we know today as Alizarin Crimson, in 1869. The chemical compound Anthracene was synthesized from coal-tar, a byproduct of the industrial production of coke, which was used as fuel for stoves and furnaces and for smelting iron. Once the chemical process for production of Alizarin Crimson was perfected, the madder root dye industry collapsed practically overnight, a sequence of events that would occur repeatedly as scientists discovered and developed synthetic versions of organic colors that were brighter, more durable and cost less to manufacture.

The original Alizarin Crimson pigment is still in use 150 years later, although its lightfastness rating is low compared to the colors that would be produced in later centuries. The newer versions are usually a mixture of two or more synthetic organic pigments labelled as Alizarin Permanent or Alizarin Crimson Hue.

The phenomenal advancements that occurred in pigments during the 20th century were largely the result of industrial manufacturing and the requirements of objects in everyday life to be brightly colored, with the application of those pigments filtering their way into the artist's palette after they had been thoroughly tested out in the world. The first leap forward occurred in the 1930's with the development of Phthalocyanine Blue, which was originally created as a more stable cyan color for the printing industry. The intensity and durability of Phthalo Blue made it suitable for all sorts of applications and sparked off a rush of research into pigments synthesized from the carbon molecules found in petroleum. The chemical structure of these synthetic organic pigments is similar to plastic, so as the plastics industry advanced, so too did the science of color production. Phthalo Blue was quickly followed by Phthalo Green, while new organic compounds helped to fill out the color spectrum. The automobile industry had a lot to do with the development of a wide range of colors, since car paint needs to be extremely durable and people like having cars that are bright and shiny. Synthetics like Quinacridone Red and Arylamide Yellow (also called Hansa Yellow), helped to fill that need.

From the point of view of fine artists, the color range was expanded tremendously, and furthermore, the synthetic organics are very pure, "clean" colors, with very little gray or brown undertones. A certain amount of "muddying up" the colors was found to be necessary to achieve a more natural look, since the real world actually has a whole lot of gray and brown in it! As these new pigments were initially being assimilated into the art materials industry, many paint producers felt that the chemical names of the pigments sounded entirely too scientific and intimidating, so Phthalocyanine Blue became Winsor Blue for the Winsor and Newton company, and Naphthol Red became Grumbacher Red for the Grumbacher company. It's worth noting that, at least in the United States, paint manufacturers are required to list the pigments used for a particular color on the paint tube or jar, so you can look there to see exactly which pigments are being used to create it.

So this is where we stand today! We've gone a long way from digging up red and yellow dirt, all the way to the modern organic chemist's laboratory, and it's unlikely to end there. Who knows what the future may hold?

(Courtesy of the Binders Art Blog,
http://bindersart.blogspot.com/2010/10/
subject-of-art-14-history-of-colors.html.
Used by permission.)

There is no way I can include all the many artists who contributed to the visual arts, such as painting, or the kinesthetic art, such as sculpture. However, I want to include the other Michelangelo, because his life represents an example of how one becomes a creative artist in spite of all odds.

## THE OTHER MICHELANGELO—THE GENIUS OF CARAVAGGIO

Boccio shows us how Caravaggio became great despite the obstacles:

Most of us are (or should be) familiar with the works of the famed and revered Renaissance master sculptor and painter,

Michelangelo di Buonarotti, and even the folks with no knowledge of art history at all will have heard of and perhaps seen photos of his most famous work—the frescoes on the ceiling of the Sistine Chapel. However, there is another Michelangelo, born into the next generation of Italians, who is much less well known, even though his influence would change the style and technique of much of European painting.[33]

This mysterious character was named Michelangelo Merisi da Caravaggio, typically known simply by his surname, Caravaggio, which also happened to be the name of the town in which he was born during the latter part of the 16th century. While the Michelangelo of Renaissance fame was a true giant in the art world whose uniqueness and genius could never be duplicated, Caravaggio developed ideas about painting that resonated with many of the artists of his day. His ideas inspired many to copy his techniques and spread his new style, which only continued to gain momentum through the centuries until the present day, where his influence can still be felt and seen in the work of contemporary realist artists.

Born in 1571 and being raised in the small town Caravaggio in the Lombardy region of Italy, Caravaggio lost both of his parents by the time he was thirteen. Fortunately, he had already demonstrated a talent for drawing and was taken in as an apprentice by a Milanese painter who had himself studied under Titian. From a young age he displayed a shockingly uncouth character that, from the point of view of our modern sensibilities, would seem to belie the evidence of deep sensitivity he displayed in his work. He was particularly prone to fighting and seems to have engaged in street brawls on a regular basis.

During one such incident in 1592, he appears to have wounded a police officer and was forced to flee from Milan, eventually ending up in Rome. In desperate straits, Caravaggio took a job as a painter of flowers and fruit for a factory-like workshop that churned out cheap paintings for the masses (perhaps like the 17th century equivalent of Thomas Kincaid?), which must have been a difficult time for someone with Caravaggio's genius and tempestuous personality! Nevertheless, it was during that time that he seems to have developed most of his major stylistic innovations and became prepared to strike out on his own as a working artist. He had become acquainted with several people who were able to help him become known in the vibrant art world of Rome and in 1594 he painted what is considered to be his first masterpiece, The Cardsharps, that immediately gained him renown among the critics and collectors. A flurry of brilliantly executed private commissions finally brought him to the attention of the Catholic Church, from which he gained the larger public commissions that cemented his reputation as a master to his contemporaries and to us as well.

Caravaggio's innovations in painting were threefold. The most obvious one is his intensified use of chiaroscuro—the transition from light to dark in a painting, which he brought to never before seen extremes. His paintings are dominated by the inky blackness of the background that give way suddenly and sharply to the brightest, most intense lightness of the foreground figures. Far from having a jarring effect on the senses, Caravaggio's technique was so highly refined that he could pull off these high contrasts in a way that seemed pleasing to the eye and had the effect of drawing one further into the complex psychological dramas that were depicted. The technique was so influential that it was given a name—tenebrism—and became a standard for many artists up into the present times.

Caravaggio was also known for eschewing the use of preparatory drawings, preferring instead to work out his compositions directly on the canvas and directly from the live models. Such practices were considered barbaric by the academic establishment at that time, but such criticisms had little effect on the headstrong painter and the immediacy of the technique was something that would be applauded by generations of future artists who came to value the spontaneity of the moment afforded by painting directly in that manner.

Lastly, and perhaps most controversially, Caravaggio was a deeply committed realist as was evident from the meticulous detail he put into all of his works. The stark realism of his style was greatly at odds with the mainstream of art at that time which preferred a classical idealism and was offended by Caravaggio's "warts and all" images, even of stories from the Bible. His realistic depictions of his subjects led to more than a few scandals that resulted in rejection of his work by the buyer, particularly in the case of the Church when in his paintings of the Madonna the features of known local courtesans (read prostitutes) could be recognized! But again, he persevered in spite of the criticism and rejection and that spirit of realism that he sparked would become a revolution in the 19th century, changing everything we know about art and opening the doors to Modernism.

Unfortunately, Caravaggio's tumultuous personal life continued to cause him great trouble. He was forced to leave Rome in 1606 after killing a man in a fight and fled to Naples and from there to the island of Malta where he was knighted. All along the way he kept on producing incredibly vibrant works and building up his reputation. But again, in 1608 he was arrested and imprisoned for brawling and was expelled from the Knights of Malta "as a foul and rotten member." Upon his release he moved to Sicily where he had friends and thrived again on his brilliant work. But he also made more than a few enemies, eventually driving him out of Sicily. Finally he hoped to return to Rome in 1610 to receive a pardon for his earlier crime from the reigning Pope who seemed to look upon him with favor. He never got that chance, however, as he passed away from a fever en route from Naples at the young age of 39.

After his death, some of the people who had been his rivals and detractors in life sought to discredit him and were largely successful. His name was, for hundreds of years, largely forgotten, even though the artists that he inspired carried on his ideas, giving birth to the great works of artists such as Rubens, Velazquez, Vermeer, Rembrandt, Courbet and Manet, just to name a few. It was not until the 1920's that art historians finally restored Caravaggio to his rightful place as a true master of Western art, bringing back some vestiges of honor to a man whose life had been ruled by so much chaos.

(Courtesy of the Binders Art Blog,
http://bindersart.blogspot.com/2010/08/
subject-of-art-10-other-michaelangelo.html.
Used by permission.)

From the realism of Caravaggio, we are now taking a bold step into abstract painting, bypassing a great deal of history that can be covered by many other sources.

## THE EXTREMES OF ABSTRACT EXPRESSIONISM

And here blogger Boccio shares history of the greats in abstract expressionism:

It took a long time for art made in the United States to gain recognition in the rest of the world. There were a few painters who made their mark early, Benjamin West and Thomas Eakins being good examples, but for the most part America was seen as provincial and it's artists lagged behind the pioneering work that was coming out of Europe.

The famed Armory Show in New York, 1913, which brought paintings and sculpture by some of Europe's most progressive modern artists, such as Picasso, Kandinsky, Matisse and many others marked a turning point as American artists discovered non-objective art and unfettered expression for the first time. Although the art culture in the United States had been very conservative up until that time, many artists embraced the new ideas they were exposed to and began to explore the as-yet-uncharted realms of Modern Art.

It took a couple of decades for the Americans to really catch up and they may not have if it hadn't been for the cataclysmic destruction of Europe that resulted from two World Wars. As Europe lay in ruins after World War II, the United States remained strong and stood ready to take the forefront, economically and culturally. In addition, there were a number of influential artists who had fled Germany, France and other countries to escape the clutches of Nazi oppression. These expatriates, most notably Hans Hoffman, settled in America and, besides creating and selling art, began to teach a new generation of American artists.

In the 1950's, those artists came of age and banded together to become known as Abstract Expressionists. Backed by rich, powerful patrons like the Rockefellers and the Guggenheims, these young artists became the new avant-garde, and their art and ideas would have a lasting impact on visual expression in both America and Europe. Though European concepts and teachers directly influenced Abstract Expressionism, it was the first truly American art movement that achieved prominence and respect throughout the Western world.

Among the most well-known and daring of the Abstract Expressionists are names like Jackson Pollock, Barnett Newman, Mark Rothko and Willem de Kooning. Pollock and Newman were born in America, while Rothko and de Kooning immigrated from Europe as children. These artists worked consistently on a monumental scale, creating huge canvases that would completely fill the visual field of a person standing before them, immersing that person in the environment of the painting. They all were also interested in bold, intense colors, often squeezed directly from the tube without mixing to maintain the saturation of the hue. However, there were major differences as well and, in many ways, the art of these painters might not seem to fit together into the same category.

On the one hand, painters like Pollock and de Kooning created works that used flowing, improvised brushstrokes to create a complex, organic composition that served to record the movements of the artist. While most of us are familiar with Jackson Pollock's method of working with long drips of fluid paint, it was actually a series of photographs by Hans Namuth of Pollock at work doing what seemed like a shamanic dance over a canvas laid flat on the floor, with drips of paint flying everywhere, that served to cement the reputation of the Abstract Expressionists in the mind of the art establishment. This was something new— a way of working that had never been accepted as art before.

On the other hand, painters like Newman and Rothko worked with geometric forms and flat planes of color to create more serene, meditative paintings. Barnett Newman systematically dissected the concept of visual composition until he arrived at the basic foundation: a ground, which was the entire canvas painted in one or two flat colors, and a figure, which was a vertical line (he called them "zips") painted in a different color that ran from the top to the bottom of the canvas. This primal figure-ground relationship served as a platform for Newman to experiment with color relationships and proportional compositions on the most basic level.

What united these two very different ideas about painting was the understanding that they were simply two different expressions, or perspectives, on the same thing: the relationship between the artist and the work of art. Abstract Expressionists helped to dissolve the traditional conceptions of what art is and how it should be made. Taking the paths of abstraction and expressionism to their fullest extremes, they brought Modern Art to its end, as it seemed there was nowhere else to go from there.

Inevitably they were eclipsed by the artists that were to come after them in the movement known as Postmodernism, which attempted (and is perhaps still attempting) to make sense of what happened during the first half of the 20th century and understand what the role of art is in society. What is your understanding of the role of art in our society? This is not an idle question. Without some understanding there is a limited amount of appreciation one can experience.

(Courtesy of the Binders Art Blog,<br>http://bindersart.blogspot.com/2010/06/<br>subject-of-art-7-drips-and-squares.html.<br>Used by permission.)

## POLLOCK'S TECHNIQUE IN THE TWENTY-FIRST CENTURY

Blogger Boccio continues here with insights into what some would call the greatest of modern artists:

Jackson Pollock became an icon of Modern Art in the 1950's by daring to break down the concept of painting to an apparently random looking assortment of drips and splatters on the canvas. A first glance at one of Mr. Pollock's paintings has often elicited the response "My kid can paint better than that!," but upon further reflection and by investigating his body of work, one can clearly see that there was much more going on than it seems on the surface and that what looked to be a simple, mindless way of putting paint on a canvas was in fact far more complex.

Although one painting by itself may not appear to make much sense, viewing several of Pollock's paintings in a row, or better yet being surrounded by them in an exhibition, one can see the repetitive motifs that run through them—the broad arcs of paint that trace the extent of his arm's reach or the sinuous, vine-like lines that echo his signature flick of fluid paint off of the brush. If one chooses to step just a little bit further into Pollock's world, it becomes clear that there was a great deal of forethought and intention behind every mark and that the use of his controversial technique was another way to break down the barriers of the viewers preconceptions about what constitutes a works of art.

Jackson Pollock's paintings began with a primed, but unstretched, canvas laid out on the floor. The fact that the canvas was not on a frame was important since the scale of the work was usually very large, so it would be necessary for him to actually step on the canvas at certain times while painting. The brushes that Pollock favored were old house painting brushes that had hardened with dried paint until they became totally stiff. These afforded him the grip and balance of a brush, while allowing for a hard end like a stick that enabled greater control over the paint as it fell off the brush. Finally, his paint had to be thinned to just the right consistency to allow it to drip and flow freely, but still be thick enough to be easily guided by his hand and to leave coherent lines on the canvas. For most of his career, he used traditional oil paints that were thinned with the right amount of turpentine, but by the height of his output he was already experimenting with other mediums, particularly enamel paints that were usually used for house painting or industrial purposes. He liked the enamels because they were just the right consistency for his dripping and pouring technique right out of the can, so no thinning was needed, plus he took an interest in colors that had a metallic sheen, that were not available as pigments for oil paint at that time. Unfortunately, oil paints and enamels don't mix together, which is one of several reasons why Pollock's paintings are very fragile and difficult to maintain. There is actually a group of conservators whose entire job is to work on Pollock's paintings and make sure they stay in one piece! The materials of his time just weren't up to the standards that he needed to fulfill his visions.

If Jackson Pollock were alive and working today, the story would be quite different! Fluid acrylic paints would have provided much of the paint consistency he was looking for, premixed into the full spectrum of colors required by fine artists and including a range of metallic colors. His techniques made no use of blending colors, so the switch from oil to acrylic paint would most likely have been very natural for him. In addition, there are now a couple of acrylic mediums that can be added to the paint that are specifically designed to create spectacular dripping effects, inspired by Pollock's example!

Tar Gel by Golden and String Gel by Liquitex are essentially two versions of a medium that, when mixed with fluid acrylics, gives a honey-like consistency to the paints. After adding the gel to the paint and mixing thoroughly, one should wait about ten minutes or so to let the air bubbles rise up and out before using it. Then, with a palette knife, or perhaps Pollock's favorite—the stiff, paint-hardened brush, you can scoop up some of the mixture and let it drip off to create long lines. Golden claims their Tar Gel has sufficient consistency to hold together in a solid line that reaches three stories! Both the Tar and String Gels are thick enough to allow for an unprecedented level of control when dripping, so the possibilities for intentional technique become much greater.

Liquitex has recently created another product called Pouring Medium which can, as the name suggests, allow the fluid acrylics to be poured more easily onto the canvas. Like the Tar and String Gels, color should be mixed into the medium first and then it should be left for a few minutes to allow the air to escape. The special qualities of the Pouring Medium will become more apparent as it hits the surface of the canvas, because the medium has been formulated to mix colors in a very special way. When one color mixed with Pouring Medium is dripped over another color mixed with Pouring Medium, the two colors will puddle together and form all sorts of organic lines and flowing shapes, an effect which is known as marbling.

These are just a few examples of the ways in which the work of a pioneering artist can help the evolution of art as a whole, opening up new techniques and methods of expression that we can all enjoy. Thank you Mr. Pollock!

(Courtesy of the Binders Art Blog,
http://bindersart.blogspot.com/2010/10/
tips-tricks-13-drips-splatters-pollocks.html.
Used by permission.)

An example of abstract painting is shown in Figure 1.1 by my friend Dr. Max North, who was using it as a way of practicing various colors but did not consider it a painting per se until I saw it in his studio. When I told him how much I liked it, he gave it to me on the spot and it now adorns one wall of my office where I observe it every day with a great deal of pleasure. Don't ask me why but I like it.

## COLLAGE: THE ORIGINS OF A MODERN ART EXPRESSION

*Collage* is a French word that means attaching and gluing various separate fragments, usually flat, to create an entire composition that is visually pleasing (to most viewers). Objects to be glued together can be almost anything from newspaper clippings to pieces of driftwood. All one needs is a pair of scissors and a vast collection of magazines to select different colors and sources. This technique has been

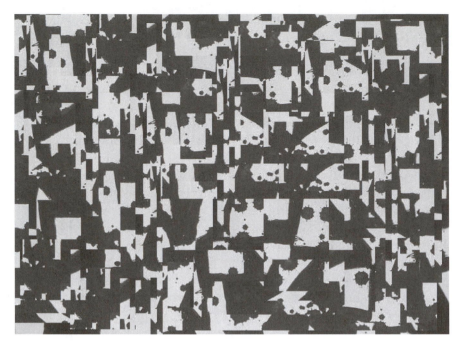

**Figure 1.1**   Example of an abstract painting by Dr. Max North: http://www
.drnorth.net/max/album.htm.

found in China and Japan as well as in Europe in the Middle Ages.
With the advent of the Modern Art movement at the beginning of the
twentieth century, collage as we know it today has come of age. Credits
for this kind of art expression have been given usually to Pablo Picasso
and especially to Georges Braques, founders of the art movement known
as Cubism. The basic notion behind Cubism was to shatter the heretofore
common view of a realistic image as the true expression of art. Painting
was no longer attempting to reproduce reality as we see. This function
can be taken over easily by the advent of photography. Therefore, the
purpose of painting no longer conformed to reproduce reality but to
reproduce parts of that reality in its components parts put together for
maximum visual impact completely independent from reality. Collage
was also a foundational component of the Dada and Surrealistic movements that greatly appreciated the value of randomness and the potential that can be found in integrating different elements into a whole.

What happens when the visual aspects of collage are connected to
its verbal aspects? This question is answered by the notions about this
connection developed by Dr. Laura G. Sweeney.

**The Connection between Visual and Verbal Arts and Writing\***

When we think of visual arts or writing, we tend to envision these two activities as being separate domains, but if the truth be told, there are many reasons why these activities are connected. Not only are visual arts and writing linked, but learning about each domain enhances the other. For example, writers must envision the setting in which their fiction or nonfiction takes place. Thus, developing drawing skills or even layout drawing benefits the writer who plans his or her scenes carefully. Writing down one's ideas in the form of a poem or narrative enables visual artists to have a clear idea of what they wish to achieve before proceeding to manipulate their medium. Additionally, some writers and visual artists opt to combine the two forms, such as when they create a collage and intersperse words throughout the design.

If you are a writer who has not utilized drawing in the past, you will definitely benefit from drawing shapes, shading, and coloring in forms to get a better idea of the sensory details you wish to depict. Take this one step further, and you will collect textures, cut them into shapes, and glue them into a collage representing the tactile details of your writing. Your writing will undoubtedly benefit from visual planning. With a little practice, you may even decide to illustrate portions of your own book.

Many a visual artist that I have known over the years has dabbled with poetry writing or with prose poetry. Many were not well-known or published poets, but they desired to express those feelings depicted in visual arts through words. Counting syllables and meter of lines puts restrictions on the visual artists' linguistic expression; however, this process of employing meter results in the production of imagery that one would not have otherwise depicted either verbally or visually. On the other hand, visual artists may employ free verse or prose poetry to express themselves without limitations. For those who find they take poetry seriously, editing it many times will be a necessity.

At Avant Garde Books we explore the combination of poetry and visual arts as a unified art form. For instance, poets illustrate their own poems, and visual artists write poems to further express the thoughts underlying their art. Between the two forms, symbolism remains a key unifier. Bits and pieces of papers are ripped and cut to form poems out of found imagery while rhythmic lines are drawn on these collages to represent the lyricism of poetry. Combined art and writing, from poems to non-fiction, may be expressed with an entire spectrum of color or in an array of gray values depending upon what one wishes to achieve. Additionally, creators often utilize software technology available to them.

As we can see, writing and visual arts enhance one another in many ways and may be employed as a team to bring about original themes. One should not be shy about integrating these two art forms in the same context. Perhaps, one way to begin doing this would be to take a quill pen and dip it in black ink, create a free-flowing ink drawing of basic shapes and rhythmical line while inserting various words that come to your mind within the drawing. Do not be afraid to take chances because the best art originates from free and spontaneous experimentation.

This comment was contributed by Laura G. Sweeney*, Ed.D. Here are some online answers to her comment published in a blog.

**Rebecca:**  I knew my graphic design background would come in handy! I love drawing—I haven't done anything lately—too much writing to do.

**Ethel:**  I find that drawing, painting with oil pastels, surrounding oneself with colors and textures helps a person to be creative, as well as arrive at solutions to problems. The images evoke stories that are often deeply submerged in the subconscious. When we can express them, they help to heal and move us forward. Also, a vehicle for creativity and healing is the use of movement and music.

**Delores:**  Thank you for this, Laura Gael. My strength is my writing. I don't have a lick of fine arts skill, but for some reason I keep trying. Your insights into the correlation between the two is illuminating, and now I feel inspired to keep at it. Knowing that my attempts to put shapes, textures and colors into context to fuel my writing gives me great satisfaction.

**Ellen:**  Anybody who is truly interested in the link between poetry and the visual arts should study the New York School. Frank O'Hara and James Scheyler worked at MOMA; John Ashbury, Barbara Guest and Schuyler were all critics for Art News. Abstract Expression art was a major influence, and many of the poets had deep artistic and personal ties with the most important painters of the time, including Pollack and DeKooning. Line breaks in modernist poetry are profoundly influenced by visual graphics, and are an important way for poets to express themselves graphically. I don't happen to agree with Dr. Sweeney that it's always fruitful for poets to try drawing or vice versa, but there are people who are talented in both arenas. I do believe that it's always fruitful for creative people to look for new ways to express their creativity.

## Summary Comment by Dr. Laura G. Sweeney

"After reading everyone's comments today, I thought about SYNES-THESIA, a synthesis of art modalities, when one stimulus has an influence upon another, whether it be visual art and writing or music and color selection. Some colors evoke unusual thoughts and so on. . . . I'm not talented at dance or anything kinesthetic for that matter, but some activity in a domain in which I am not proficient seems to stimulate creation—not to mention mathematics." Another example of how visual and verbal arts can be combined in visible in a production by Dr. Sweeney where poetry and painting are combined in a collage with letters taken from newspaper (see Figure 1.2 and poem that follows).

### CONSTRUCTIVIST VISION

Fast and fresh vision
facing resurgent urgency
due to the first taste of summer.
You can't pass up
the unrestrained, Constructivist paradigm,
nature's affirmation of life,
fast and fresh, raising the day
with expansive revisions.

Impulsive decisions about ideas newly arisen
in paper collage reflect indecision,
but by intent they are driven to rebirth.

Research shows Constructivists reject derision
of ideas in amusing daydreams.
Rather, expressions cut out of papers
grow into unrestrained diagrams,
where ingenuity first began
growth and appealed to outer vision.
Words tossed across the paper for self-actualization

**Figure 1.2**   Example of a collage and matching poetry by Dr. Laura G. Sweney: http://www.avantgardebook.com.

> in the colorful mosaic-collage
> reinforce budding, communicative bricolage.

By Dr. Laura Gail Sweeney from the New Dadaist Collage Poetry
Chapbook (http://poetryartandstories.blogspot.com/)

At the bottom of this chapter, the basic channel to enjoy arts is a good eyesight. Vision allows us to view and to observe artistic production and reading is how we can become aware of masterpieces as well as heroes and heroines. As Bryant and Veroff[34] in their book on savoring reviewed in greater detail in Chapter 8 of this volume, suggested that "reading remains one of the most reliable activities for savoring artistic expression" (p. 60).

## ART AS THERAPY

The fact that art can be used as one of the many forms of therapy[35] illustrates how important art appreciation can become once we start producing something. I remember when I was a single young man in Greenville, North Carolina, as a distraction from my first job as a clinical psychologist at the Pitt County Health Department and teaching at the Extension Division of what was then East Carolina College (now University), I participated in the local theater group (as the Greek landlord in *My Sister Eileen* and the Italian smuggler in Agatha Christie's *Three Blind Mice*). I took also a course in pottery. At the end of the course, we were supposed to show off our masterpieces for a public exposition. My work was so limited and poor that my classmates donated some of their pieces to me to make sure I would not be ashamed of my work (and bring shame to them!).

Nonetheless, the relationship between health and the arts has been reaffirmed and validated by the recent publication of a journal on *Arts & Health: An International Journal for Research, Policy and Practice*, It is published by Routledge of New York in collaboration with the Society for the Arts in Healthcare. Society members receive the journal as a membership benefit. There are other journals that publish research and practice about the use of art as a form of therapy, as the *Creative Art Therapies Journal, Body Movement and Dance in Psychotherapy, Nordic Journal of Music Therapy, Journal of Creativity in Mental Health, International Journal of Art Therapy: Inscape,* and *Journal of Poetry Therapy,* all published by Routledge. By the same token, movies can be used to understand psychopathology, that is, mental illness. Whether they can be used to treat mental illness is another questionable story.

More specifically, Johnson and Stanley[36] reported on a VicHealth-funded research project that aims to enhance the knowledge of community arts, a field of increasing importance in mental health promotion. The research explores social capital and social inclusion, which underpin the VicHealth Mental Health Promotion Framework.[37] The framework seeks intermediate outcomes in attainment of the social determinants of mental health, defined as social inclusion, freedom from discrimination and violence, and access to economic and social resources. This article reports on early findings as measured by the instrument Most Significant Change in the evaluation of the community arts project, The Torch Project. Findings include the development of the social networks of participants and of trust and reciprocity between members of the project group.

Self-awareness, self-expression, constructive behavior, and communication skills are fundamental to successful behavioral change for inmates in correctional institutions. Without interventions to promote such change, most treatment programs prove to be unsuccessful. The arts have gained increased attention as being effective tools for overcoming obstacles to, and promoting, learning and self-awareness. This article will introduce what has been, and will be, an effective model to bring about healthy change in those who participate. Much of the proposed program will rely on the visual and expressive arts. The first part of this article will explain why introducing the arts is not only desirable, but natural given the setting, and inmates' propensity for creative expression. The next part will present the program's predecessors and the development of the Interdisciplinary Wellness Arts Education (IWAE) program. The article will conclude with a proposed application of this model in a juvenile detention facility in rural Florida.[38]

Engaging people in treatment is a primary concern at a community outpatient day treatment program serving 280 adults with severe mental illness and chemical dependencies. Goals include stabilizing one's life to remain out of the hospital and gaining skills to live more independently. The immediate focus is directed toward monitored medications and attendance at the weekday program that provides breakfast, lunch, and a variety of educational and therapeutic groups and activities. The art therapy program consists of two weekly groups, a gallery for exhibiting client artwork, and a quarterly newsletter for sharing art and writing produced by the community. Case material from a 36-year-old patient with schizophrenia in the program is also presented.[39]

Reynolds[40] reviewed

previous research into the meanings of textile art making for people living with long-term illness. Qualitative accounts of the creative process suggest that textile art making is a multi-dimensional experience. Some practitioners regard textile artwork as a means of coping with discomfort and other symptoms. For a minority, it enables expressions of anxiety and feelings about loss. Nevertheless, participants place more emphasis on the role of textile art making in rebuilding a satisfactory identity and restoring autonomy and quality to life. It fills occupational voids following early retirement and enables social contacts. Textile artwork also stimulates learning and personal development. Reynolds analysed qualitative accounts from seven participants to identify whether textile art making has any distinctive experiential qualities. As a creative occupation, it seems to be quite distinctive in being readily accessible even to those who do not consider themselves as artistic. Further enquiry into the distinctive influences of different creative occupations upon well-being is recommended.

Reynolds, Vivat, and Prior[41] attempted to

understand the meanings of art-making among a group of women living with the occupational constraints and stigma of physical diseases. The study explored their initial motives for art-making, and then examined how art-making had subsequently influenced their subjective well-being. Ten women with a physical disease were interviewed; three provided lengthy written accounts to the interview questions. These researchers found that illness had resulted in devastating occupational and role loss. Participants took many years to make positive lifestyle changes. Art-making was typically discovered once participants had accepted the long-term nature of the disease, accommodated to illness, and rep-rioritized occupations. Several factors then attracted participants specifically to art-making. It was perceived as manageable within the constraints of ill-health. Once established as a leisure activity, art-making increased subjective well-being mainly through providing increased satisfaction in daily life, positive self-image, hope, and contact with the outside world. Conclusions: Creative art-making occurs as part of a broader acceptance and adjustment process to physical disease, and allows some psychological escape from a circumscribed life world.

Soden[42] in a doctoral dissertation challenged

the accepted notion of art-making as goal-oriented and com-modified. By contrast, spontaneous image-making, coupled with reflection on the art product, is presented as a process-oriented activity and viable means to self-discovery, personal growth and health. The author examined two case studies within the context of Insight Imagery, an approach to art-making that involves direct expression and image-contemplation in the com-pany of an empathic other. Through them, the reader is witness to a personal transformation experienced by the participants and the facilitator. As well, ideas in arts education, psychology, holistic learning, art therapy and wellness, as related to the topic, come under review. Spontaneous art-making as a wellness vehicle within the general population is strongly urged. Unless we begin to see image-making as a normal, everyday, necessary personal expression, a language akin to verbalization, we are limiting our life experience. The unfortunate consequences of ignoring our inner life include emotional and spiritual fragmen-tation, and a disconnection and lack of purpose in an increasingly alienated world. . . . Insight Imagery becomes a fundamental path to emotional, psychological and spiritual "fitness" for the future.

## CONCLUSION

This chapter has tried not to repeat information easily available in any public or private library or on the Internet. Therefore, it did not follow a linear sequence, with considerable gaps in its progression, especially in its jarred historical perspective. This means that there was little sequence in the various topics covered in this chapter, except the history of color. There is no way all the arts can be included in this chapter except as lists for masterpieces, heroes, heroines, and nothing else. I just hope the reader was not bored by it.

## EXERCISE NO. 1

From the two lists of arts presented at the beginning of this chapter rank-order arts according to the one art you enjoy the most to the one you enjoy the least. Please give one or more reasons why you ranked-ordered these arts the way you did.

# 2

# Avocations: Doing Whatever You Like When You Want To

Avocations or hobbies are completely voluntary activities. Nobody is pointing or putting a gun to our head to make us do them. Some avocations, such a volunteering, prolong lives.[1] As shown in a great deal of evidence in the literature, hobbies and avocations in general tend to improve the quality of life.[2] The variety of avocations is large but direct and indirect references to physical and mental health will be considered. Unfortunately, I did not find any entries for hobbies in either Azinov[3] or Fuller.[4] Therefore, I will have to rely on personal experience, which is quite limited as far as hobbies are concerned (collecting art stamps) but extensive in other sources of pleasure in most chapters, including play and exercise (see Chapter 6 of this volume). What do we do with our leisure time if and when we have it?

Through history and religions there has always been an emphasis on "taking care of one self" in surplus, discretionary time, that is, leisure.[5] This is why leisure means whatever extra, discretionary time we have to choose what to do, including doing nothing except watching television, which is next to nothing. Leisure, therefore, can be used to devalue self, spending time in a bar getting drunk or doing it by ourselves in the privacy of our homes, or watching TV aimlessly or cruising on the Internet trying to find something juicy and exciting. Leisure, on the other hand, can be used to enhance self and improve one's view of oneself.

A great deal of our choices about avocations depend on our feelings and emotions, that is, moods. Clearly we might not be interested in doing something unless it improves our mood.

There are many ways to spend our leisure time, passively or actively, constructively or destructively, by ourselves or with others. Hobbies, therefore, represent how we use our leisure time actively doing or producing something productive (sorry, but watching TV won't cut it!), solitarily or socially. Play is such an important hobby that an entire chapter (Chapter 6 in this volume) is devoted to it. Consequently, we will need to expand on leisure without play and consider other alternatives to play.

## THE ADVANTAGES OF HOBBIES

There are at least nine advances of hobbies to the extent that they are active and constructive.[6]

1. Improvement in body growth, greater coordination of motor or movement-oriented activities, such as sports or just regular exercise. If a hobby requires passive acquisition of information, such as reading, it might help brain functions as well. However, active and interactive reading as in following written instructions to develop a piece of wood or construct anything, including painting (as discussed in Chapter 1 of this volume), would ensure a more lasting hard-wiring of brain functions than just passive reading.

2. Camping or outdoor recreation that requires active moving out of one's house even for just weekends, such as hiking. For instance, my good friends Charlotte and Rubin Battino, now well-retired, like to travel to places where they can hike, be they the Appalachians or the Rockies or mountains in the South Island of New Zealand.

3. Active entertaining that requires cooking, organizing, and preparing food and recreations for friends. For instance, Bess (Mrs. L'Abate to you) and I, when we were younger and more energetic, used to celebrate February 17 as the Independence Celebration for Waldenses (or Waldensians), when the King of Savoy in 1848 granted us freedom to cross a river in Piedmont that allowed proselytizing in the rest of Italy. Years ago, Bess cooked for a great many guests who helped us celebrate this special occasion paired with little Italian flags to put on one's lapel. We had to give up this celebration as we became older and handicapped. However, I have been able to be promoted from helper

first class (*sguattero* in Italian) to beginning cook with the help, directions, instructions, and suggestions from Bess. Fortunately, I have still lot to learn in this newly acquired hobby, apparently following in the footsteps traced by my father (see Chapter 4 in this volume).

4. The number of simple activities one can indulge in is practically infinite, as drawing and painting (as discussed in Chapter 1 of this volume), doing many crafts, including a simple activity as organizing a photo album for no special reason or for a special occasion.

5. Now one no longer needs to read. One can listen to tapes, CDs, and attend plays and movies. My most favorite hobby when I go to bed at night is reading an interesting (usually professional or scientific) book while listening to music from the Atlanta Classical Music Station (WABE). Years ago, when I thought I had plenty of time, I used to read all the possible spy books by LeCarre and similar others, until I got tired of all the conspiracies that no longer appealed to me as much as professsional and scientific books. Who needs to read about conspiracy theories anymore? All we have to do is to listen to crazy conspiracy theories spawned by our own in-grown domestic Taliban and Al-Queda right-wing hate groups, militias, and so-called patriots. These groups need those theories without evidence whatever to justify their existence. Furthermore, with aging, my time perspective has become shorter and shorter and I have to use my time more usefully than read about conspiracy or spy stories, or listen to them.

6. Attending lectures or events related to museums, special places, special occasions, or walk to see a garden. When we were young enough to travel OPM on Other People Money or on our own money, Bess and I loved to see the beautiful gardens in Vancouver and Vancouver Island in British Columbia, as well as those in Mobile, Alabama.

7. Practicing and playing music, either by oneself or with others, represents one of the most select and highest level of leisure-time activity. Listening to music can be just as enjoyable.

8. Starting or being part of a reading club would be just as important as practicing on and playing a musical instrument.

9. As mentioned from the outset of this chapter, volunteering is one way to prolong one's life.[7]

Can you think of anything else that was left out from this list? All I can say is that leisure is just as important as work. Actually, I would argue that having something positive to do in our leisure is really more important than work. What are we going to do and how are we going to spend our time once we retire from work?

## COLLECTING AS A HOBBY

Hobbies can become obsessions and in some exceptions magnificent obsessions that replenish many museums in the United States. For instance, Bridget Booher, in *Duke Magazine*,[8] describes how one wealthy Duke alumnus, David M. Rubinstein, at an auction bought the last remaining copy of the 1297 Magna Carta in U.S. soil for $21.3 million. This valued document became part of Rubinstein's collection of seminal historical documents. In 2008, for instance, he bought a rare 1823 copy of the Declaration of Independence now on permanent loan with the U.S. State Department. These philanthropic impulses spring from a deep sense of patriotism and profound gratitude for how Rubinstein started from blue-collar beginnings in Baltimore to attending Duke on an academic scholarship and eventually succeeding in the upper echelons of the international business world.

Another example of a collector given by Booher is Blake Byrne in talking about his recent acquisition of a latest piece of contemporary art that includes works by artists such as Jasper Jones, Sol LeWitt, ED Ruscha, and Claes Oldenburg, among many others. He described collecting as a form of energizing that he did not find anywhere else.

Another type of more active collecting is producing a garden from nothing else on the ground. Nancy Sanders-Goodwin,[9] for instance, transformed her 61-acre property in Hillsborough, North Carolina, into a series of gardens that attracts horticulturists and gardeners from around the world. Eventually she had to build a deer-proof fence around the whole garden to keep animals from intruding and destroying some of the interesting plants and beautiful flowers she planted over the years.

As I said earlier in this chapter, I used to collect stamps during my adolescence but I had to give my collection away once I moved to the United States. Since I married I did start to collect only art stamps from all over the world. Eventually I plan to trade the generic stamps just for art stamps that I have collected over the years but not yet catalogued. I am reserving that chore to when I really retire and no longer will read professional or scientific books, but I do not know when I will do that.

## RESEARCH TO SUPPORT AVOCATIONS (HOBBIES)

Interestingly enough, a great deal of the research about hobbies is linked to subjective well-being (SWB) already reviewed in the Introduction of this volume. For instance, quite ahead of his time, Beiser[10] reported a six-year study of 112 rural Canadian residents that examined the formulation of the process through which psychological, that is, SWB, is maintained. Evidence is presented that at least three affects may take part in this process: negative affect, positive sense of involvement, and long-term satisfaction. Different patterns of association were demonstrated between these affects and variables such as social participation, cultivation of hobbies, planfulness, emotional reactivity, physical health, and expert ratings of psychiatric disorder. It was suggested that these associations demonstrate the heuristic value in attempting to conceptualize and measure the dimensions of psychological WB, rather than assuming that WB can be considered as a one-dimensional, global construct.

Dik and Hansen[11] described the relationship between interests and WB by conceptualizing interest as both an emotional state and a stable disposition. First, interest is explored as a distinct emotion or affective state, itself a form of WB that also leads to other forms of WB by facilitating the development of diverse life experiences and competencies. Next, the theoretical linkage between affective interest and stable, enduring interests (or what interest inventories measure) is summarized. Finally, evidence suggesting that interests predict WB in the domains of work and leisure is reviewed. Part of living the good life, the authors conclude, means living the *interested* life.

Meir, Melamed and Abu-Freha[12] examined the interrelationship among three aspects of congruence (vocational, avocational, and skill utilization) and their relationship to several well-being (WB) measures (occupational satisfaction, job satisfaction, work satisfaction, anxiety, burnout, somatic complaints, and self-esteem). This study extended a previous study hypothesizing that (1) the three congruence aspects were not inter-related and (2) each of them was related to WB. Participants in the previous study (74 Jewish female teachers) were compared with 51 female and 66 male Arab Bedouin teachers in Israel. Both hypotheses were confirmed on both samples, excluding avocational congruence among the Bedouins.

According to Coster and Schwebel[13] experienced professional psychologists identified factors that contributed to their ability to function well in Study 1, through interviews with six well-functioning psychologists, and in Study 2, through questionnaire responses from 339 randomly selected licensed psychologists. Collectively they highlighted self-awareness and monitoring; support from peers, spouses, friends, mentors, therapists, and supervisors; values; and a balanced life, including vacations and other stress-reducers. Discussion focuses on stress-management enhancers to maintain well-functioning, especially at times of deep and pervasive change, like the present and the foreseeable future.

Heintzman[14] attempted to develop a model of leisure and spiritual well-being and to investigate, from a social science perspective, the relationships between various dimensions of leisure style (activity, motivation, setting, and time) and spiritual well-being, as well as the processes linking leisure and spiritual well-being. Study 1 involved secondary analysis of data from the 1996 Ontario Parks Camper Survey, which asked a question concerning the degree to which introspection/spirituality added to satisfaction with the park experience. It was found that more natural settings, participation in nature-oriented activities, and being alone in these settings and activities were more likely to be associated with introspection/spirituality adding to the satisfaction with the park experience. Study 2, in-depth interviews with eight people who had an expressed interest in spirituality, explored the relationship between leisure and spiritual well-being. There was unanimous agreement that participants associated their leisure activities and experiences with their spiritual well-being. Participants saw leisure as providing the time and space for spiritual well-being. An attitude of openness, balance in life, nature settings, settings of personal or human history, settings of quiet, solitude and silence, and "true to self" activities were all conducive to spiritual well-being while busyness, noisy settings and activities, and incongruent activities were detrimental to spiritual well-being.

Study 3 was a survey (n = 248) that explored the relationships between the various dimensions of leisure style and spiritual well-being, and the processes linking them. There were significant relationships between spiritual well-being and the following leisure style components: personal development activities, cultural activities, outdoor activities, hobbies, overall leisure activity participation, intellectual motivations, stimulus-avoidance motivations, overall leisure motivation, leisure settings of quiet urban recreation areas and one's own home, and solitary leisure activity participation. Statistical step-wise regression analyses showed that *participation in personal development activities* was the best predictor of spiritual well-being, followed by stimulus-avoidance motivations and a setting of one's own home. Through cluster analysis (another statistical method), it was discovered that a leisure style of low leisure activity participation and low leisure motivation (Mass Media Type) was associated with lower spiritual well-being. A "Sports/Social/Media" leisure style, characterized by stimulus seeking, was associated with a moderate level of spiritual well-being. More than one type of leisure style ("Personal Development" and "Overall Active") was associated with higher levels of spiritual well-being. A Leisure-Spiritual Processes (LSP) Scale, developed from the literature review and findings of the first two studies, examined the 12 processes (grounding, working through, time and space, sacralization, attitude, busyness, being away, nature, sense of place, fascination, compatibility, and repression) hypothesized to link leisure with spiritual well-being.

A statistical procedure called Factor Analysis of the LSP Scale suggested a three factor solution. These factors were labeled SACRALIZATION (leisure sensitizes one to the spiritual), PLACE (setting factors where leisure is occurring), and REPRESSION (leisure represses the spiritual tendency of a person). Another statistical procedure called Path Analysis suggested a series of models that linked leisure style components directly and indirectly through the leisure-spiritual processes, from the behavioral to spiritual well-being both directly and indirectly related to subjective spiritual well-being. In summary, these findings suggested that the leisure style components of time, activity, motivation, and setting, both individually and through the interplay of all the components, have the potential to, either directly or indirectly, through the processes of SACRALIZATION, PLACE, and REPRESSION, enhance or detract from spiritual well-being. This topic will be discussed further in Chapter 7 of this volume.

## CONCLUSION

This might well be the shortest chapter in the whole volume. However, the list of avocations and hobbies we can indulge in is practically limitless.

**EXERCISE NO. 2**

List and then rank-order avocations or hobbies according to those you enjoy the most to those you enjoy the least. If you do have hobbies or interests, please give one or more reasons why you ranked-ordered those hobbies the way you did. If you do not have any hobbies or interests outside of your job or work, ask yourself why, write your answer, and discuss it with whoever you consider a friend.

# 3

# Being, Doing, and Having:
# The Triangle of Life

In this chapter I plan to distinguish among whatever is exchanged among human beings, that is, the modalities of being or presence that includes the bestowal of importance and sharing of intimacy, from doing or performance, such as proffering and receiving information and services, and having or production, such as possessions, things, and money. These modalities of exchange are helpful because they have been already covered in Chapters 1 and 2 of this volume and will be covered in the remaining chapters of this volume. These sources of pleasures are reciprocal to the extent that involves love and intimacy in being present versus exchanges that are based on possibly non-reciprocal doing or having. In being present is where esthetic and spiritual pleasures may more likely occur, even though there may other pleasures where spirituality may occur, as discussed in other chapters of this volume, and discussed in greater detail in Chapter 8 of this volume.

Ultimately, what do we exchange and share continuously among intimates and non-intimates, all the time of our lives? To survive as well as to enjoy we continuously exchange with others, activities and possessions according to these three modalities: being, doing, and having. These modalities are the major sources of pleasure and displeasure and each, as we shall see throughout this chapter, is composed of two resources. The six resources are necessary whether we choose to live a pleasurable or an unpleasurable life.[1] The choice of how to live our lives is entirely ours and we cannot make others tell us how we can or should do it.

## BEING = PRESENCE

At first blush, being may seem an abstract, almost strange, and ephemeral notion, hard to understand, reach, and to obtain throughout the course of our lives. Especially when we equate being with presence, we add one more abstract word that may confuse us. On the contrary, *being present* consists of two clear, easy to define and easy to observe concrete resources we exchange mostly with intimates and non-intimate. Some people choose to exchange them with pets.[2]

### Importance

Importance is how we feel and think we are worth as individuals in our own rights, regardless of our performance, production, and problem-solving. Synonymous terms for this resource in addition to *self-worth* have been *self-esteem* and *self-regard*. Especially in the past a frequently used and even enthusiastically fashionable synonym for importance has been self-esteem. To this point, educational programs, popular, professional, and scientific books have been published to bolster and legitimize this notion, another one of the many fads and fashions that complement the field of psychology, such as happiness reviewed in the Introduction to this volume,[3, 4, 5] including a self-administered workbook.[6] The rationale behind those sources was that self-esteem is good for you and the more we have of it, the better off we are and will be if we spend time to increase it.

Unfortunately for those who supported this resource, there were a great many shortcomings that came to life in the last decade. First, self-esteem is an orphan psychological notion without any established connection to any reputable psychological theory or model. Self-esteem was accepted and uncritically used as the sinecure for the world's ills without making any negligible dent in that area. Second, self-esteem is such a ubiquitous notion that shows inconsistent and paradoxical connections to other behaviors. The inconsistency, variability, and contradictions in self-esteem practice and research raised serious questions about whether it is worthy of professional and scientific acceptance and practical use. For instance, inmates in prisons show much greater self-esteem than noncriminal individuals.[7] Even individuals with schizophrenia seem to show high self-esteem!

Over the last decade, therefore, self-esteem lost some of its cache and influence, even though it is still used, at random and not systematically, in the scientific literature. Third, and I think even more crucially from the viewpoint of human relationships, self-esteem is the remnant of what is called the past, intra-psychic, intra-individual psychological view of behavior, that is, the individual as emerging and developing in a vacuum of human relationships. Even though this view may seem incredible to the layperson on Main Street, up to recent times, psychologists, uncritically and blindly, studied individuals as if they did not live with other individuals. I tried to fight this viewpoint but to no avail.[8, 9, 10] Perhaps recent advances in attachment[11] and relational competence theories[12, 13, 14] may have laid that viewpoint to rest, but I doubt it. It is still deeply ingrained in the psyches of many psychologists.

In keeping with the notion of self-importance advocated here, would you accept an invitation to a wedding on the basis of either your self-esteem or the self-esteem of whoever invites you? If you voluntarily attend the funeral of a loved one, a dear friend, or a known colleague, would you attend the funeral on the basis of your self-esteem or the self-esteem of the deceased one? If you are invited to a party, would you attend on the basis of your self-esteem or the self-esteem of the host? As you see, there is no way that anyone can use self-esteem to explain these choices because there is no way to estimate and use the notion of self-esteem rationally and relationally.

On the contrary, I have advocated for years that a sense of importance is bestowed on us by ourselves and by others as much as we bestow and exchange it discriminately and selectively on loved ones and others. If we have it, we choose to give it and to receive it. We share it continuously within ourselves and with others, intimates and non-intimates. We are invited to a wedding, attend a funeral, or accept an invitation to a party because we feel that we were deemed sufficiently important to be invited and for our hosts, or deceased persons and their loved ones, to be significantly important to accept being with them in happy as in sad occasions.

Furthermore, this bestowal can be observed relatively easily when we see it working in intimate and non-intimate relationships. Self-esteem, on the other hand, is difficult to evaluate and observe, since it is usually measured by a paper-and-pencil, self-report questionnaire. We cannot see how it works, while we can observe how a sense of importance works for us and for others readily and directly. For instance, when we bestow a sense of positive self-importance constructively on ourselves and others we are demonstrating liking and even loving ourselves are well as others.

A well-known child psychologist and columnist in the *Atlanta Journal and Constitution*,[15] John Rosemond added unexpected support to my years-old negative position about self-esteem. In a column titled "The Downside of High Self-Esteem" he concluded that "[t]he notion that adults should do all they possibly can to advance the self-esteem of children is dying a slow but hopefully unavoidable death." He cites the research mentioned above by Roy Baumeister at Florida State University about criminals showing high self-esteem. He goes on to remember how his parents would instill in him a healthy dose of humility, lest he grew up to act "too big for his britches." One way to put a child in her and his place is to keep in mind priorities of self-importance first, partner-importance second, and child-importance third.[16]

Priorities include our attitudes, goals, likes, needs, dislikes, and wishes, in short, our motivation to be, do, and have whoever we want to be, do, and have. Priority implies a continuous rank-order of who, what, and when we like, want, and need, as discussed in greater detail in Chapter 8. These priorities can be organized according to urgency, appropriate stage in the life cycle, agreement with partner, friends, and parents, and for older folks, one's adult children. Priorities can be personal, related to self and others, or survival and enjoyment related to work and to leisure time, dealing with the necessary chores and responsibilities we all have to meet at various ages and stages of our lives.[17]

If you want to call "love" as what makes us bestow and exchange reciprocally this importance on ourselves and selected others, you may. If you want to use Christ's (Matthew 22:39) command to "Love your neighbor as yourself," you may do that too if you want. If this sounds like preaching, please forgive me, but if you keep reading you will find that (1) We are our best-known neighbors. Therefore, (2) we need to take care of ourselves if we want to take care of others;[18] and (3) that command or suggestion has been the basis for attempting to prove it conceptually and empirically. It is a free country and, fortunately or unfortunately, we can choose or not choose to love or not love our neighbors, literally or otherwise. We fall in love, marry, and mate with individuals that we deem important in our lives, leading to what I have called *selfulness: We both must win.* Usually, selful individuals tend to be attracted and eventually marry other selful individuals. Pleasant feelings of compassion, contentment, joy, and happiness underlie this condition. If you want to learn more about love from its various, multifarious aspects, I would recommend Sternberg's[19] small, possibly already outdated, but well-packed work on this topic. If you want to find out why and how we are attracted by people with similar interests you may want to consult much more technical and hard-to-read models of Relational Competence Theory.[20]

The process of bestowing a sense of importance to ourselves and intimate others is supported from a variety of sources, too many to cite here but cited frequently in my past writings. Hegi and Bergner,[21] for instance, claiming to have found the Holy Grail of Love, defined it as a process of "investment in the well-being of the other for his or her own sake." These authors cited Singer[22] who wrote the definitive three-volume treatise on love. Singer emphasized that "[h]e bestows importance to her needs and her desires even when they do not further the satisfaction of his own."[23] I have problems with both definitions because to make their definition acceptable scientifically as well as professionally,[24] Hegi and Bergner need to define what they mean by "investment" and "one's own sake." We have already reviewed "well-being" in the Introduction to this volume. This is a remnant of what has been called a previous psychological view about the individual-in-a-vacuum of other relationships in contrast to a more up-to-date relational view of the "individual-in-a-context."[25] Both "investment" and "sake" could be thought as representing a past view, while bestowal of importance represents a more current, observable relational process, giving and receiving something to and from somebody, a reciprocal exchange.

However, the most glaring omission in both definitions given above is their failure to consider self-love as a crucial component of love. If we do not love ourselves, that is, if we do not consider ourselves as important individuals in our own rights, how can we bestow importance on others? I shall demonstrate how the process of bestowing importance to self is crucial in understanding love in its most functional as well as in its most dysfunctional expressions. This differentiation was not considered by either Hegi and Bergner and even Singer. They considered only normative expressions of love. How about non-normative expressions of love, love in less than functional relationships?

To wit, there is a downside to love as a positive bestowal of importance to self and intimates present that is easy to see, for instance, in individuals with criminal records and personality disorders. These individuals bestow importance to themselves but deny this importance to others. This relational propensity, which I have called *Selfishness*, is seen easily in cheating, stealing, and, in its extremes, in murder: *I win, you lose*. When you cheat, steal, or even kill another person, you do not believe that what belongs to that person is sufficiently important for them to have, including, unfortunately, their lives. Their goods, possessions, money, or lives are less important to the cheater, thief, or murderer than importance bestowed on oneself. Anger is the feeling often underlying this condition.[26]

When importance is bestowed on others more often and positively than on ourselves we reach a condition called *Selflessness: You win. I lose.* In its extremes, this condition leads to depression and, worse, to suicide. Sadness is the underlying feeling in this condition.[27] When importance is not bestowed and denied and seemingly absent in individuals with certain severe conditions, mental illness occurs. Here, fear is paramount in doing or saying anything other than withdrawing from reality and others as the best escape. I have called this condition *No-self: We both lose.* No one can win when the no-self individual is not even aware or unable to admit being sick. Denial of being sick is one of the first signs of being sick. Catch-22.

Additionally, love is a multidimensional notion that cannot be encapsulated in a uni-dimensional definition. What does that mean? It means that love comes into different packages, each with its own address. My collaborators and I[28] defined love as being a redundant notion in the sense that comes up as a package with many different addresses in many different ways. For instance, it could be defined by (1) *closeness* and *distance*, that is, we approach and live with those we love and who love us, and we avoid those we do not like or love; (2) *availability,* we are available to ourselves and intimates emotionally and instrumentally, that is, we do things for and with them; (3) *successful problem-solving and negotiation*; (4) *sharing* common grounds in similar belief and value systems, interests, hobbies, etc.; (5) *commitment* to being together no matter what: "Until death does us part"; and (6) *intimacy* as defined below.

In case readers wonder whether what I am presenting is pure fantasy coming down from the blue sky, my colleagues at the University of Padova administered a self-report, paper-and-pencil test, the Self-Other Profile, to a variety of participants in more than a dozen studies that supported the validity of what is called the Selfhood Model. The bestowal of a sense of importance, in and of itself, however, is not sufficient to lead to being present. It takes another condition to complete the redundant process mentioned above, and that is: intimacy.

## Intimacy

So much has been written about this resource in the popular, professional, and scientific literature that it would be useless and redundant to review it here, especially when the literature on intimacy has already been thoroughly reviewed.[29, 30] Intimacy, like love, seems such an ubiquitous process with so many meanings and dimensions that make it difficult to define and to even use in practice. Like love, most psychologists including myself and my collaborators[31, 32] have produced paper-and-pencil self-report questionnaires trying to get to this condition indirectly rather than directly. As a result of this process, a plethora of intimacy-related scales have been published.[33, 34]

I, for one, decided that using paper-and-paper self-report questionnaires raises more questions than it solves by taking us away from observing intimacy directly in real-life situations. For instance, how can we be sure that we are getting at this condition if participants are not aware of what it is? What about their biases or desire to make a good impression and orient and skew their answers in a direction that makes it impossible for a professional or a layperson to get to this behavior? Furthermore, if there are so many different questionnaires directed to evaluate the same condition, that is, intimacy, which one is "better," more reliable, more valid, and more useful than other questionnaires?

However, denying the importance of such questionnaires does not mean writing them off the face of the earth. On the contrary, those relatively inert questionnaires can be transformed in dynamic and useful written interactive practice exercises or workbooks, just like many other psychological tests and questionnaires, as already suggested in the Introduction of this volume in relation to Prof. Fredrickson's positivity.[35]

Long ago[36] I decided that *intimacy is a process based on the sharing of joys and hurts and fears of being hurt.* Instead of relying on paper-and-pencil, self-report questionnaires that deal with intimacy indirectly, why not rely on the direct, specific, and concrete observation of how people share their joys, hurts, and fears of being hurt with each other? Can we see ourselves when we laugh, when we share joys, triumphs, and happy events, and when we cry while sharing painful, even tragic, losses and events? Aren't these direct observations more useful than relying indirectly on questionnaires?[37] Intimacy also means acceptance of oneself and significant others, warts and all, without demands for perfection, performance, production, or problem-solving. It means forgiving one's own transgressions and those of our loved ones. Indeed, I wrote about forgiveness long before it became an acceptable and now accepted psychological process.[38] However, the process of forgiving cannot occur unless there is a sharing of joys and hurts beforehand.[39] Something "forgiveness" experts seem to have forgotten.

What happens when some individuals are unable and even fearful and unwilling to share their hurts with a loved one or even with a professional? We have to go back to the definition of bestowal of importance given above, because importance and intimacy as defined here are connected. In selfulness there is an appropriate, constructive, and reciprocal sharing of joys, hurts, and fears of being hurt. In selflessness and selfishness, there may be intimacy thus defined at special occasions, such as weddings and funerals, but nowhere else, and if there is it may be a one-way street, without reciprocity. In no-self there is no intimacy thus defined. This is why there have been treatises written about fear of intimacy.[40, 41] Some individuals cannot bear sharing their hurt feelings with others, because very likely, expressing and sharing them with others might have been taboo in their families of origin or they are fearful of being judged negatively and even rejected for such an admission.

Once these two resources have been defined, we can expand on them freely.


## THE FOUR ADVANTAGES OF BEING PRESENT

*Being alive* means using all our senses, sensibilities, sensualities, and sexualities for our advantage as well for the advantage of those we love and who love us. Even though this advantage may seem obvious and simplistic, not all individuals are able to rely on all the resources available to us within our body, as discussed at greater length in Chapter 7 of this volume. Handicap, sickness, and traumatic experiences may blunt any of the four resources listed in the first line of this paragraph. Think of the many women who were sexually abused during childhood and who carried emotional scars from those experiences for most of their lives. Think about the abused and neglected children who carry inside the burden of such experiences throughout their lives. In one way or another we are all hurt human beings whose senses, sensibilities, sensualities, and sexualities may have been impaired by past negative and painful experiences. We may be physically alive but emotionally handicapped and scarred.

*Being aware* means being and becoming cognizant and knowledgeable of our strengths and limitations, including being able to reflect on our past behavior and thus becoming insightful enough to correct whatever errors and transgressions we may have produced to ourselves and to loved ones. Being aware is not as easy as it seems. That is why I suggested homework assignments at the end of each chapter to teach willing readers to practice becoming aware through repetitive experiences.

*Being available* implies not only being alive and aware but also being in touch with ourselves to the point of being available to ourselves first and to those we love and who love us, not only emotionally but also instrumentally, doing for them what we would like to have them do for us. If we are not available to ourselves emotionally and instrumentally, it is going to be difficult to be available to others.

*Being attentive* is a process based on the three previous advantages, enjoying the company of loved ones without any demands for performance, perfection, production, or problem-solving. Being attentive also implies meditation and reflection about one's own pleasure in doing absolutely nothing, as in the Italian *"Dolce far niente."*

More specifically, advantages of being present include, among others, the following: (1) being *able* to feel and to enjoy the moment; (2) being *appreciative* of the importance of self and of intimate others, including being grateful for what one is, does, and has, gives and receives; (3) being *mindful* of self and of intimates; (4) being *motivated* to change if and when it is necessary, including asking for professional help; (5) being *supportive* of self and of intimates as well as selected others.

## DOING = PERFORMANCE

While *being* might appear quite difficult to define and achieve, because of the seeming complexities involved at first blush, it was reduced to specific and concretely visible operations and processes. *Doing* consists of two separate activities, acquiring and dispensing *information* and providing or being provided *services*.

Bloom[42] cites the importance of context in the evaluation of performance using the world-famous violinist Joshua Bell[43] as an example. As an experiment for Gene Weingarten of the *Washington Post*, Bell, dressed in jeans and T-shirt, performed at the entrance of a DC subway. While he would command thousands of dollars for any performance in the world's greatest music halls, he was essentially ignored by passersby who threw a few dollars in his violin case that he has already seeded with his own change.

Think about working conditions in a mine where the dread of death is constantly present versus working in a safe building with sprinklers where natural light comes through large windows without any dust, smoke, or gas, with air-conditioning keepings the temperature constant. It is a marvel that some people work and perform well in unpleasant and even dangerous environments. Said this, one must be aware about the importance (did you count how many times this word is used in this chapter?) of context in determining not only performance but also production.[44] For one, I have emphasized the importance of immediate and distant context in human relationships since 1986.[45]

## Information

We acquire and dispense information through talk, hearing the news and music on radio or television, going to the movies, and reading books, magazines, and newspapers, including iPods and more recent technological advances. As Walter Isaacson, President and CEO of the Aspen Institute, concluded "... information wants to be paid for."[46] Information is free but it is becoming more expensive, especially when newspapers had to slash their contributors due to the decrease of readers who rely on TV, cell phones, computers, iPads, and the like. Information may not only be free but is immediate. We can get it any time we want or need it. However, if we want detailed and specialized information we may need to pay for it, to the point made by Walter Kim.[47] Boredom is extinct. He notes[48] that commodity is no longer possible: "Thanks to Twitter, iPads, Blackberries, voice-activated in-dash navigation systems, and a hundred other technologies that offer distraction anywhere, anytime, boredom is losing its grip on us at last." However, Kirn makes a good point by asking "But what else has been lost?" I agree with his answer:

> Creativity, just maybe. Because when one thinks about the matter—though we really have no reason to think about the matter, or to think about anything since boredom disappeared—the keypad and the touch screen now do the work that used to be the business of the daydream. Remember daydreams? No, of course you don't. How could you? Three more text messages have just arrived and another three, in one moment, will go out.

I did and still do daydream a great deal and one of my preferred lines is from the wonderful American musical *South Pacific*: "You have to have a dream to have a dream come true." However, I never dreamt in my wildest dreams that I would be able to publish as much as I have been able to do, including this volume. Nonetheless, the same point made by Walter Isaacson above was made also by Chris Anderson[49] in his discussion about the many political, economic, and professional implications of the World Wide Web. Anderson argued that the Web will be here forever, but it is questionable whether it will be free and available to whoever has a computer. It may become "colonized" by the interests that profited by its phenomenal growth. I, for one, have been putting many of my professional chips on the use of programmed distance writing, through computers and the Internet, since information is power and can be used to help many troubled people at a distance without ever seeing them in addition to face-to-face talk and exercise.[50, 51]

Unfortunately, the flip side of all the good that can be achieved through the Web includes the mushrooming of absolutely wild, incredible conspiracy theories, near-death experiences, alien abductions, and witch hunts,[52] including paranoid propaganda from hate groups, holocaust deniers. so-called patriots and militia arming themselves fearing that the government is going to arrest and detain law-abiding citizens, etc.

According to Michael Hirshorn,[53] even though the Web will last "forever, it will hardly be the delightfully free-form open plain of the early years. Its colonization is inevitable" (p. 80). He argued that the browser of the computer has now giving way to the applications of the smart phones that can now do almost everything that a computer can do: "Meanwhile, video-content services are finding that they don't even need to bother with the Web and the browser. Netflix, for one, is well on its way to sending movies and TV shows directly to TV sets" (p. 80). Essentially, the browser will be replaced by thousands of applications (apps) that will allow one to have whatever one wants informationally wherever one wants it. The future is here. Consider the nuances spotlighted on these web sites:

> Virtual Reality food could be used in therapy for eating disorders according to the UK Telegraph—Sufferers of anorexia and bulimia could reduce their fear and anxieties around food by visiting a computer generated restaurant and pretending to dine, a study shows. Researchers believe that the technique could reverse their unhealthy relationship with food to the point where they can eventually be reintroduced to the real thing. The novel approach could be developed after scientists found that food

presented in a virtual reality environment causes the same emotional responses as real food.

*To read more, visit* http://bit.ly/9Z04T9.

How many times have you logged onto Facebook only to find that (fill in the name here) has updated their page for the umpteenth time with yet another entirely forgettable, wonder-of-me moment? It would be easy to assume from the anecdotal evidence that a legion of insufferable narcissists has found the perfect sounding board. But maybe it's not just your impression. A new study by researchers working at York University in Canada has indeed found that Facebook users were more likely to be narcissistic. It also found that those Facebook users who checked the site frequently throughout the day tended to be more likely to suffer from low self-esteem.

*To read more, visit* http://bit.ly/dxg77q.

A Russian research team is attemptingan unprecedented study. Six volunteer astronauts will spend 520 days locked in a room, and perform different tests in what will be a simulated trip to Mars. "This is the Mars space program 500, in which the participants inhabit a 'capsule' specially designed in Moscow. There, in addition to living together for about a year and a half, need to consider how factors such as stress of work overload, boredom and limitations of social contact alter cognitive functioning, emotional and even the overall moral of the team."

*To read more, please visit* http://bit.ly/94QG3v.

It's inevitable that wave of new gadgets, such as smart phones, answering machines, Internet-connected computers, thousands of applications (apps), etc., promises to make boomers' golden years better and cheaper. For instance, power wheelchairs may have been around for decades. Instead of being controlled by manual commands, they can be controlled verbally and even just through thinking! Here and now is where, with the help of aging-related technology, we are nearing science fiction territory.[54] Senior Living, Version 2.0. *Smart Money: From the Wall Street Journal*[55]

Nonetheless, computers and online information are getting to be cheaper and cheaper. When I bought my first 512 MacBook and rotary printer in 1985 for $4,500 to replace what I was spending in secretary help ($9,500) in one year for typing countless revisions of the same pages (and references), I paid half as much for a more powerful and useful MacBookAir and a multiple-function printer (fax, copier, etc.)

that I have not yet learned to master. According to Anderson[56] what cost \$10 for a single transistor in 1961, one can buy the latest chip with two billion transistors for \$300! In fact, Anderson argued that some businesses might give some products for free to advertise other products, hence the title of his book.

Free, however, has two meanings. In Anderson's book[57] it means inexpensive. However, on the world stage it means available to almost everybody. In an editorial by *The Economist*[58] there are now many countries who want to curtail such a freedom to make sure ostensibly that "ordinary people's computer systems are not co-opted by criminals or cyber-warriors." However, in most cases, and especially authoritarian countries, such as China and Iran, to name a few, the countries want control of the Internet to restrict access to political dissidents. In fact, the mouse and the keyboard may become new weapons of conflict in future cyberwars.[59]

Information in its exchange nature (giving and receiving) cannot not be delivered and received without the use of services.

## Services

Services to provide and receive information imply action of some type, ranging from cleaning and dressing oneself to studying or working as well as participating actively in all the other commercial, industrial, financial technologies necessary for our survival and enjoyment, including electricity, water, taxes, hospitals, and clinics.

There have been various classifications of work, such as (1) manual versus intellectual;[60] (2) single, working alone versus social, working with others; (3) indoors versus outdoors; (4) aggressive, as in producing a weapon versus pacific, as in producing a statue; (5) creative as in producing completely new objects versus routine, as in working from already available blueprints and drawings.

This classification, as useful as it might be, does not really deal with the meaning of work. After all, both information and services are based on work, an activity that Diener and Biswas-Diener[61] classified usefully according to three different orientations: (1) work as a job; (2) work as a career; and (3) work as a calling. In a job, leisure is more important and money is the main motivation but the job would not recommend it unless it were required. In this orientation, one looks forward to the end of the shift, while doing what one is told, working hard for monetary incentives. In a career, there may be enjoyment in working hard to advance. However, a great deal of time is spent thinking about vacations while taking initiatives to impress superiors. In work as a calling, there is a great deal of enjoyment in work with a feeling of making a contribution and recommending it to others. Here thinking is focused on the work and not on the clock. By doing a job well, work is its own reward. In this way one works harder than if it were a job or a career.

There may be little enjoyment in a job, especially if the job entails routine repetition of parts and objects. There may some enjoyment in a career especially of one is appreciated for performance and production. There may be even more enjoyment in a job if in addition to appreciation there is the feeling of contributing to the direct welfare of others. However, I would like to add a fourth job-orientation to the three suggested by Diener and Biswas-Diener, and that is work as a *mission*, which goes above and beyond work as a calling because in a mission the motivation to work consists of multiple reasons for working. The goals of a mission are not only immediate or delayed but imply reaching a wider audience than can be done in a calling. For instance, my professional mission has been to help effectively as many people at risk, and in need and in trouble as I possibly can at the least possible cost.[62] I do not know whether I have ever fulfilled that mission. That judgment is left to others to decide, but I have had lots of fun trying to fulfill it, including writing this volume.

## HAVING = PRODUCTION

Having consists of producing or collecting and gathering money, goods, or possessions.

### Money

In a homework assignment or a take-home test about the California Gold Rush, one question asked of my 10-year-old granddaughter in the fifth grade at Fernbank Elementary School in DeKalb County, Georgia, was: "Do you think it was right for storeowners to raise prices when miners came to town? Explain your answer." She answered emphatically: "Yes. Because the miners aren't the only people who need money, the store owners need money too!" To which her teacher wrote a side note: "Remind me not to shop at your store."

As the saying goes: "It's not how much money one makes. It's how one spends it." I have seen millionaires living in posh houses in the best part of town end up in a trailer in a meadow owed by a son-in-low. I have seen frugal people allow themselves luxuries that not even some millionaires can afford, the luxury of a well-lived life with family and friends. For instance, once my wife and I, when we were practicing together years ago, saw a millionaire who brought to the session her parents. During this session, the daughter accused the (workaholic but extremely successful) father of not having told her whether he loved her. To which he replied: "But I have given you seven millions last week!" In response the daughter took her checkbook out of her purse and said: "Do you want them back?" For her, being told by her father that he loved her was more important than any millions he might have given her.

Cash, as we know it, is no longer the major mean of exchange. Think about checks and credit cards. In some social and ethnic circles, money as a gift is considered as a crass way to show appreciation, care, and importance for special occasions. On the other hand, at least in the Greek and Polish cultures, it is perfectly appropriate to give envelopes stuffed with dollar bills or even checks. Years ago, my son went out of his way to find a perfect gift and a perfect card for my birthdays. Once it was established that there was no object that would be necessary or acceptable, he sent me through e-mail an Amazon gift coupon instead: quick and easy. I do not think that my son loves me less because his gift is a coupon.

## Goods/Possessions

In a competing work related to this volume, where he considered topics overlapping with those included here, such as art (Chapter 1 in this volume), food (Chapter 4 of this volume), sex (Chapter 7 of this volume), music (Chapter 5 in this volume), fiction (Chapter 1 of this volume), Paul Bloom[63] at Yale argued that

> pleasure is deep. What matters most is not the world as it appears to our senses. Rather, the enjoyment we get from something derives from what we think that thing is. This is true for intellectual pleasures, such as the appreciation of paintings and stories, and also for pleasures that seem simpler, such as the satisfaction of hunger and lust. For a painting, it matters who the

artist was; for a story, it matters whether it is truth or fiction; for a steak, we care about what sort of animal it came from; for sex, we are strongly affected by who we think our sexual partner really is. (p. xii)

In other words, people, money, goods, and possessions are important to us according to their internal meaning, not according to their extrinsic value but according to their intrinsic value to us. Since Bloom's position (called thesis in academic circles) is especially relevant to goods and possessions, it will be useful to expand on it according to his view, which he calls *essentialism*, the philosophical viewpoint (called paradigm or theory in academic circles)[64] that we need to go underneath the surface of people and objects to find their intrinsic nature. It's the basic essence or nature of a person or an object that counts, not its superficial qualities, such as how we present ourselves to others to make a good impression, as found in some personality disorders.

For instance, Bloom[65] asks (rhetorically), How much money would you take for one of your kidneys? You would not accept money from a stranger but if the life of your partner, your parent, or your child were at stake, I am sure you would not hesitate to donate one. Kidneys, such as many other goods and objects, are irreplaceable but become replaceable under special circumstances.

I was making this point years ago in Wellington, New Zealand, during a workshop my wife and I were giving to counselors. I was using the tie I wore as an example of an object that is complete replaceable. One member of the audience took me up on that claim and I had to make good and exchange my beautiful tie for another tie not so beautiful. However, if that tie had been given to me by my wife or a loved one, I would have insisted in keeping it and exchanged something for something that did not have the same meaning to me. The extremely large card I received from my grandson for my birthday that adorns one side of my chest of drawers in my bedroom is much more important to me than diplomas and degrees I received over a lifetime.

Even money may represent something different for different people or reasons. For instance, Bloom cites the case of someone, very likely of small stature, who did not steal any money or jewelry in his house, but did steal only the Xbox machine and all of its games. He also cited research[66] whereby Harvard MBA students, given the opportunity, are more likely to steal cans of Coke than dollar bills.[67] Think how much people spend to buy something that belongs to a celebrity. The object in and of itself may not cost too much. However, its belonging to a live or dead celebrity increases its cost tremendously.

If I may be allowed to differ from Bloom, instead of how people just "think" about themselves, that is, being, doing, and having, I would also emphasize also how we feel about the same topics. I happen to think that feelings exist before thinking and I have argued and cited evidence to support this position.[68, 69] Developmentally, the infant is born is a world of feelings, not of thinking. Only with time and with proper nurturance can the child learn to think. The infant is born in a world of space where approach and avoidance by caretakers determine pleasure or pain, abuse or warmth. As the infant becomes a child the child learns to think and to either inhibit and delay or to express and discharge pleasant and unpleasant experience. This delay or discharge occur in a world of time, that is: speed.[70, 71]

As noted, gifts are one way to show the importance of an individual to the giver. One of the most unusual and thoroughly unexpected gifts I ever received in my life happened a few years ago, when I was invited to visit my alma mater, Tabor College in Hillsborough, Kansas. After a whole day of talking, lecturing, and meeting a variety of students and old-timer city residents, my last meeting at the end of the day was with the entire faculty. After completing our conversation, I was given as a present a rather heavy package. When I was asked to open the wrapping, to my complete amazement I found it to be a set of "bocce," the most popular game that Italians play. Even in Atlanta, members of La Societa' Italiana have been able to get two bocce courts built right in Piedmont Park, the largest one in the middle of the city. Many members of this society do have bocce courts in their backyards. After my granddaughter Alessandra learned the rudiments of the game we participated as a team in two bocce tournaments sponsored by this society. That game allowed me to bond even closer with my beloved granddaughter. What else can an old man ask for?

To answer that question, the ubiquitous editors of FC&A Publishers from Peachtree City, Georgia, who will be cited repeatedly during the course of this work in Chapters 4 and 8, provided a whole volume dedicated to *Free Stuff and Bargains for Seniors: How to Save on Groceries, Utilities, Prescriptions, Taxes, Hobbies, and More!* According to the claims made in this volume, if you buy it, you will be able to "Save as much as 80% no matter where you shop; Slash your electric bill by 30% or more!"; "Get prescriptions drugs for up to 65% off!" This is just the beginning. As the usual free gift given with this kind of hyperbole,

I also received a booklet entitled *The Little Book of Big Savings: How to Save on Everything from Automobiles to Zip-Lock Bags*.

If you are a senior on a fixed income, and you want to control your spending on goods and possessions, this may be one place to start. If you want to follow my advice, however, to save money, get your local library to buy it, so that more people will be able to use it. And, if your local library is unable to order it, for whatever reason, perhaps you may convince a group of friends to chip in their share of the cost. OK?

## Advantages of Doing and Having

Without performance there would not be any production. However, the two should not be equated. One could perform a lousy job and produce a poor product repeatedly, as shown in various chapters of this volume. How about the many car recalls we see every day, for instance? Let alone medications, foods, vitamins, etc. whose quality I question in Chapters 4 and 7 of this volume. Quality and quantity do not necessarily go together. However, the combination and control of doing and having produces power: Who controls doing and having, as in authoritarian regimes or autocratic systems, countries, industries, the military establishment, has power.[72] The power can be used for good or for bad, as we have seen consistently in past history.

## Disadvantages of Doing and Having

We Americans are so enamored if not obsessed with the importance of performance and production at the expense of being present that, in my past clinical practice, I had to teach couples and families learn how to *be together* without any demands for performance, production, or problem-solving by prescribing hugging, holding, huddling, and cuddling with each other without talking, possibly in the dark, to minimize any other interferences, including the doorbell or the telephone.[73]

Not all couples and families can or should be prescribed this process, however, because in some couples and families there is (1) an underlying, hidden agenda, such as physical or sexual abuse that may preclude being able to follow this prescription; (2) so much hurt that makes it impossible for some couples and families to be intimate in this fashion; and (3) resistance to anything seen as dangerous and threatening, that is, the fear of physical and emotional intimacy.[74,75]

Normality in this triangle of life is found when it is ideally equilateral, with importance given to the three modalities flexibly at different stages of the life cycle. For instance, studying and learning to get a job may be a primary priority at the beginning of one's life. However, once a job, marriage (or its alternatives), and a family have been established, one may devote time and energy to enjoy life through recreational, surplus-time activities, as described in Chapter 2 of this volume.

## THE PATHOLOGY OF LIFE

Pathology means sickness, within this context *mental illness* in one degree or another and of one type or another. This deviation from the norm is achieved when these three modalities of Being, Doing, and Having are used and exchanged in lopsided ways, without a proper balance among them. For instance, one could use doing to the point that both being and having will suffer, as in compulsive workaholics or driven personalities, including persons with addictions. On the other end, doing nothing for the pleasure of hanging around might be nice but it won't lead to anything except dependency on others and on the welfare system. Yet, in India, I am told, there are holy men who lie and live all the time on beds of nails surviving on the food offerings of the faithful.

Extremes in one modality, therefore, lead to extremes in the other two modalities in a triangle. If one side is too long, it decreases the length of the other two sides of the triangle. For instance, there are packrats who like to amass things compulsively, such as newspapers, shoes, fetishes, etc.,[76] as seen in the Collier brothers, who in 1947 died of starvation and suffocation by the trash they had hoarded for years.[77] More recently in Las Vegas,[78] a story detailed how the body of a woman whose house was cluttered garbage was found in the house after an initial evaluation failed to find the body there. Instead, the months'-long search was oriented outside the house where even search dogs were unable to enter because of the smell and impossibility to move around piles and piles of refuse generated by animals, decomposing garbage, food, clothes, and other stuff.

There are tycoons who have amassed incredible amounts of money even though they are and will never be able to enjoy the fruits of such acquisitions. At the other end of having, there are individuals in some religious orders who give away their material goods for a more rewarding life by attending to the needy and poor in preparation for a better life in heaven. My historical predecessors, the Poor of Lyons, did that in the twelfth century and thereafter. The recent movement among tycoons to get rid of at least half of their holding may be a correction in the right direction.[79] Let's see how many tycoons are willing to part with half of their billion-dollar estates and then see how they starve to death!

## CONCLUSION

Being together with family members and friends while eating good food and drinking a liquid of our choice (mixed with some soft background music?) is one of the greatest pleasures of life because it combines all three modalities, presence, performance, and production. To share this pleasure one must have sufficient number of family members and friends to share the meal with and amounts of either goods or money to be together, eat, and drink with intimate others. Food as a source of pleasure will be discussed in the next chapter.

## EXERCISE NO. 3

From the major headings of this chapter rank-order the six resources according to how you enjoy them, from the most to the least enjoyable ones. Please give one or more reasons why you rank-ordered these resources the way you did.

# 4

# Food: For Survival and for Enjoyment

> I confess. I am a foodoholic. I find it hard to control myself. I am addicted to dark chocolate. Once I start eating one nugget, it is hard for me to stop! Please help me!

Food is composed of solid and liquid aliments ingested through the mouth. Food is the fuel and force that allows us to survive and to enjoy. By the same token, food can be used for a variety of purposes, such as withdrawing it as punishment or giving it as a reward, or as an addiction when too much is consumed. It can become an obsession to the point of producing obesity and with that increasing the risk that obesity will be likely related to diabetes, coronary heart disease, and a shortened lifespan. By the same token avoiding food might produce alimentary sicknesses such as anorexia and bulimia nervosa. Consequently, this chapter will be divided into two sections: solid and liquid food, including the downside of hucksters who prey on the naive but needy American public to sell worthless vitamins and supplements as panaceas for all sicknesses real or imagined.

It seems like we Americans are obsessed with food, judging by the cult status of many famous chefs, including an elusive one, who tries to escape his devotees and is difficult to locate anywhere in the United States.[1] Isn't everybody on earth elusive? Since I came to the United States in 1948 as an exchange student in the Midwest (Kansas), food was either boiled, fried, or baked with few if any condiments. With the influx of veterans returning from foreign countries after World War II, Korean and Vietnam wars, and eventually immigrants from other countries, especially Asia, Central, and South America, the range of foods available to us in the United States has exploded to incredible heights and widths (pun intended, if you get it!).

Additionally, as a representative of this obsession, the relative affluence toward the last quarter of the past century produced an explosion in recipe books (estimated to be upward of 50,000), sophistication in food preparation, and eventually creation of a Food TV channel with competitions and promotions about super-chefs, culinary heroes who are now household icons. This growth includes also a variety of food-related magazines, such as *Bon Appétit* and *Cook's Illustrated*. I subscribe to and love the latter, especially for its introductory columns, drawings, and the detailed instructions on how to make food more appetizing.

If you revisit the triangle of life introduced in Chapter 3, you will see that it can be applied also to food as goods or possessions as something pleasurable eaten when being together with friends and family, savoring it leisurely with a preferred drink and even background music, that is, *being* or *presence*. Here is where conviviality is the major reason for eating rather than food itself and when food is another reason to *be together* and is more important than what is eaten, as, for instance, cooking on a grill outdoors with the company of family and friends.

I did just that for a party when I invited many of my colleagues during the 1962 meeting of the American Psychological Association in St. Louis. It was very hot (100 degrees!) and the sun was beating right from the west into our backyard where I was grilling chicken. I kept on grilling by myself while all my buddies were indoors enjoying our air-conditioned house eating all the chicken I was grilling and all the drinks we had in the fridge. As you can see, I still remember vividly an episode that taught me never to grill in the sun and make sure you have company next to you while you are grilling in the shade, or else.

When food becomes just fuel and something to eat, digest, and get over as quickly as possible, without any pleasure either in the tasting or in its substance, we can think of food eaten in this way as *doing* or *performance*, as seen also in those who are fanatical about the food's nature (calories, weight, provenance, and composition) including possible health benefits without emphasis on pleasure. When food is eaten obsessively in as many quantities as possible without any limits as to cost, thinking, and knowledge of its composition and outcomes, and certainly without any savoring and pleasure, then food could represent *having* or *production*, as seen in obesity.

## SOLID FOOD

Solid food is composed by any alimentary substance that usually needs biting, crunching, chewing, and digesting. However, I plan to add three sections to this chapter: (1) foods for pleasure; (2) foods for thought; and (3) foods for health. Extremes in too much solid food, leading to obesity, or too little food, leading to anorexia nervosa and bulimia, prompted a review of diets and the whole diet market in the United States, and the incredible advertising from phony or seemingly real doctors who sell nostrums to the gullible, naive, and needy American public. This is done without evidence except enthusiastic testimonials and self-aggrandizing descriptions of their superior abilities, education, and knowledge with no proof whatever except superlative descriptions about the incredible health-producing goodness of their products. The chapter will end, like in any meal, with liquid food.

### Food for Pleasure

If one were to list all the cookbooks that are published in the United States, one would think that food is the most important pleasure in American life, not to mention a whole TV channel completely dedicated to food, with its heroines and heroes parading their wares in front of enthusiastic audiences and awestruck funs. In the last 60+ years, since the end of World War II, Americans have become much more aware of food. In the last 30+ years a variety of foods heretofore unknown to most Americans have become available practically anywhere in the country. If you cannot find it in your neighborhood grocery store, you can find in an ethnic one, and if you do not have an ethnic grocery store in your community you can find anything you want, solid and liquid, on the Internet.[2]

For pleasure, Asimov[3] and his wife once ordered Lobster Fra Davolo in an Italian restaurant but he was the only one served ceremoniously while his wife's order was apparently ignored or overlooked. When he asked "And my wife's?" everybody in the restaurant thought that this question was funny and everybody laughed. But there was no laughter in the case of the guest who commented to the hostess about the deliciousness of the meal, adding "what there was of it." Sensing the hostess' hurt expression on her face, to make amends, the guest hastened to add: "there was plenty of food, such as it was."

There are at least six if not more recent "movements" in the field of food for pleasure. Do I dare say fads and fashions in most elegant and expensive restaurants instead? (1) *fresh* food, obtained from local providers (read: farmers) within driving distance from a restaurant; (2) *slow* food, as a reaction to the already-established American fast-food practices; (3) growing emphasis on a more *vegetarian* fare; (4) *organic* food; (5) *smaller portions*; and (6) *molecular* cooking.

Let me expand on each of these movements:

- *Fresh* food is now fashionable because of the interest in eating non-frozen, not too distant and therefore possibly dangerous foods imported from foreign lands, as in the case of recent salmonella in eggs, spinach, and tomatoes epidemics.
- *Slow* food is a movement especially developed in Italy where eating is a pleasure to be shared with a minimum of time and work restraints and where the main meal, contrary to American customs, is eaten in the middle of the day. One variation on this movement is cooking with feeling, that is, cooking with a minimum of rules and a maximum of freedom and creativity against the traditional and repetitive nature of most European cuisines.[4]
- More *vegetables* and less meat is now the new fashion among big name chefs such as[5] (a) John Frazer of Dovetail restaurant in New York City, who on Mondays gives his patrons a choice between a vegetarian or vegetable-based prix fixe meal for S42; (b) Jose Andres with six restaurants in Los Angeles and Washington DC where two of his best-selling tapas items at the Bazaar in L.A. are spinach and asparagus; (c) Quinn Hatfield of L.A. who emphasizes small-plate dining with greater variety of courses to avoid serving big hunks of protein ("Meat is boring"); (d) Wolfgang Puck with 24 restaurants in nine states often orders veggie-intensive appetizers and only 8-oz steaks at his steakhouses in L.A. and Las Vegas; (e) Mario Batali with 15 restaurants in three states offers extra vegetarian options on Meatless Mondays while his newer eatery in NYC will be strictly vegetarian; and (f) Bill Teleplan of New York City gives top billing to his monthly harvest menus.

Abend[6] commented on the cult of food illustrated by iconic food gurus ("kitchen gods") who started behind the counter and ended up in the spotlight of celebrity food TV channel. According to her, these chefs have transformed the restaurant industry and even changed the way we eat. She listed among them the perennials Wolfgang Puck, Paul Bocuse, Marco Pierre White, Gordon Ramsay,

Emeril Lagasse, David Chang, Tom Colicchio, Padma Lakshmi, Mario Batali, Thomas Keller, Rocco DiSpirito, Dan Barber, and Rachel Ray. Other kitchen luminaries will be cited below.

*It was difficult to see a difference between *organic* and non-organic food, except in the price, until Doctors Health Press published *The Smart Shopper's Guide to Organic Foods* (undated) and Jeffrey Kluger[7] made a detailed comparisons of pros and cons between the two types of food. For instance, Kluger cites a study that "found no nutritional difference between organic and conventional produce-and conventional even squeaked ahead in one category." On the other hand, "grass-fed cattle have higher ratios of omega-3 to omega-6 fatty acids, a balance that's believed to reduce the risk of cancer and heart disease." However, "a freakishly large, overly engineered tomato that is designed to ripen on route to the store, will never match the taste of its natural, vine-ripened tomato." According to Kluger, there is broad agreement that biopesticides are not as dangerous as synthetic pesticides, but less toxic doesn't mean nontoxic. He compared organic versus conventional eggs, milk, beef, and fruits/vegetables, where he recommended to go organic in the first three and conventional in the fourth.

Additionally, Kluger asked a panel of well-known chefs to compare chicken, carrots, steak, white nectarines, pork, eggs, and goat cheese for their flavor and taste. Most of these judges chose organic, four for organic and three for a draw between the two choices. However, readers should not consider those comparisons as final or reliable. As a psychologist, to make such a comparison really scientific, I would have judges blindfolded and choosing between two types of food given in alternative order.

In spite of the information given above, I do not know of any evidence, and if there is, I would like to know it, that eating organic food makes one healthier or live longer than eating non-organic food. Therefore, I wonder whether eating organic food is one of the many fads or status enhancers that have grown quite frequent in the last half century. Remember the non-eating-eggs fad years ago? Admittedly, some of these fads might have been fueled by the medical profession. Nonetheless, one cannot help wonder whether there is a difference in taste between organic and non-organic food. If one can detect and claim taste differences between organic and non-organic food, make sure you do it blindfolded.

- *Smaller portions*. Due to the present economic crunch, many restaurants have resorted to serve smaller portions to maintain the price of a dish. The other influence in reducing portions has been trying to retain quality by decreasing the quantity of the food, as in the use of *tapas*, appetizer-portions favored in Spain or the Chinese breakfast din sum.

- *Molecular gastronomy* (MG) is the latest fashion in cooking that is a combination, coupling, and mixture of science in finding and defining the basic chemical nature of any food with its delicious aspects (remember "essentialism" in the previous chapter?). This combination means that science has now entered in the kitchen where chemistry and even physiology have become part of the process of food preparation and presentation. To achieve the goal of combining science with kitchen, MG also emphasizes the chemical components of traditional foods to see whether their flavor and healthfulness can be enhanced.

One more trend in food was added recently by the Food Critic of the *Atlanta Journal and Constitution* John Kessler, on Sunday, October 3, 2010. He argued that the age of artisan food is here because "the best food stories are about people who aren't chefs at all, but who learn to make something well and then run for it. . . . We've moved from the age of the chef to the age of the artisan. Today's brightest culinarians are distinguishing themselves not with their creative moves in the kitchen, but with the commitment to providing a unique product."

It's hard to believe, but a more recent fad that is absolutely prehistoric in its haute cuisine origins is *foraging*[8] where individuals obsessed with getting or doing something exceptional or unusual will search for food in woods, sea, and parks such as bull kelp, morels, stinging nettles, elderflowers, and ramps, among many other earthy choices.

I cannot forget our recent seating at the table for supper with my brother Alberto, his wife Anna Luisa, and their daughter, Alessandra, visiting with us in Atlanta from our hometown of Florence (Italy, not South Carolina). As we were enjoying our meal, my niece, with tears in her eyes, started to reminisce about my father, her grandfather. He would cook for her and her brother and sister when my brother and his wife were away from home fighting for peace and lying down in front the American missile bases in Sicily. She then gave me orally the favorite recipe that was much liked by all three children that my father cooked for them often:

On an oven-resistant large pan laced with olive oil, put one layer of sliced onions, one layer of already cooked slices of potatoes, one layer of sliced tomatoes, one layer of sliced eggplant, all covered with mozzarella cheese and olive oil. If you want to add some oregano, pepper, parsley, or other aromatic herbs, be my guest. One variation on this recipe is adding spicy tomato source. Cover and cook in the oven at 400 degrees for at least half an hour and more, depending on when the dish looks cooked. *Buon appetito*!

## Food for Thought

Pesticides are now becoming more frequently thought of in the American food consciousness. For instance, the Environmental Working Group listed foods lowest in pesticides, and they are onions, avocado, sweet corn, pineapple, mangos, sweet peas, asparagus, kiwi, cabbage, eggplant, cantaloupe, watermelon, grapefruit, sweet potato, and honeydew melon. Those foods tested with the highest level of pesticides were celery, peaches, strawberries, apples, blueberries, nectarines, bell peppers, spinach, kale, cherries, potatoes, and imported grapes.

According to a special supplement (another awful pun!) to Healthy Years in the Newsletter from the University of California at Los Angeles, "evidence is growing that certain supplements [get the pun?] maybe beneficial for the brain." However, this conclusion does not mean that supplements should be taken in mega-doses, the more we digest the better off we are, i.e., beware of food and vitamins fads. Many vitamin supplements can interact negatively with prescription medication. By now, knowledgeable readers do know the importance of omega-3 fatty acids and fish with a variety of whole grains, fruits, vegetables, legumes, nuts, and seeds together with foliate, B, C, D, and E vitamins.

## Food for Health

We all have become conscious of the influence of our eating habits and about the nature of the food we ingest to the point that food and health have become practically synonymous: "What you eat is who you are." Not only are eating habits and foods linked to physical health but also to mental health.[9] The Mediterranean Diet, for instance, consisting mainly of plant foods, plenty of vegetables, fruits, whole grain cereals, legumes and nuts, as well as wine, has been considered as the ideal way to eat and apparently related to lower rates of depressions in the Mediterranean basin countries (France, Greece, Italy, Portugal, and Spain). It may well be an established possibility. However, I would add one variable that has not been considered in all the evidence accumulated to proclaim this diet a winner, and that is: People in those countries tend to walk much more on the average than we Americans do. Just by itself this factor needs to be considered before electing and raising this diet to an exemplary position.

The glycemic-index and load have been found responsible for the production of blood sugar and insulin, and related to negative moods, such as depression and irritability, as well as physical effects, such as diabetes and heart disease. Hence, a low glycemic-index and load are good for you. High glycemic-index and load are bad for you. Additionally, my physician told me years ago to avoid caffeine in coffee and tea and I am glad he did, because caffeine may well be related to anxiety.

Certain minerals, called also with a technical term as "micronutrients" (impressed?), have been found to be related to possible mental health effects, such as iron, zinc, magnesium, and chromium, while vitamins B and D have become recognized as important components of healthy food possibly related to a positive mood and a lowered risk of anxiety and depression. Overall, however, the important function of omega-3 fatty acids to decrease inflammation and discomfort, and consequently, negative mood, has been recognized widely.

The Harvard Medical School released a list of 26 health "revelations" that may be useful for us to know:

- Olive oil does not turn into trans fat when cooking.
- Niacin, B3 lowers bad LDL cholesterol and triglycerides but increases good HDL cholesterol.
- Blood pressure pills are best taken in the morning after getting up to lower blood pressure's build up during the night.
- Moderate alcohol consumptions over 65 years of age may reduce the risk of dementia. However, heavy drinking increases health risks for heart and mind.
- St. John's Wort, supposedly a treatment for depression, does not work for severe depression.
- Hiccups are usually minor and short-lived but if they persist they may be associated with an underlying medical condition.
- Coffee may have anti-cancer properties for liver and colon.

- Caffeine, as found in coffee, tea, and soft drinks, can linger in the body up to 12 hours.
- Lowering the number of calories we use every day may lengthen our lives.
- The trans fats found in cookies, margarines, and fast foods may raise bad and lower good cholesterol.
- Sudden and excessive sweating prior to or at the beginning of a heart attack may be the main reason for asking for help.
- Sunscreen lotions are supposed to last up to three years.
- Decaffeination in tea reduces flavonoid content drastically, no matter what tea companies claim to the contrary.
- These are the six prevention tips for macular degeneration: don't smoke, wear sunglasses, eat kale and spinach, exercise, eat fish and nuts, and keep your weight down.
- You do not need to go overboard with supplements to ingest potassium; fruits and vegetables supply plenty of this mineral.
- Three or four miles of daily walking is just as good at reducing heart disease as marathons.
- Vitamin D does more than strengthen your bones, it may protect against colon cancer and autoimmune diseases such as multiple sclerosis and heart diseases (possibly lowering the level of depression).
- Early treatment of Bell's palsy with a steroid anti-inflammatory such as prednisone increases the chances of a full recovery.
- Red wine may protect people against the common cold.
- Dark chocolate (hurrah!) contains flavonoids and may even lower blood pressure.
- Sleeping on the back is the worst position for snorers. Try sleeping sideways or on your stomach.
- Certain exercises may keep you from shrinking as we age.
- Aspirin and ibuprofen may be cancelling each other's effectiveness.
- The risk of obesity jumps almost 25 percent with each two-hour increase in daily TV watching.
- Seventy-year-olds today apparently are equivalent healthwise to 65-year-olds who lived 30 years ago.
- The alternative physician who prescribes chelation therapy should be aware of serious side effects, such as kidney failure and convulsions.

If you are ready for straight, reliable answers about food and health instead of wildly speculative news stories likely to be contradicted the following morning, check out the *Tufts University Health & Nutrition Letter*. Listed below are 25 key facts to bring the sanity back to cooking, eating, and enjoying good food. These are precisely the kind of facts you would discover each month if you were to subscribe to that letter. They represent just a sampling of what that letter reports to its readers in recent issues:

- Here is a supplement you should take: A daily dose of vitamin D to guard against colon, ovarian, breast and possibly prostate cancer.
- Diet sodas get an unfair "bad rap." They are safe (and part of normal food intake) as long as they use FDA-approved non-caloric sweeteners.
- Eating plenty of carrots, sweet potatoes, and spinach can protect your eyes from age-related macular degeneration.
- To eat smarter, stay out of the center aisles in the supermarket next time you shop. That's where salt- and sugar-laden packaged goods are stacked.
- Ninety-four percent of news media reports on health *do not* point out that the results may not apply to humans.
- Replacing regular salt with potassium-enriched salt can lower the risk of cardiovascular disease.
- Eating breakfast helps control hunger and binge eating later in the day.
- Frequent exercise *does* appear to delay the onset of Alzheimer's disease.
- Those low-carbohydrate fad foods may cause constipation, nausea, weakness—and ultimately lead to heart disease.
- Brightly colored produce—oranges, bell peppers, pumpkins, tangerines, papayas—help protect against arthritis.
- Consuming more than five portions of fruits and vegetables per day can cut the risk of stroke by 25 percent.
- A diet rich in chicken is associated with a lower risk of colon cancer.
- At the doctor's office, five minutes of quiet breathing in a chair, *just before* the nurse puts on the cuff, can lower your blood pressure and the chance of a false high reading.
- Avoid fish prone to containing mercury—shark, swordfish, tilefish, and king mackerel. Approach fish low in mercury—shrimp, salmon, Pollock, catfish, and canned light tuna.
- Ignore TV commercials. No food can "burn" fat. Such claims about grapefruit, celery, and cabbage soup are false.
- There is *no* connection, as many believe, between your blood type and the foods you should eat.
- Along with containing lots of added sugar, dried fruits lose much of their vitamin C.

- Never microwave food in margarine tubs or whipped-topping containers—chemicals may leach into the food.
- What's the recommended dose of Glucosamine and Chondroitin for arthritis? Zero. They don't work. Period.
- Regular coffee is *not* linked to hypertension—bur decaf coffee seems to raise levels of LDL, the "bad" cholesterol.
- Urban legend: Peanut butter is laden with evil trans-fat. Reality: Testing of 11 brands of peanut butter found no detectable trans-fats.
- They may look like "health food," but raw alfalfa sprouts (just like improperly cooked meat and fish) are frequently linked with food-borne illness outbreaks.
- Do *not* take antioxidant vitamins if you're undergoing radiation or chemotherapy for cancer. They may do more harm than good.
- It seems to be true—the more complex your work, the less the risk you may have for Alzheimer's or dementia.
- Low-fat dairy products help lower the risk of type-2 diabetes in both men and women.

If you subscribe to this letter you will get a list of 51 healthy foods and the Tufts University Blacklist of unhealthy foods. Below I will use various sources to compare, contrast, and report on which foods are the healthiest (Table 4.1). You have the choice of selecting which food fits into your personal tastes.

The Doctors Health Press (DHP) published by Lombardi Publishing Corporation of Boston, Massachusetts, in magazine-format booklets, after an introduction to the nature of pain, lists the top 10 pain-relieving foods. To their credit DHP also published booklets about *The Smart Shopper's Guide to Organic Foods, Lifesaving Recipes that Will Blow Your Taste Buds Away,* and *Deserts for Defeating Heart Disease* (see Table 4.1) for information and comparisons among these sources. Additionally, DHP, on the basis of extensive analysis, recommends eggs, nuts, spelt, barley, and rye bread, shellfish, and lean beef.

Dr. David Perlmutter with the help of Carol Colman[10] gives the best tools for improving memory and sharpness and preventing aging in the brain. Reading this book will allow you to (1) discover hidden brain toxins in your medical cabinet, household products, and the food you eat; (2) bring back clarity and mental vigor; and (3) find what your doctor won't tell you about preventing and treating stroke, Alzheimer's, Parkinson's, and other neurological conditions. Once you pass the hype, you will find detailed information about the effects of most known foods and vitamins, including a whole recipe list of

**Table 4.1  Most Healthy Foods Ratings from Various Sources**

| NAH[a] | CSPI[b] | DHP[c] | Pain-Relieving DHP | Heart Disease DHP | Brain-Boosting DHP |
|---|---|---|---|---|---|
| Broccoli | Apples | Dark Green Leafy Veggies | Blueberries | Dark Chocolate | Berries |
| Butternut Squash | Basil (O) | Asparagus | Avocados | Walnuts | Fatty Fish |
| Crisp-breads | Bell Peppers | Blueberries | Curry Bread | Bananas | Green Tea |
| Garbanzo Beans | Blueberries | Other Berries | Cherries | Peanuts | Dark Chocolate |
| Leafy Greens | Broccoli (O) | Cantaloupe | Figs | Strawberries | Grape Juice |
| Mangoes | Kumquats | Spelt Grain | Dark Chocolate | Blueberries | Apples |
| Sweet Potatoes | Lemons | Broccoli | Ginger | Maple Syrup | Leafy Greens |
| Watermelon | Lime | Lentils | Papaya | Molasses | Avocados |
| Wild Salmon | Onions (O) | Black Beans | Salmon | Honey | Curry |
| | Peaches | Brussels Sprouts | Soy | | Coffee |
| | Red Cabbage (O) | | | | Olive Oil |
| | Strawberries | | | | Barley |
| | Tomatoes | | | | |

[a]Nutrition Action Health letter published by CSPI.[b]
[b]CSPI = Center for Science in the Public Interest.
[c]DHP = Doctors Health Press(O) = Organic.

meals that will improve your mental and physical strength. This book is praiseworthy because it does not sell anything, contrary to practices detailed below.

A "food" doctor who apparently follows the path of recommending but not selling food supplements is Victor Marchione, who in his newsletter suggests, among others, how to put "the breaks on allergies," "Fructose can raise your blood pressure," the "Secret Healing benefits of Essential Oils," "How Rubard helps digestion," a Secret Japanese food for weight loss, how pecans could protect your brain, a juice to help Alzheimer's disease, and even the Italian national condiment olive oil coupled with healthy assortments of recipes. He also includes some scientific sources for his suggestions. However, there is no free lunch (awful pun!). If you want to receive this newsletter, you have to pay for its subscription.

Another doctor who will sell his newsletter full of recent discoveries in the health industry is Robert Jay Rowen. I have subscribed to his newsletter *Second Opinion* for years to keep in touch with alternative medicine, which he seems to represent. However, I have never believed his sensationalistic claims about any nostrum he sells because he does not show or publish research to substantiate his claims. Apparently, he has quite a following and he is willing to admit to mistakes, reversing his original objections to the PSA test and recommending that "every man should have this prostate test done today."

Dr. Rowen does sell products he recommends through a separate company and is available for consultation through telephone appointments. He is also editor and only writer for the *Journal of Natural Medicine*, where he sells through Advanced Bionutritionals of Norcross, Georgia, his Advanced Memory Formula and if you buy three jars of this product for one month ($39.95 + $5.95 S&H), you will receive three gifts, a standard operating marketing ploy for many alternative medicine representatives, as you will see repeatedly in the rest of this chapter: "for his Advanced Joint Support," and for his Super Sudoku for memory problems.

Through the *Journal of Natural Medicine*, Dr. Nan Kathryn Fuchs explains to us why our stomachs still hurt. We can do that by stop putting temporary band aids on our digestive problems. Instead, she is willing to give us a simple solution that will strengthen our entire digestive system. Time after time, she has seen it work wonders when all else has failed us. She informs us about how to get rid of gas, indigestion, and similar problems by buying her Integrative Digestive Formula for $34.95 and $6.95 S&H.

Dr. Robert D'Amico with Schweiz Health of Kankakee, Illinois, recommends the Billion-Dollar Secret for Superhuman Health to look, feel, and perform as if we were 10, 15, even 20 years younger. What is this "new approach to stress, super energy, and total health"? You should already know! It's Adaptogenics now available in the United States through EVH Supreme! You can get a free trial sample and if it "does not do everything they say it does then you do not pay!" Sound familiar? This refrain is repeated *ad nauseam* from most companies that sell products reviewed here. In case you do not understand Latin, those two words mean "it makes us vomit."

Dr. Mark Stengler, with the support of BottomLine Books, offers us for *free* a book that will tell you how you can heal yourself with today's best fast-acting natural cures, thus reversing diabetes, cancer, arthritis, and Alzheimer's without drugs or surgery. Get rid of pain, fatigue, flu, high blood pressure, and high cholesterol faster than before. Heal wounds, cuts, and bruises in minutes. Avoid worthless supplements that don't work. I hope someday someone will sue good Dr. Stengler and BottomLine for making false claims.

What can I say in the rest of this chapter that would not be repetitious of information already commonly available to most readers through reading, watching TV, and consulting the Internet and one's health professional? To answer this question, and to keep with the purpose of this work, for my pleasure and the pleasure of my readers, I thought that it might be a distinct pleasure for them to read my exposé of most hucksters, scammers, and cons that plague the food industry and especially the vitamins and minerals billion dollar food market.

I went over all the food advertisements, brochures, and blandishments I have received in the mail during the last years, trying to convince me to buy miraculous vitamins and fantastic supplements supposed to improve my health and prolong my life. Let us consider—seriously, logically, and scientifically—whether or not there is any real evidence that these can and do work, or whether they are more a "buyer beware" line of products.

## THE MERCHANTS OF "GOOD" FOOD

I do not know about you but in the last few years I have been deluged by colorful, expensive brochures promoting all sorts of healthy foods, diets, and foods as medication for practically every disease in

**Table 4.2  Sample List of Selected Products Sold to Improve Health**

| Company | Address | Areas of Body Advertising Says Will Be Improved | Name of Product | Cost per Unit in Dollars and S&H |
|---|---|---|---|---|
| Advanced Bionutritionals | Norcross, GA | Bone Density | Ultimate Bone Support | 29.95 + 6.95 |
| | | Arteries and Immune System | Advanced Resveratrol Formula | 39.95 + 6.05 |
| | | System Detoxification | Pectasol Chelation | 39.95 + 6.95 |
| Bel Marra | Boynton Beach, FL | General Health | Daily ORAC Power | 99.95 + free |
| Bel Marra Nutritionals | Boston, MA | Health | Omega-3 Miracle | 89.00 + free |
| Best Life Herbals | Boise, ID | Blood Pressure | SetaCuorenol | 50.95 + 9.00 |
| | | Weight Loss | Acai Berry | 21.17 + 4.95 |
| | | Prostate | ProstaRye | 16.95 + 4.95 |
| | | Incontinence | Colostrum | 23.76 + 4.95 |
| | | Cardiovascular Health | Nattokinase | 23.76 + 4.95 |
| | | Vision | Visonal | 25.45 + 4.95 |
| | | Circulation, Memory | Resveratrol | 16.96 + 4.95 |
| | | Energy, Vitality | Invigoral | 47.52 + 4.95 |
| | | Heart Functioning | OmegaGel | 33.96 + 4.95 |
| | | Sleep | SlumberSPRAY | 21.17 + 4.95 |
| | | Sleep | Delta/Som | 27.95 + 4.95 |
| | | Pain | Desinol | 23.76 + 4.95 |
| | | Cramps and Spasms | Ointment | 16.96 + 4.95 |
| | | Bone, Lower Back Pain | OsteoD-Fend | 2.76 + 4.95 |
| | | Detoxification | Flora DSF | 16.96 + 4.95 |

(continued)

**Table 4.2** (Continued)

| Company | Address | Areas of Body Advertising Says Will Be Improved | Name of Product | Cost per Unit in Dollars and S&H |
|---|---|---|---|---|
| | | Belching and Flatulence | GAS | 16.96 + 4.95 |
| | | Colon Cleansing | Colo-Cleans | 25.45 + 4.95 |
| | | Lungs | Clear Lungs | 16.96 + 4.95 |
| | | Tinnitus | TinniSPRAY | 16.96 + 4.95 |
| | | Multi-vitamin | Men and Women Daily Formula | 33.96 + 4.95 |
| | | Energy | 8 Hour Energy XP | 42.45 + 4.95 |
| | | Memory | Memory SPRAY | 16.96 + 4.95 |
| | | Skin Aging | Dermisen Crème | 42.46 + 4.95 |
| Biocentric Health | Centreville, MD | Energy | Alexin | 49.95 + 6.95 |
| | | Joint Pain | Hydraflexin | 39.95 + 6.95 |
| | | Digestion/Gas | Digelin-3 | 34.95 + 6.95 |
| Biomolecular | Manteno, IL | Painful Joints | Rejuve-A-Joint | Not given |
| | | Memory | Memitol | Not given |
| BioNutrax | Manteno, IL | Old Age | Proxergen | Not given |
| Biowell | Canfield, OH | Unclog Arteries | Cardio Vital | 39.99 + 7.95 |
| | | Vision | Oculing | 39.90 + 7.95 |
| Dr. Earl Mindell | | Anti-aging | Life Extension Kit | 90.00 + 14.95 |
| Dr. Frank Shallenberger | Norcross, GA | Arthritis | Prolozone | Not given |
| Dr. Michael E. Rosenbaum | Torrance, CA | Aging | Sun Chlorella | 39.95 + 6.00 |
| Dr. Victor Marchione | Boynton Beach, FL | Colon | Healthy Colon | 49.95 + free |
| | | Vision | 20/20 Vision | 99.95 + 4.95 |
| | | Aging | The Red Wine Pill | 99.95 + free |
| Goldshield Direct | West Palm Beach, FL | Aging | Ultimate Anti-oxidant | 39.95 + 4.50 |

**Table 4.2  (Continued)**

| Company | Address | Areas of Body Advertising Says Will Be Improved | Name of Product | Cost per Unit in Dollars and S&H |
|---|---|---|---|---|
| Hampshire Labs | Minneapolis, MN | Joint Pain and Stiffness, Cartilage, Skin | JointFlex | 39.95 + 4.95 |
| | | Sleep, Weight Loss, and Muscle Growth | Collagen | 29.95 + 5.95 |
| | | Diabetes | Circulation Booster | 19.95 + 7.95 |
| | | Vision | Vision Choice | 39.95 + 5.95 |
| | | Diabetes, | Ultimate Diabetic, | (all three products together) |
| | | Blood Sugar, | Circulation Booster, | |
| | | Blood Circulation | Glyco-Betic | 39.95 + 4.95 |
| | | Artery Circulation | Artery Cleanse | 127.90 + 4.95 |
| | | Artery Circulation | Nerve Rejuvenator | 39.95 + 5.95 |
| | | Heart | Asian Heart Health | 29.95 + 4.95 |
| | | Everything | Collagen VIP | |
| Harmony Company | Northvale, NJ | Joints | Flex: Solve 24/7 | 39.95 + 9.95 |
| Health Resources | Hueytown, AL | Longevity | Advanced ResV Plus | 29.95 + 6.95 |
| HomeCures | Mesa, AZ | Thyroid | ThyActive | 29.95 + 6.95 |
| Immunocorp | Mira Mar, CA | Immune System | Immutol@ | 59.95 + 6.95 |
| Institute for Vibrant Living | Camp Verde, AZ | Strength | Energy Greens | 39.95 + 7.95 |
| Juvenon | Manteno, IL | Healthy | Natto BP Plus | 49.95 + 7.95 |
| Life Extension | Ft. Lauderdale, FL | Anti-aging Pill | Juvenon | 46.90 + 6.95 |
| Miracle Breakthrough Labs | Coral Gables, FL | Brain Aging, Depression, Fear | Cognitex | 37.00 + free |
| | | Anxiety, Stress | FeelGreat 2020 | 39.00 + free |

*(continued)*

**Table 4.2 (Continued)**

| Company | Address | Areas of Body Advertising Says Will Be Improved | Name of Product | Cost per Unit in Dollars and S&H |
|---|---|---|---|---|
| Nature City | Boca Raton, FL | Health | AloeCran | 29.95 + 6.95 |
| | | Pain and Inflammation | TrueAloe | 24.97 + 6.95 |
| Natures Wave | Leesburg, VA | Illnesses | Energy Booster | 200.00 + 10.00 |
| | | Poisons | Detoxifier | Unspecified |
| NorthStar Nutritionals | Frederick, MD | Bloating and Cramping | SMARTShip | 89.95 + 6.95 |
| | | Painful Skin | IncrediCream | 27.95 + 6.95 |
| | | Prostate | ProSense | 59.94 + 6.95 |
| | | Sleep | V-calm | 34.95 + 6.95 |
| | | Pain | Soothanol X2 | 49.95 + 6.95 |
| | | Restless Leg Syndrome | LegSense | 59.95 + 6.95 |
| | | Aging | Healthy Aging | 54.95 + 6.95 |
| | | Stiff Joints | Flexanol | 34.95 + 6.95 |
| | | Bladder Control | UroLogic | 49.95 + 6.95 |
| | | Immune System | PureImmune Plus | 39.95 + 6.95 |
| | | Prostate | Prostate Defense | 39.95 + 6.95 |
| | | Vision | Vision Sense | 24.95 + 6.95 |
| | | Energy Level | Natural Energy | 19.95 + 6.95 |
| | | Body and Heart | CoOMelt | 49.95 + 6.95 |
| | | Aging | RegeneCell | 399.95 + 14.95 |
| | | Blood Sugar | Gluco-Sure | 39.95 + 6.95 |
| | | Hair Loss | Restore FX | Free trial |
| | | Pain | Soothanol X2 | 49.95 + 6.95 |

**Table 4.2** (Continued)

| Company | Address | Areas of Body Advertising Says Will Be Improved | Name of Product | Cost per Unit in Dollars and S&H |
|---|---|---|---|---|
| Nutri-Health Supplements | Cottonwood, AZ | Pain | ArthroZyme | 39.95 + 6.95 |
| | | Prostate | Prostaleve RX9 | 39.95 + 6.95 |
| | | Sinus | Flora Sinus | 46.90 + free |
| | | Constipation | Flora Source | 36.90 + free |
| NutritionExpress | Torrance, CA | Health Products | Various Products | Different costs |
| Primal Force | Royal Palm Beach, FL | Weight Loss | Primal Lean | 42.26 + 6.95 |
| Real Advantage Nutrients | Frederick, MD | Strength | Ultimate Bionic Plus | 34.95 + 6.95 |
| Rejuva Naturals | Manteno, IL | Digestion | DyflowGEST | 39.95 + 6.95 |
| Rejuvenation Laboratories | Cadillac, MI | Osteoarthritis | Medi-Collagenics | 34.00 + 6.95 |
| Schweiz Health | Manteno, IL | Everything | KurZyme | 59.95 + not given |
| | | Aging | Phyteva | Not given |
| Stop Aging Now | Orlando, FL | Health | Superfruit Fusion | 19.99 + not given |
| | | Joint Pain | Super Osteo Gold | 29.95 + not given |
| Tabak | Irvine, CA | Joint Pain and Stiffness | Arthritis-Ease | Not given |
| Targeted Nutrients | Phoenix, AZ | Energy Booster | D-Ribose | 29.95 + 7.95 |
| True Health | Hueytown, AL | Toxins, Plaque, Blood Clots, Pressure, Cholesterol | Advance Artery Solution | 59.85 + 6.95 |
| UniScience | Bridgeport, CT | Memory | Mem-Plex | 46.90 + 6.95 |
| Vitamin Science | Huntington, NY | Vision | VisiVite | 39.95 + 6.95 |
| WellMed | Encino, CA | Thyroid | Thyroid Control | 49.90 + free |
| Wellness Research and Consulting | Royal Palm Beach, FL | Lungs | PACE Program | 39.95 + 6.95 |

111

existence or in nonexistence, not to speak of minerals, supplements, and vitamins. More specifically than what has been presented above, during the last few decades there has been a movement toward finding the relationship between certain foods and their relationship to improve health. As a result of this movement, all sorts of food are proclaimed to be the real source of health. A prime example of this movement is the publishing house of *Prevention* magazine sold in practically all grocery stores in the United States. In their latest book edition[11] they give nutrient prescriptions for most common conditions, ranging from acne to wrinkles. They also give detailed descriptions of essential nutrients, minerals, and vitamins. For instance, they admit that diabetes is a serious condition and the individual with this condition should be working with a physician to keep the disease under control. Then, they list alpha lipoic acid, B vitamins, Chronium, CoEnzyme Q10, Magnisium, N-Acetylcytine, Omega-3 fatty acids, vitamin D, and Zinc as possible ways to deal with that disease. No scientific source or reference is given. The reader has to accept such prescriptions on faith, assuming that they are correct and based on reliable research evidence.

In a recent brochure, Rodale Books, at the same address as *Prevention* magazine, advertised to sell at no risk to readers the *24 Hour Pharmacist* for four easy installments of $7.99 each with three gifts: "Dermatologist's Secrets for Sensational Skin," "77 High-Speed Home Healers," and "Test Your Health Yourself," as well as "The Gluten Connection" and "Diabetes without Drugs." How can you bypass such bargains? If you want to purchase vitamins and minerals at discount prices, perhaps you may consult reliable references given in Table 4.2.

Take, for instance, this advertisement by a Charlotte Garner who asks whether you (the reader) suffers from bloating, abdominal cramps, constipation, diarrhea, digestive spasms, or irritable bowel syndrome. She has good news for you. According to Charlotte, now there are amazing new solutions you may not have has a chance to see. Because she really does care about your health, good, old (?) Charlotte wants to be the *first* (emphasis hers) to give you information that even your doctor may not have heard—about *natural* solutions to all kinds of troublesome, even embarrassing, digestive problems. Charlotte thinks that Gayle K. Wood's new book *Guide to the Complete Digesting Health* is one of her best—especially when it comes to finding relief from "tummy troubles." But you, dear reader, do not need to take Charlotte's word for it, you can have it, and start using it, right away at no cost or risk. What do you have to lose? In this book you will find how some simple changes in food intake will, among others, (1) help you get rid of gas; (2) find effective ways to ease stress and calm digestion; and (3) select fruits that can fix constipation (two prunes and five almonds a day do it for me, thank you).

Most specifically, Gayle herself tells us about "Foods that explode in your bowel!" including honey to "conquer" constipation, herbs (unspecified) to get rid of gas, and cinnamon to banish bacteria. According to Gayle, there is just one nutrient that can prevent, ease, or help heal at least 22 health problems—including high blood pressure, irritable bowel syndrome, diabetes, and weight gain. This is just a small sample of what food can do for you. This is the hype and oftentimes the hoax. To support her claims, Gayle uses four testimonials from three older women and one man who testify to the almost miraculous outcome derived from her book. Furthermore, you have nothing to lose; Gayle will refund your money if you are not 100 percent satisfied. If you order your volume before the expiration date we, lucky prompt readers, will receive a booklet entitled: "Eat to Beat the Top 27 Health Problems." How lucky can we get? For instance, regulate your digestion with honey, soothe your stomach with peppermint, and ditch diarrhea with bananas.

Hampshire Laboratories of Minneapolis, Minnesota, for "just three easy payments of only $9.99 each" will send you a "Complete Guide to Digestive Health" to examine without an obligation and will also send you a free booklet, "Eat to Beat the Top 27 Health Problems." If we want to learn all we want to know about "foods that heal" "35 times faster" than others, it is easy to find this information. For a miserly $77 paid to Dr. Frank Shallenberger, MD, of Norcross, Georgia, we can subscribe to his *Real Cures* for two years and save $117 and receive 17 free reports. If we are tight with our money, just send only $39—save $57—and receive just 12 issues. Mind you, this is information "we won't find anywhere." Dr. Shallenberger wants to sell us a two-year subscription to his *Real Cures* newsletter and his reports will give us ways and means to take care and "cure" as many illnesses as you can list in one minute, ranging from a permanent cure for arthritis, how he cures his allergies for good and so can you, how to end insomnia for good, etc. including prostate cancer, arteries, interstitial cystitis, type-2 diabetes, blood pressure, etc. All of this from the privacy of our own home. We better hurry up or we will miss a good deal.

Good, old Jerry Baker of Wixom, Michigan, wants to send us his book about *SuperMarket Super-Remedies* for free to examine it with a

Lifetime Guarantee. If we keep the book all we have to pay is four installment of $7.69 each (total $30.76) plus shipping and handling. In this book, we will find how we can beat arthritis with cherries, banish back pain with chamomile, wipe out age spots with horseradish, tame ulcers with cabbage, and smooth away cellulite with grapefruit. All of this in the palm of our hand.

If you want to really live longer and healthier you should use an amazing health secret, you should use Sun Chlorella, as recommended by Dr. Michael E. Rosenbaum in a 10 ½ × 13 ½ inch 24-page brochure with lots and lots of colorful testimonials. You can get 300 tablets of this miraculous product for just $24.95 that comes with a free gift of a booklet about the "Life Diet Book." If you order within 10 days (from when?) you will get another extra free gift for promptness: "Nature's Fountain of Youth." I tried this product for three months and all it gave me was what it was supposed to cure: constipation.

Recent book acquisitions (returned to the source after careful perusal) include *Eat and Health* published by the editors of FC&A Medical Publishing from Peachtree City, Georgia, tells us how to cure practically everything through food. If you buy this book (which I did not buy and returned immediately), on page 11 there is a substance that fights heart disease, stroke, impotence, and cancer. On page 298 we will fight Father Time with an "humble dried fruit. Research shows it could help stave off the diseases of aging, including Alzheimer's and Parkinson's disease." I could go on and on, but we get the drift. Woods advocated without any scientific or professional evidence, proof, or bibliographical reference would have to be indeed miraculous.

The same publishers sell also a book about *Super Foods for Senior* to "Rejuvenate your veins and arteries." In this book on page 140 you will find that "Just two servings of this [food] each week will bolster your body against heart attack, stroke, type 2 diabetes, depression AND cancer" and "Lose weight, reduce stress, and even treat diabetes with this amazing remedy found on page 166." Need I to go on? Apparently, if we use all the foods included in this book we would not need any medication, reverse the effects of aging, and keep our brains sharp for the golden years. To be fair, these publishers at the end do list a great many popular, professional, and scientific sources. However, there is no way one can trace one single source to one specific food. Then why list all these sources, except to give a certain degree of legitimacy to a questionable enterprise? The intentions of these publishers may be good, but in spite of their use of biblical references, or perhaps because of them, we know where the road of good intentions leads to.

## Vitamins and Minerals: The Great American Scam

The multi-billion market for minerals and vitamins is so popular that every day I receive expensive advertisings about all the miraculous breakthroughs and incredible cures that such products can produce. This phenomenal number of advertising is probably due to my buying some products and their manufacturer selling a list of addresses to new companies. There are, however, different types and degrees of scams, some with legitimacy, that have research and evidence to support the product, some evidence at the borderline of legitimacy, and some evident scams without any kind of evidence or legitimacy, except the word of one practically unknown individual.

How are we going to discriminate among all shades and degrees in legitimacy? I will go over the information I have received to bring readers up-to-date about what is going on in these areas of vitamins and minerals. Here we enter the world of scams, where vitamins and minerals are sold, in some cases with a seemingly great deal of research,[12] in some cases with some research background, as in the book published by Rodale[13] and in many cases without any kind of research background except testimonials of individuals who apparently make a living by appearing in some of the brochures peddled by these scammers.

In Rodale's[14] *Healing with Vitamins: The Best Nutrients to Slow, Stop and Reverse Disease*, the editors of this volume list supplemental prescriptions for 90 common conditions, with a large, introductory section detailing all the vitamins and minerals that are necessary for health, followed by a vast section of most diseases that supposedly can be "cured" with vitamins and minerals as well as food, from age spots all the way to yeast infection. The amount of detail given about each prescription is quite large and impressive, except for one particular point: the scientific bases for each prescription, usually consisting of references in peer-reviewed journals, are not given. Some physicians are quoted but no other information is given, raising the question of whether the information given is reliable, that is, to be believed, or whether this information is coming from unreliable sources: not to be believed. If the reader is willing to take a chance, this volume may be one place to start.

However, it would be important to check on another source that does use medical references and that attempts to integrate traditional mainstream with alternative medicine.[15] Using an impressive roster of physicians as its editorial board, this Life Externtion Foundation is a veritable encyclopedia of health-related information that claims to have introduced life-saving medical discoveries from 1980 to 2004. After an introduction to scientific medicine, a wider range of medical conditions are detailed ranging from acetaminophen poisoning to wound healing.

There is, unfortunately, one troubling spot that concerns me about the Life Extension Foundation, and that is: selling and advertising its own products, a practice that mainstream medicine or professional associations do not do. Why? Because there would be a conflict of interest. That conflict would not allow an objective prescription and administration of any mainstream and questionably alternative medication. This is what quacks do, as discussed below. For instance, after reading in their magazine an article on Vitamin K and called in to check on the appropriateness of this vitamin, I was assured that it was appropriate for me to use. However, after a murmur was discovered in my heart and after extensive tests, my cardiologist recommended that I no longer should take that vitamin because it acts as blood thinner inappropriate for my condition.

Nonetheless, if one were to overlook such a concern, the information given in the Life Extension encyclopedic text and its monthly magazine is rather remarkable and certainly useful to an advanced reader. But I doubt whether an average, mature layperson could read and use what is printed. Who am I to judge who is average and who is mature? Let the reader decide. I still found the information interesting and in some cases useful. More about the Life Extension magazine below.

*Prevention Magazine* from Emmaus, Pennsylvania (same address of Rodale books), advertises for Dr. James A. Duke, "legendary founder of the world-famous *Green Pharmacy*." In this book, you will find how to lose 62 percent weight with a handful of almonds a day, drop your blood pressure by 10 points with a tomato, beat high cholesterol with blueberries, beat hot flashes with black beans, erase arthritis pain with ginger, soothe irritable bowel syndrome with salad greens, beat osteoporosis with a serving of salmon, and magnify your memory power with mint. These cures and more for just four easy payments of $7.99 plus S&H.

The "Vitamin Doctor" David Juan writes in a newsletter published by Doctors Health Press (DHP). In the issue I read, he does not sell any vitamin and supplements. His information seems timely and useful, sometimes giving full scientific references to bolster his conclusions. He seems to adhere to the exemplary Mission Statement of this newsletter:

We believe that better health can be achieved through education, informed decision making, and proactive motivation. Our goal at "The Vitamin Doctor" is to provide a balanced and unbiased newsletter, featuring new and established information on vitamins, minerals, and supplements. Everyone can lead a long, healthful and active life, and this is attainable through solid nutrition, healthy choices, and educated consumption.

Unfortunately, DHP also sells products such as *Secret Herbal Cures to Combat Sickness.* Another member of the same group advertises "five powerful cures" for incontinence. There are three words that should alert curious and suspicious readers to spot questionable advertising such as this: (1) why "secret" if it is now advertised? Apparently, it means that mainstream medicine either does not know about it or does not use it because there is no evidence to support its use; (2) no single product in science and medicine can "cure" anything because cure means eliminating a disease and no evidence is presented to support the use of the word "cure"; and (3) "sickness" is too general and non-specific to the point that one should know what kind of sickness. Sickness can range from an occasional cold to a persistent cancer. As we shall see later on in this chapter, there are definite guidelines to spot questionable and false advertising that apply not only to food, minerals, supplements, and vitamins but also to products that are supposed to enhance sexual impotence and increase penis size, as discussed in Chapter 7 of this volume.

In a *Journal of Healing Discoveries,* Dr. DicQie Fuller tell us to forget about all the herbs, supplements, vitamins, minerals, and even prescription drugs or healthy eating; they won't work and will not cure your health problems. What the good doctor wants you to do is buy her amazing KurZime for just $59.95 a month. You better hurry because this special introductory offer is for the first 500 customers who will call immediately.

In the *Journal of Modern Health* from Cottonwood, Arizona, using evidence by over 40 clinical trials and one lengthy testimonial,

Nutri-Health Supplements will sell you a bottle of AthroZyme (see Table 4.2) that will do away with any arthritic pain you may have.

One doctor, Jonathan V. Wright, who publishes the newsletter *Nutrition & Healing*, does give prescriptions for minerals and vitamins to treat specific conditions. However, to his credit, he is quite an exception, i.e., apparently, at least in the copy of his newsletter I have in my files, he does not sell what he prescribes. Readers are free to buy whatever he prescribes anywhere they want. Wow! Furthermore, he also lists alternative health resources that can also be found on the Internet. The Health Sciences Institute of Frederik, Maryland, will send you "uncensored" truth about natural cures that the medical establishment won't let us have. If you become a member for $49 you will receive as an extra bonus volume *Vital Health Secrets*. Aren't getting sick of all these "secret" cures? Just read on and you will become sick!

However, in a booklet written by Matthew Simons and published by Healthier News LLC of Baltimore, Maryland, that writer bemoans how Dr. Wright's clinic was closed by a "band of terrorists," i.e., federal agents from the FDA, who attacked it by kicking the door down, and with guns drawn, including sticking a revolver in the receptionist's face and ripping phone lines from the wall, holding the staff at gunpoint for two hours, kicking them out of the clinic, and ransacking the clinic by destroying medical equipment and pawing through confidential patient records. The reason: apparently using preservative-free B vitamins. No charges were ever filed and two federal grand juries didn't return an indictment.

Following this information, Mr. Simons precedes to praise Dr. Wright's "leading the way to an amazing new kind of medicine ... doing with food, vitamins, and minerals things that drug companies never imagined possible" (p. 27). For example, "The 26-cent miracle that knocks out Alzheimer's," that is, lithium carbonate, aspartate or orotate to treat bipolar disorder. Other recommendations are: "Stop diabetes in its tracks with cinnamon," an "astonishing cure for cancer," an extract from eggplant called BEC5, spectacular sugar cane cures outdo cholesterol drugs, ultimate prostate treatment shrinks swelling, may prevent cancer, and protect manhood with a mineral to be added to selenium. You will find the name of this mineral and many other food, mineral, and vitamin cures if you subscribe to Dr. Wright's 12-issue newsletter for just $49 and if your reply within 11 days you will receive a free bonus booklet about "The Miracle Mineral." What are you waiting for? You can use a check and most credit cards. Aren't you lucky that I gave you this information? I just hope you do not take me seriously because Dr. Wright advertises "secret cancer cures and effective steps to cancer prevention."

In another issue (No. 17, 2010) of his *Nutrition & Healing* newsletter, Dr. Wright tells readers the secret that "mainstream medicine does not want you to know to reverse osteoporosis by actually rebuilding bone without the side effects of patent medicines." If you want to promote male fertility Dr. Wright suggests Tribulus Leaf, Korean Ginseng, and Withania root. To his credit, Dr. Wright report research studies to support the use of these three herbs! However, he undoes himself by then recommending magnetic energy to decrease pain. No wonder FDA agents raided his clinic. With claims of this kind without any evidence, the good doctor should be in jail.

A special report from a Health Sciences Institute will give us "for free" a complete encyclopedia of miracles cures if and when we become members of that institute. This volume will give us "100 medical discoveries that cure what nothing else will." These discoveries will "dry up cancer with liquid bread" (p. 5), "Romanian secret expels depression in days" (p. 7), " Stop smoking without will power within 5 seconds" (p. 9), "3,000 year-old secret found" for "stronger bones" and "fractures," "Sinful miracle chocolate. It's caffeine-free, yes, but boy will it keep you awake!" (p. 15). That's just a sample of the hyperbole these companies use to entice us poor, naive, gullible Americans.

Another scam, unfortunately apparently supported by "Legendary Newscaster Hugh Downs," is *Bottom Line*, which sells books entitled *Ultimate Healing* and *SuperHealing Unlimited*, which are replete with standard information easily available to whoever is interested and curious to know about it. For instance, one of their "medical team members" found an answer to Alzheimer's disease by "making brain plaques nearly disappear." Supposedly, a Nobel Prize winner "scoops drug firms and releases heart-healing breakthrough. His FREE secret could wipe out heart disease and replace some of today's costly new drugs." That's not enough: Cancer's cause unmasked and conquered! Shocking breakthrough could save millions from chemo and radiation! How about this: "Blacklisted breakthrough beats prostate cancer." Not enough? "Arthritis abolished in minutes by doctor's astonishing speed cure." Plus: "You too could lose 172 pounds in 7 months and keep it off for 7 years." Finally, the coup de resistance: "One spray & hurray! Amazing sex at any age is just a sniff away." However, "does your spouse snore? Stop the roar! Free treatment halts cause in 10 days," or "Maverick doctor reveals the tea he would drink if he had cancer." In a separate advertising booklet Bottom Line recommends that you follow direction on page 13 you will get an answer instantly for an Alzheimer's Home Test and if you buy the *2009 Bottom Line Yearbook*, you will have as many solutions to your health problems to last you a lifetime. If you believe all of this sensationalistic malarkey I can sell you the Brooklyn Bridge for a good price. Negotiable.

Another source of information that I have not checked out that may be on the borderline between legitimate and illegitimate practices is Dr. Bruce West's two-volume *Encyclopedia of Pragmatic Medicine*. If you subscribe to his Health Alert newsletter for two years at the miserly cost of $77 for two years, you will receive the two volumes of this encyclopedia. If you subscribe within 10 days since you received the advertisement, you will also receive an additional special report about *Bad Drugs and Big Lies: Big Pharma's Secret Assault to Your Health*. All total a $2,217 value that you can save by subscribing to his newsletter. See how much you can save?

How can you let go of such an opportunity? The good doctor informs us that your health is his number-one concern and he gives an "iron-clad" (Get it? Minerals? I love this pun within this context) 100 percent money-back guarantee if you are dissatisfied with his newsletter. He will give you a prompt refund for the full subscription rate and if your medical problem is not featured in his newsletter or in his encyclopedia, he will make sure that you will receive the information you need. On top of that, if you decide to cancel the subscription you may keep the encyclopedia as a gift. What do we have to lose?

However, "New evidence shows that the most life-giving organ in your body—your colon—is totally out of whack! ... Death begins in the colon. ... Tick, Tick, Tick. ... The Bomb in your Gut is About To Go Off! Most colons are swollen and too blocked to pass regular bowel movements! ... Gas and Bloating are your body's way of screaming SEND HELP NOW." You are reassured by the picture of a man in a white coat and 36 colorful pages chockfull of testimonials that the solution to all your real or imagined colon problems is supported by no less than Yale Medical School that "Says Yes to Probiotics!" If you order now up to a six-month supply of Flora Source from Nutri-Health Supplements from Cottonwod, Arizona, with a 100 percent iron-clad (I can't help myself, I love this pun!) money back guarantee of satisfaction, you will receive two extra free bottle of the stuff. Aren't we lucky?

In case you want to live a longer life than what is expected by your age, gender, and health condition, just order Dr. Michael Ingraham's

Phytenol's Extended Life Formula from Biomolecular from Manteno, Illinois. And if you want to live an even longer life, order CHO-WA from Kumato Labs of Signal Hill, California. If you want to "switch" and "Shut off Pain" three tiny drops from a bottle of Vital3 sold for a paltry $13 by Dr. Eugene R. Zampleton from Lindon, Utah, will do the trick.

An Adverse Drug Reaction Bulletin published by the Doctors Health Press of Boston, Massachusetts, warns readers about the dangers of legitimate medications for allergies, arthritis, and back pain all the way to ulcerative colitis. Instead, for just $49 Drs. Victor Marchione, Richard M. Fox, David Juan, and Jeffrey Shaprio recommend buying and subscribing to the five-volume *Library of Traditional Chinese Medicine Healing Miracles* based on herbs and their mixtures. The same press also publishes *Doctors' Vitamin Cures That Work: A Special Report.*

On the other hand, the September 2010 issue of *Consumer Reports* (*CR*) lists 12 supplements that should be avoided because they are dangerous to health: Aconite, Bitter Orange, Chaparral, Colloidal Silver, Coltsfoot, Comfrey, Country Mallow, Germanium, Greater Celandine, Kava, Lobelia, and Yohimbe. In addition, in the same issue, *CR* informs us that there are (1) at least 1,500 estimated U.S. supplement manufacturers; (2) only 55 estimated FDA inspections for good manufacturing practices; (3) 170+ supplements found to have hidden drugs or steroids since 2008; and (4) 33 percent of supplements in Natural Medicines Comprehensive Database with scientific evidence of efficacy that are likely safe. By the same token, *CR* listed 11 supplements that are safe enough to consider using: Calcium, Cranberry, Fish Oil, Glucosamine Sulfate, Lactase, Lactoba-cillus, Psylium, Pygeum, SAMs, St. John's Wort, and Vitamin D. Most multivitamins sold on the market by reputable companies seem equally safe except for the price. Additionally, synthetic food dyes should be banned because they may be responsible for a great many conditions, such as attention deficit hyperactivity disorder where these dyes may be the culprits.[16]

Another "legendary" (in whose mind?) doctor Julian Whitaker in a Health & Healing booklet from Lancaster, Pennsylvania, warns us about the "astonishing story of how an absurdly easy-to-treat disease (like diabetes) became America's most out-of-control epidemic." He also tells us ignorant readers, "What your doctor won't (and can't) tell you about how to heal diabetic heart disease, neuropathy, vision loss, incurable wounds—and escape inevitable kidney failure and amputations." His brand-new special report about *The Seven Greatest Secrets of*

*Beating Diabetes* can be had for *free* if you subscribe to his Health & Healing for just $29.99 with other free gift books. If you respond promptly you will get an extra bonus. You better hurry!

## How to Spot a Quack

By now you should be getting the drift about where I am going. I have already written in the professional literature about charlatans selling nostrums to a unsuspecting, gullible and naive, if not needy public.[17] In the same work, I have included chapters by reputable researchers and scholars about diets,[18] food,[19] preferable herbs to use as medications,[20] vitamins and supplements,[21] and omega-3 fatty acids.[22] However, because what I wrote might be considered an exposé for professionals, it is time to expose charlatans and quacks to a much wider audience of nonprofessionals, as I have done in Table 4.2. Hopefully you, the reader, are part of this wider audience.

Since I wrote that exposé, however, the amount and quality of quackery in the United States has grown exponentially. If the amount of mail I receive every day is an indicator of such an incredible growth, it shows why the U.S. Postal Service may go broke for mailing expensive brochures as printed matter. If this information were to be subjected to higher postage, perhaps our great American USPS may be able to survive financially.

Furthermore, there is no way the beleaguered, impossibly under-funded Federal Drug Administration can oversee and regulate a plethora of products as listed in Table 4.2 here. This is why we have such an incredible number of products based on extraordinary claims about their fantastic outcomes. These charlatans know no one will evaluate the usefulness of their products; a few testimonials and color-ful pictures will do the trick. More importantly, the same charlatans rely on the power of suggestions, what is now better known as the pla-cebo effect. Some placebos, sugar pills with no alimentary or health value in and of themselves, have been found to produce as many results as the medications they are supposed to compare with.

This effect does not work in every case. Reputable researchers in some disciplines and with some medications do still use placebos to evaluate the comparative usefulness of many medications. Hucksters, however, rely on the power of suggestions that, "If I bought it and I paid good money for it, it must be good." Additionally, these scammers rely on the power of self-evaluation by giving us lists and lists of possible signs of discomfort and even illness. Who has ever not experienced a cold, a congested chest, a temporary constipation or diarrhea? As I wrote earlier, if we do not have an illness, we shall find one after we read brochures published to entice us to develop one.

These charlatans have no scruples. They do not care whether their customers benefit or do not benefit by their products. Bottom line, the sales are to make money, not really to improve our health. If they were really interested in our health, they would evaluate their products according to standard research techniques and not just sensational testimonials.

There are sure-fire ways to spot fraudulent quacks or charlatans, as already illustrated and listed above. These scammers use pretty much the same techniques to lure us naive and needy costumers to fall prey to their enticing offers. As shown in this chapter and in Table 4.2 I have and will name them in the hope that they will sue me and take me to court for calling their bluff. That is the only way I know I will ever become known outside myself ("I am a legend in my own mind") and a small circle of family and friends. Let me list their practices to make sure you can learn to spot a quack.

1. *Expensive* and explosively colorful brochures advertising a new discovery or a new method of treatment that will solve most if not all medical and physical problems that imply self-diagnosis. For instance, do you want to live longer? Simple: buy one bottle or more of Advanced ResVPlus formula that supposedly includes the miraculous vitamin Resveratrol found in red wine and you will live to the ripe age of 122 years, such as the French woman used as an example to advertise this vitamin.

Using Harvard University's research as a supporting background, an outfit called Health Resources from Hueytown, Alabama, promises that if you buy 12 bottles of this stuff, you receive a $406.40 discount in the price and you will receive up to five *free* reports about (a) the Secret Power of Resveratrol anti-aging miracle, (b) 100 years and beyond, the secret of a healthy and long life; (c) the miracle brain nutrient that can restore 12 years of memory loss; (d) seven new health secrets for aging skin; and (e) the shocking truth about gray hair and other aging myths. Ordering is easy, by phone, mail, fax, and Web. What are you waiting for?

Thanks to the powerful youth-enhancing secret discovered in the wilderness diet of Alaska's giant Kodiak bears we can all become as healthy as a bear! This "secret" formula Proximas, sold by BioNutrax of Manteno, Illinois, will take care of all the signs of old age, and you know them well: wrinkles, fatigue, poor eyesight, memory fog, lackluster skin tone, low stamina, joint aches, sleepless nights, weight gain, low sex drive. Proximas will give you 10 to 20 years of life, guaranteed or your money back!

If you think this is just one example, how about the Goji-Vitality treatment from, of all places, the Himalayas! According to a colorful advertisement, there are seven good reasons for such treatment:

1. If you feel that your memory is failing
2. If you can no longer take feeling exhausted
3. If your physical strength recedes by the day
4. If you can no longer take these pains that are messing up your life (lumbar, sciatic, rheumatism, arthritis, etc.)
5. If your test results (cholesterol, hypertension) worry you
6. If sexual pleasure is but a fond memory and you want that to change
7. If your skin is drab, loose, and full of wrinkles and you want to take action

All you have to do is read the enthusiastic testimonials from individuals who supposedly took this nostrum and you will be convinced that you fit into at least one of those seven reasons. If you order it immediately you will receive this food extract with a 100 percent (iron-clad, of course!) money back guarantee.

2. *Self-aggrandizement* through real or phony doctors with various degrees, years of experience, and apparent recognition on well-known TV shows. For instance, these doctors oftentimes wear a white coat and sometimes a stethoscope wrapped around their necks. What could be more authoritative than that!

3. *Unproven personal claims* supported by testimonials from paid individuals of unknown origin. For instance, a Natural Health Report from Hampshire Laboratories from Minneapolis, Minnesota, in a 16-page brochure claims that the famous doctor Linus Pauling, MD, who won the Nobel Prize a record two times, recommends this supplement for a healthy heart. Now available to you (lucky reader) is the same supplement, The Ultimate Artery Cleanse for relief from many health problems, namely:

• lower your risk of heart attack by removing dangerous plaque from your blood
• lower you risk of stroke—from stopped blood flow to your brain
• end fatigue by giving you more energy each day
• lower your blood pressure because now blood flows more freely through your heart arteries.

- lower your cholesterol and triglycerides so you can have a longer, healthier life
- end sexual performance problems from more blood to your penis
- lose weight faster and easier
- end frequent urination trips at nighttime as prostate problems subside
- pain relief—as blood flows better through the entire circulation system of your body
- reverse loss of memory and mental functioning
- normalize blood sugar levels
- fight off infections, colds, and flu
- remove wrinkles, bags, and old-looking skin
- end sleeping problems
- end digestion and bowel problems
- enjoy vision and hearing improvement
- reduce anxiety, stress, and worry

All of these problems are taken care of by one single pill, sent to you on a no-risk basis, and if you are not satisfied, you will receive an extra $10 cash guarantee. Isn't that great? How could you turn down such an offer?

4. *An ambivalent love-hate dislike* for traditional medicine and Federal Drug Administration (FDA) as the major impediment to their practices even though relying on some (not all scientific) sources of evidence to support their claims. For instance, the FDA, called disparagingly "los federales," is accused of the most nefarious deeds, such as shutting down offices and procedures not deemed acceptable to the general public. In spite of these attacks critical of FDA practices that link this agency with large pharmaceutical companies, I have to admit that I found such a critique in one issue of the Life Foundation magazine quite credible and informative, and it makes me wonder whether we can trust such an agency to be working for us or for helping pharmaceutical companies accrue billions in financial gains.

In a booklet entitled *The Cure Conspiracy: Medical Myths, Alternative Therapies, and Natural Remedies Even Your Doctor May Not Know*, the editors of FC&A Medical Publishing from Peachtree City, Georgia, suggest all the possible ways most physical illnesses can be cured by eating the proper food, herbs, honey, etc. To their credit, these editors do debunk a great many myths and suggest supposedly better ways to address common illnesses. What I find difficult to digest (forgive another awful pun) is their recommending special food or vitamins solutions on the basis of little if any evidence and the existence of a huge *conspiracy* as if all pharmaceutical companies and the FDA were in cahoots to cheat the American public. Is that possible? In "An urgent message from the Executive Director of Health Sciences Institute," Executive Director Jenny Thompson warns readers to "Discover the secrets even most alternative doctors are scared to tell you." It's not enough to hear about conspiracies without a shred of evidence from extreme hate groups; apparently we have conspiracies within alternative medicine as well!

In a recent article in *Time* magazine[23] reporters Massimo Calabresi with help of Alice Park and Susan Weill documented how the FDA succumbed to pressures from GlaxoSmithKline to continue marketing blood thinner for diabetes Avandia in spite of numerous and consistent reports of its producing a significant number of heart attacks. As these reporters concluded, substantiating what Life Extension has been saying for years:

> Over the past two decades, as drug after drug has been recalled after winning FDA approval, it has been hard not to wonder if FDA regulators have been captured by the drug industry (p. 25) . . . the drug approval process is too easy for pharmaceutical companies to game. . . . The results of this broken system may prove *criminal* as well as *fatal.* (p. 26; italics added)

An even more chilling and frightening report about the relationship among pharmacological companies and the academic community, one must read exposés by Elliott and by Mayer[24] about the influence on the health industry by the infamous billionaire brothers Charles and David Koch. It is absolutely frightening how their money has corrupted the body politic and decision making at the highest echelons of power in Washington.

Traditional medicine is also the target of many attacks. For instance, in a booklet written by William Campbell Douglass II, MD, described as a "colorful, rebellious crusader," he is now broadcasting to us from somewhere outside the United States. He lists the biggest medical lies of the last 50 years plus nine more medical lies that can wreck our lives. Among them: cholesterol does not cause heart disease. Lower your cholesterol and die faster. No-salt diet may increase your blood pressure: a medical myth. Statin drugs are a threat to your life. Drink (alcohol) to your health and do it often! Eight glasses of water? Sez [*sic*] who? Exercise won't add even one day to your life! Medical tests cause cancer.

However, if you subscribe to *The Douglass Report* for two years for $77 you also receive 10 free gifts consisting of booklets about a variety of ills. If you subscribe for one year and pay $47 you will receive only seven free gifts. In another large 20-page brochure Dr. Douglass warns us about the "vicious conspiracy designed to keep us sick" perpetrated by Big Pharma that is "not our friend and is run by irresponsible lunatics." If we were to believe what a recent *Time Magazine*, quoted earlier in this chapter, had to say about the FDA, perhaps this conspiracy may no longer be a secret. It is now well known that pharmaceutical companies work to make money for their stockholders and their upper-echelon directors. If I were making a salary close or more the $2 million as a CEO of a pharmaceutical company, I would fight any change myself. Would you? These companies have spent millions to wreck any new health program that may allow most Americans to be covered for being sick. However, the claims made by the Douglass report about curing diabetes, arthritis, and other sundry conditions need to be substantiated, no matter what the FDA does or does not do.

5. *Inordinate claims of cure-alls* for just about any condition. For instance, if you want to know about "The Two Most Powerful and Important Health Discoveries of Our Time" send a check for $15 to Beacon Hill Publishing and you will receive this information with a money-back guarantee if you are not 100 percent satisfied. Hurrah! I was able not to add "Iron-clad guarantee here." How controlled can I be? You are not told what these amazing, exceptional, and remarkable nutrients are. However, you are told that they will "turn back time and make your body's cells younger!" All of this "super-food" comes in a pill "that puts your body in perfect balance."

6. *Scare tactics*, such as those from Colon Medical News from Proper Health Systems in Newbury Park, California, that informs the reader that "Autopsies don't lie" and that colon autopsies show it and now studies prove it: Toxic bowels triggered by hidden constipation have become an out-of-control and *deadly* epidemic. According to colon expert Dr. Dana Churchill (a nice young man in a while coat and a stethoscope over his neck), "millions of Americans are lugging around 6–12 pounds of thick, accumulated toxic fecal matter without knowing it! 90 percent of adult American are walking around with a clogged colon." This claim is supported by a colorful, detailed 12-page brochure promoting the sale of Coloxin, a compound composed of psyllium seed, fennel seed, buckthorn bark, golden-seal whole herb, cascara sagrada bark, rhubarb root, licorice root, ginger root, and N-Acetyl Cysteine. For $33.16 a bottle you get also five free extra

reports about detox secrets from colon experts around the world, what you need to know before your next colonoscopy (that gastroenterologists don't know), how to get rid of gas quick, how to undo years of weight gain caused by stress, and finally, the piece *de resistance*: the art of sex and seduction after 50. I can't wait to get it but I am too cheap to pay for it. More about the latter in Chapter 7 of this volume.

## What Makes a Product Legitimate?

When we go to the supermarket we shop with a certain degree of security that whatever food we buy is covered by the Federal Consumer Protection Agency. That agency requires companies to give and label the breakdown of chemicals that make up the composition of the product, including also its calories. This method might not be perfect but is sufficient for us to be confident in the relative safety of the food we buy.

Nonetheless, Blumenthal and Volpp[25] attempted to answer the question why current approaches to food labeling in restaurants may be largely unsuccessful, a question that may be also asked in regard to food labeling in most alimentary products: (1) Consumers may not underestimate caloric content; (2) consumers may not understand caloric information; (3) the problem may often lie on self-control on the part of consumers rather than on lack of information. These writers made the following suggestions for making food labeling more useful: (1) Make information provision more easily understood; (2) focus on information framing; and (3) use defaults to favor healthy food choices. Even better, to make sure consumers understand what they eat, make this information easily available in the menus.

These requirements are completely absent in most of the products listed in Table 4.2 as well as in Table 7.1 of this volume. This means that usually we do not know (1) what chemical components make up the product, even though in all fairness some companies do; (2) research supporting the use (safety) of each particular component, especially in regard to side effects; (3) whether the product was evaluated with a sufficient number of animal and/or human participants using an experimental group that was administered the product and a control group that was not given the product or was given a dummy placebo pill instead; and (4) comparative evaluation of the product with similar products that claim to "cure" the same condition. Given the same the results for any two comparable products, all things being equal, the cheaper one wins. Unless a product fulfills all these four requirements, there is good reason to believe that the product is illegitimate and should not be used.

## DIETS AND WEIGHT-CONTROL

The same criteria just outlined above apply also to all the commercial companies that sell diet and weight-control programs.[26] There are more than a dozen such companies. To stay in business they must provide customers with reasonable and reliable (that is, legitimate) information about their programs. In spite of these requirements, some companies indirectly use research, such as the glycemic index, to advertise their programs and in some instances sell their food products directly to the public. There is no need to use precious page space to list all these companies. I am sure the curious reader can find them all on the Internet. However, the best diet program is composed of two requirements: (1) a fierce willingness to lose weight and (2) where there is a will, there is a way to follow a definitive routine to eat less but make every bite count, literally. Just remember LESS and see whether you can follow it on your own. If you cannot, then rely on a choice of a program, not a pill, after evaluating many programs using the criteria given above to spot a charlatan. Above I gave also the requirements necessary to evaluate the legitimacy of any pill or program.

If you are interested in "The Changing American Diet," as a starter, consult the article by Bonnie Liebman in the March 2010 issue of *Nutrition Action Health Newsletter*. However, if you are looking for a healthy, anti-aging, heart-brain-connected diet, keep in mind the acronym DASH that stands for Dietary Approach to Stop Hypertension. In terms of servings a day it consists of (1) seven to eight of whole grain products; (2) four to five vegetables; (3) four to five fruits; (4) two to three low-fat or fat-free dairy products; (5) one to two meats, poultry, and fish; (6) four to five nuts, seeds, and dry beans; (7) two to three fats and oils; and (8) five servings per week. You can go back to Figure 4.1 for more specific suggestions.

The Editors of FC&A in Peachtree City, Georgia, have published since 1995 a booklet that claims you can take off 20 pounds and 20 years in 20 weeks or less, naturally. You can obtain that outcome by first measuring your body mass (chart enclosed) if you exercise regularly (listing 20 more activities you can chose from), by eating

**Vegetarian Health Diet**

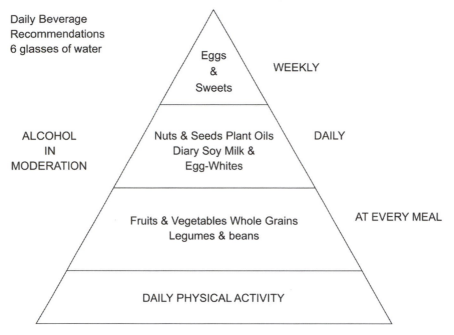

Figure 4.1    Traditionally Healthy Diet Pyramid.

certain foods and avoiding some others, and by limiting calories to no more than 1,200 a day. Included are tables of sizes for breads, cereals, grains, and starchy vegetables, fruits, meats, fish, and poultry. A great deal of relevant information for a 47-page booklet. All we need is motivation to change. That's the most important ingredient in all the diets.

## LIQUID FOOD

We need water to survive. Practically any other liquid that does not contain water and is not a liquid medicine is for enjoyment. The most enjoyable liquids that contain a minimum of water and a maximum of alcohol range from beer, to wine, and to what is called "hard liquor," containing various degrees of alcohol, up to 100 percent alcohol. Think about how many millions of people buy bottled water that is undistinguishable from tap water. Think how many people now drink red wine since reports about the supposedly healthier life of French people discovered the resvital was most responsible for such an outcome.

By the same token, think about how many alcoholics are produced every year by people who cannot control how and how much they drink. However, Kare Possick, for an undisclosed amount, will send you a free bottle of juice from the Nopal Cactus Fruit that will make you pain- and inflammation-free in five days. You can see this amazing product on a video at www.KaresCactusJuice.com. Please do not take this information as an endorsement of this product. It is included here as another example of a product sold on the basis of one personal testimonial (Kare's husband Charles) and absolutely no evidence to support its use. Nonetheless, as a drink from fruit, it may be pleasurable to drink.

If you drink hard liquor, do you know who invented the cocktail? This trivia question was answered by Curtis,[27] who traced its origins to a pioneering and flamboyant American bartender who published the first bar manual in 1862. Hurrah for a first to be proud as an American!

The last decade has seen the growth of new "energy" drinks that rely mostly on caffeine to give a "boost" to tired workers. Under the technical name of "functional beverages" they attempt to offer minerals, supplements, and vitamins in a liquid and supposedly pleasurable form. This one takes the cake. A newsletter from Heath News (Volume 17, Number 4, 2010) sells a metal container that will change the composition of your water and include through some kind of arcane process needed "alkaline antioxidant" for your body. This miraculous water will take care of Type I diabetes and will make any osteoarthritis pain disappear. If we follow all that these hucksters try to sell us, there should be thousands of miracles every day.

Italians usually do not drink hard liquors except grappa. However, they do have a weakness for mostly homemade limoncello that rates as the Italian National Drink. My Italian American buddy Gabe Pascarella introduced me to that drink as well as a more interesting version of limoncello called Basilcello, which I reproduce verbatim with his kind permission.

### Basilcello Recipe (Liquore al Basilico)

15 large basil leaves
1 lemon's zest
2 cups Everclear grain alcohol (190 proof)

2 ½ cups granulated sugar
2 ½ cups water, filtered

### Step One. Alcohol, lemon, and basil infusion

Clean the basil leaves by patting them with a dampened towel. Don't wash the basil as you don't want to lose any of their oils. (This is a lot quicker and easier that peeling lots of lemons!)

Into a glass container add the basil leaves, the lemon zest, and the grain alcohol. Cover the jar tightly and place it in a dark place at room temperature for 2 weeks.

Every few days, shake the container gently with a circular motion for a few moments. During this infusion period, the alcohol draws out the flavor and deep green color of the basil.

### Step Two. Make sugar syrup

After the infusion period, in a sauce pan, heat the filtered water and the sugar to a low boil and gently stir until sugar is completely dissolved and the mixture is clear. Continue a very low boil for 5 minutes. Remove sugar-water syrup from heat and let it cool to room temperature.

Remove the basil leaves and lemon zest by straining, then filter if necessary.

Mix strained infused alcohol with the cooled sugar-water syrup mixture.

### Step Three. Store and age

Put it away for at least another 3 weeks and it will mellow and smooth out, and will continue to do so for the next five or six months. Keep in the freezer and service ice cold! To your health!

## CONCLUSION

As we have seen throughout this chapter, food can be the source of many pleasures, including mental and physical health. However, if you look for health in all the many advertised products listed in this chapter, look for reliable information about food in the major sources given above and below, not in the sources listed in Table 4.1. What is contained in this chapter about minerals, supplements, and vitamins constitutes only the tip of a large iceberg. I tried to give the flavor (bad pun!) of what hucksters are trying to do to make money, not to improve our health.

Certain advertisers are aware of the dangers in making false claims. Consequently, they cover their backs with a statement that should get them out of legal trouble with federal regulatory agencies, such as "These statements have not been evaluated by the Food and Drug Administration. This product is not intended to diagnose, cure, mitigate, treat, or prevent any disease." These advertisers may make this claim. However, the way they advertise is usually contradictory of the disclaimer they make. In this chapter, after covering legitimate concerns about food, I have covered and included only about half or just one third of the information I have available in my file drawer. Some it's repetitive and redundant. What I tried to present is a sample hoping that the sample is ample enough to satisfy your hunger and thirst for knowledge about survival and enjoyment through food.

If you want reliable and specific information about food in general then do consult the *Nutrition Action Newsletter* from the Center for Science in the Public Interest, Suite 100, 1875 South Connecticut Avenue, NW, Washington, DC 20009-5728, as the best objective source you can get on food. I would rate second best the *Environmental Nutrition Newsletter for Food, Nutrition, and Health* published monthly by Belvoir Media Group LLC, 800 Connecticut Avenue, Norwalk, CT 06854-1631, and Tufts University *Health & Nutrition Letter*. A far fourth might be Dr. David Juan, the Vitamin Doctor, from Boston's Doctors Health Press, who does not advertise and does cite relevant references. A far fifth is the *Life Extension* magazine that does review selected vitamins and minerals. Unfortunately, it does advertise heavily and sells the products it reviews.

If you are concerned about health in general, then consult *Consumer's Reports on Health*, and if you want additional and recent information about treatments for various conditions and disorders, please consult reliable sources, newsletters such as the Cleveland Clinic, Duke Medicine Health News, Harvard Medical School Health Letter, Harvard Men's Health Watch, Johns Hopkins Medical University Newsletter, Massachusetts General Hospital's Mind, Mood & Memory, Focus on Healthy Aging by Mount Sinai School of Medicine in New York, UCLA Newsletter on Aging, and many other reliable clinics across the United States. If you can, by all means get, steal, beg, or borrow Johns Hopkins Medicine's Quick Reference Prevention Tips. In its four chock-full-information pages you will find all that you need to know about how to avoid so many possible illnesses.

Keep in mind "better safe than sorry" as your daily reminder. If you want and need reliable information, in addition to checking carefully on the Internet, do consult reliable sources and not charlatans and scammers included in this chapter and in Chapter 7 of this volume. Check with your physician before doing anything.

## EXERCISE NO. 4

From the list presented in Table 4.1, rank-order foods according to the one you enjoy the most to the one you enjoy the least up to as many as 10 items but no more than 10. After you have rank-ordered foods, do the same with liquids but no more than five, from the one you enjoy the most to the one you enjoy the least. Give one or more reasons why you ranked-ordered these foods and liquids the way you did.

# 5

# Music Does Not Need to Be Loud to Be Enjoyable

Music of any kind covers an immense range of possibilities, from classical, chamber, musicals, opera, choral, popular, be-bop, etc. With *American Idol* competitions on TV to iPods and even telephones one can listen to anything anytime one wants to demonstrate how music is important to millions and millions of people.

A colleague and collaborator, Dr. Laura Sweeney (see poem and comments and Figure 1.2 in Chapter 1 of this volume), asked me why I did not put music together with art and here is my answer: (1) I wanted to keep a balance among the seven sources of pleasure and give a fair shake to the seven I selected; (2) I cannot think of a seventh pleasure substituting for music that could take its place; (3) putting art (as covered in Chapter 1 of this volume) and music together would have produced a mammoth chapter, too big and too confusing to read; and (4) these two pleasures are based on two completely different processing channels—one is eyes and the other is ears. Furthermore, there may be some people who are more visual than others, just as there may be some people who are more auditory than others.

For instance, I am conservative as far as music is concerned. I prefer chamber, classical, symphonic, and baroque music. I do not really know popular music since the Big Bands era, such as Glenn Miller and the like. However, visually I am modern, as discussed in Chapter 1 of this volume. I love abstract art but I do not get much pleasure from anything artistic before the twentieth century, perhaps because I lived in it and took it for granted. Besides chamber, classical, and symphonic music, I love the American musical from which many popular songs originated and, recently, bluegrass. I love opera to the extent that my wife married me because she loved Italian opera and is quite knowledgeable of it. She hoped that I would sing Rigoletto's *La Donna e' Mobile qual piume al vento* ("The woman is as fickle as feathers in the wind") in the shower. However, she begged me to quit soon after the first try.

A fellow called Bernie who was extremely interested in listening to music and especially opera had a brother-in-law Jack[1] who was extremely wealthy but also extremely ignorant of culture and especially music and opera. To see whether he could change and enlarge Jack's extremely limited cultural and musical horizons, Bernie decided to invite his brother-in-law to hear Carmen. He provided an excellent box for him and the whole family. Anxious about what Jack's reactions would be, he held his breath waiting for the conclusion of the opera. On the way out, Bernie heard his brother-in-law actually mouthing the Toreador Song and excitedly asked Jack what he thought of the experience, to which Jack replied: "I tell you, as a business man, I am sure, this song is going to be a hit!"

My mother would take me along (against my loud protests) to piano, violin, or chamber music recitals in the Pitti Palace in Florence, and when she received complimentary tickets from our relatives with diplomatic status, at the Comunale theater. Occasionally, she would play the piano, usually Albeniz and Chopin. Once, for 50 cents, I played a guard in the great march of Aida at the Pergola Theater. One cannot live in Italy and not been influenced by music of all kinds. I still remember romantic and sentimental songs from the 1930s brought back to life by the greats Richard Tucker and Luciano Pavarotti.

It took me some time to appreciate my mother's insistence in taking me along to musical events. However, the greatest influence on my music appreciation was helped immensely right after World War II when we started to receive American films, such as Sun Valley Serenade with skating by Sonia Hernie and music by Glenn Miller and his orchestra. Seeing Disney's *Fantasia* was one of the most influential musical experiences of my entire life. I consider Walt Disney a genius at the same level as any grand composer, coupling both visual and auditory channels to make the whole experience unforgettable for me. Any music appreciation course should start with that film.

However, my life might have been saved, if not literally pretty close to it, by a song. Bear with me. This long story is going back to World War II, as a near-16-year-old boy wanting to save my country, I volunteered to join the Fascist Youth founded by Benito Mussolini as a form of recruitment for Italian children when they grew older. As a recruit with other boys, we were shipped from Florence to Northeast Italy on a train with a disabled German tank and cattle cars, to a camp in the Dolomite Alps north of Venice. Because of these clearly visible armaments, we were machine-gunned by two American P-38s on the Po' valley where four boys lost their lives. We were in that camp at the time that Rome fell to Allied Forces and the landings by the same forces in Northern France on June 6, 1944.

To make a long story short, to show you how grown up we were (most officers deserted us after the June 6 landings), we were told that we could be released only to our parents. My mother was alone with my younger brother and my father was missing in action. He came back safe after Florence was liberated by the Allied Forces. Therefore, I wrote my beloved aunt Delia who was a refugee from Leghorn where she and her four children had been bombed out of their house. She was the widow of a war hero who went down alive with his destroyer according to the best traditions of the Italian Navy (tradition that I was supposed to follow) and lived within relatively short distance from the camp in the town of Asiago (not the cheese).

She came down wearing the blue ribbon with a gold star given to her by the king of Italy and Benito Mussolini. I was in charge of the sentry welcoming visiting dignitaries. I trained to present our toy guns in seven seconds flat. We presented arms to her as she was passing by. She went directly to the HQs of the camp. After a couple of hours, I received my discharge and went to see my aunt in the HQs to go back to her house. She was alone in a large room littered by weapons on the floor. When I asked her how the process of discharge went, she answered: "They did not want to release you to me but I told them that I would not move unless they did."

After buying civilian clothes and resting for a couple of days with her and my four cousins, I embarked on a train trip all the way to Bologna among chaotic conditions of trains not running on time, refugees everywhere, and many railroad lines bombed out of existence. Once in Bologna, where I stayed with some other cousins, I learned that the train to Florence no longer ran and that the highway controlled by the Germans was the only way to reach Florence after dusk. During the day anything moving on the highway was attacked by American airplanes. Therefore, one of my cousins walked me to the beginning of the highway but left once we were in view of the entrance manned by three German paratroopers with machine pistols. As an 18-year-old he could have been picked up by Germans and sent to work in a camp in that country.

Here the patient reader should know that a couple of years earlier I had flunked German in my eighth grade and I had to take remedial lessons during the summer of 1942 to pass the fall examination. That summer, we were staying in the beautiful little island of Lussino (that now belongs to Croatia) where my father was in charge of the naval anti-aircraft base. My instructor was a German woman whose son was in a Panzer division (tanks). She taught me German by my having to sing military songs from World War I with her playing the mouth organ.

I do not remember how I learned a song that came out of the Spanish Division sent by Franco to Hitler to fight in the Russian front. Nonetheless, the song was about a shady lady from Rio de Janeiro who was quite free with her favors. I still remember the refrain: *Amigos, ich drinke kein beer und kein vein. Ich drinke ten wishey nur allein. Caramba, carraco, eigin, farflucht, sacramento dolores, und alles was wieder in.* "I do not drink either beer or wine, I only drink whiskey (assorted cuss words I do not know) and everything is going to pot." P.S. I do not like whiskey; as a good Italian American, I like grappa.

That song came in handy in talking to the three German paratroopers who laughed after I explained them who I was and the purpose of my going back home, asking them if by chance they knew this song. Once they heard the song and the refrain, they stopped the first truck that was starting to drive for Florence and told me to get in. The next morning I arrived home safe and sound to help my mother and brother get water from wells since we did not have water during that summer. What happened between Bologna and Florence that night is another story. I want to spare the reader's time. But that part of the trip might be of interest to my grandchildren (someday).

## THE TRIUMPH OF MUSIC

As I said at the outset of this chapter, I love music and whenever I can, I listen to WABE, the classical music station in Atlanta, during the day when I cook or wash dishes and when I am in bed reading at night. However, I am strictly a passive listener. I do not know musical notes. I do not play any instrument. I am not obsessive about basic information about music. I do follow the information in the booklet handed out to customers attending Atlanta's Symphony Orchestra, where I have a season subscription. However, at my age I retain little of it. My only small pleasure sometimes is to guess the composer of the music I am listening to. I am correct perhaps 50 percent of the time.

Having said all that, lately the greatest pleasure I received most recently about music was reading Blanning's[2] book by the same name as the heading of this section. In this beautifully written and extremely well-documented book, Blanning traced the historical roots of music for as close as he could find to the present.

Originally, before the fifteenth and sixteenth centuries, musicians were thought to be and dealt with as slaves and servants. They were hired and fired as their masters liked and wanted. These usually were kings, dukes, barons, and nobles who could afford to have musicians in their courts and who eventually gave moneys to build music halls and theaters. Musicians gained more status through the influence of Handel and Haydn who assumed a much greater status with their close associations with their benefactors and supporters. Mozart and Beethoven followed this trend but oftentimes they were left to the changing and capricious whims and wills of their masters. Nonetheless, their music began to attract attention outside the courts of the nobility and started to trickle down to the bourgeoisie. Musicians such as Rossini, Paganini, and Lists began to be viewed as charismatic heroes. With the bombastic music of Richard Wagner the musician began to acquire great status and wealth. Wagner's success was strengthened by Adolf Hitler making his music not only acceptable but supported as the official music of that regime.

Consequently, at the end of the nineteenth century, musicians began to achieve the status of iconic celebrities and shared the world stages together with famous politicians, such a presidents of countries, well-known movie and opera singers, becoming extremely wealthy by the royalties accruing from their compositions.

Louis XIV of France was one king who combined love of music with the love of power, establishing opera and music as the best representations of social status. Since its outset, especially up to the seventeenth century, music was essentially sacred, with many references to the deity, as found, for example, in compositions by Bach and Handel. Sacralization changed as music became increasingly secular and this quality allowed for music to be heard by the masses, even more when music was transformed from sacred to secular. From the limits of noble courts, music entered in the public sphere, especially with the construction of music halls and theaters. One aspect of a trend toward secularization in music was equivalent to a romantic revolution, as seen also in other arts, such as poetry and painting.

With this change from sacred to secular, musicians such as Beethoven achieved the status of geniuses and heroes. Music then was becoming part of the culture of a country, and in some cases defined it, such as la Marseilles in France and "Deutschland Deutschland uber alles" in Germany. The secular trend, however, of music began to acquire a profane aspect moving from the invention of baroque and classical to jazz, musicals, and eventually rock and be-bop.

In the beginning, music outside of noble courts and palaces was played in churches, but with its secularization, it started to move into pubs in England and then in French, German, and Italian Opera Houses, and lately in stadiums to accommodate increasing crowds of enthusiastic fans. With the advent of technology, first records and record players, then radio, and then television, and now portable small devices, music is available everywhere to everybody and is entertainment that is mostly relatively free.[3]

One aspect of music that Banning emphasized and documented with great originality was music as a patriotic expression of liberalization in some nations, to represent a country's pride as well as prejudice, as the two examples for France and Germany given above and with "Rules Britannia, Britannia rules the waves" in England. In Italy, Verdi's operas represented the oppressions of one country or nation over another, as Austrians were dominating Northern Italy. It so happened the Verdi's name was used as the initials for a sign of rebellion, known to all Italian school children, to mean **V**ittorio **E**manuale **R**e **D**'Italia, drawn at night on many house walls in Milan. The same happened in other countries oppressed by another as in Bohemia, as well as in Russia under the despotic dominance of the tsar.

Within some nations, music was used as a form of rebellion within one ethnic group or race against a dominant group. Think about the music of Guthrie in the 1970s, for example. Eventually the profane became to dominate popular music where sex, violence, and even crime have been glorified to become one major source of expression.

I wish I could have more space to dedicate to Banning's book. However, if you can, steal, beg, borrow, or, heaven forbid, buy it if you love music the way I do. I can assure that it will be worth going to jail if you steal it. In this way, you will be able to read it in a secluded space, unfortunately without music as company.

## MUSIC AS MAGIC

In the last two generations, the idea that listening to music made you smarter or more sensitive to almost anything in the world, especially when we are in the[4, 5] womb, brought about a plethora of books supposedly written to promote this idea. Using mantras and other gimmicks without any evidence was one of the major characteristics of this fashion. Drury,[6] for instance, recommended "music for inner space" by promoting techniques for meditation and visualization. Halperin and Savary[7] indicated that "music and sounds make us whole." Bonny and Savary[8] recommended listening to music with a new consciousness achieved through various individual as well as group exercises. Beaulieu,[9] for instance, is one representative of this fashion. This trend culminated with the proclamation of "music as medicine."[10, 11] Miles,[12] in another instance among many, proclaimed to "Tune your brain by using music to manage your mind, body, and mood." All of these testimonials, some reaching mystical extremes[13] without one shred of evidence, culminated in the book of sound therapy.[14]

Fortunately or unfortunately, depending on how you look at it, this brief background is the anecdotal base for using music as therapy. As we shall see, the empirical base for such therapy is questionable at best and without evidence at worst. I love music and it gives me a great deal of pleasure. I question, however, whether it has or will change my behavior or my judgment. You will be the judge after I summarize some, not all, of the most recent clinical applications of music to various populations of patients.

## MUSIC THERAPY

In the last decade, the public use of complementary and alternative therapies for the solution of various health problems has increased dramatically. Listening to music can be considered a support to the traditional medical practice for the reduction of anxiety and stress related to chemotherapy.[15] Music reduces stress and induces relaxation in both healthy and ill people. Those receiving treatment for coronary heart disease—which can cause tremendous stress—desperately need interventions to reduce the distress and anxiety. Here, physiologic and psychological responses from people with coronary heart disease regarding the effectiveness of music therapy, compared with standard care, were elaborated.[16]

### Mental Illness

As stated by Silverman,[17]

while the music therapy profession is relatively young and small in size, it can treat a variety of clinical populations and has established a diverse research base. However, although the profession originated working with persons diagnosed with mental illnesses, there is a considerable lack of quantitative research concerning the effects of music therapy with this population. Music therapy clinicians and researchers have reported on this lack of evidence and the difficulty in conducting psychosocial research on their interventions. While published studies have provided suggestions for future research, no studies have provided detailed propositions for the methodology and design of meticulous high quality randomized controlled psychiatric music therapy research. How do other psychotherapies accomplish their databases and could the music therapy field borrow from their rigorous "methodological best practices" to strengthen its literature base?

In a study by Grocke, Bloch, and Castle,[18]

a 10-week group music therapy project was designed to determine whether music therapy influenced quality of life and social anxiety for people with a severe and enduring mental illness living in the community. Ten one-hour weekly sessions including song singing, song writing and improvisation, culminated in each group recording original song/s in a professional studio. Statistically significant improvement was found on five items of one scale. Themes from the focus groups were: music therapy gave joy and pleasure, working as a team was beneficial, participants were pleasantly surprised at their creativity, and they took pride in their song.

Another study by Silverman[19] compared

group-based psycho-educational music therapy to psychoeducation in measures of satisfaction with life, knowledge of illness, treatment perceptions, and response frequency and type in acute psychiatric inpatients during a randomized and controlled clinical trial. Participants (N = 105) took part in a scripted single session controlled by a treatment manual and facilitated by a Board-Certified Music Therapist. Implications for psycho-educational music therapy and suggestions for future research were provided, raising questions about whether music therapy really works or whether just one single session would make any different in the outcome.

## Physical Illness

The following auto-ethnography reveals the author's physical struggle with being confined in bed after laser eye surgery.[20] She reflected on living simultaneously in a culture of temptation and a culture of control. The challenge causes her to shift back and forth within her personal experience while listening to music being played at her home. At a deeper level, she found inner strength to resist using her eyes as the music therapeutically addresses her social, physical, emotional, and cognitive needs. In the end, writing the auto-ethnography transformed her self-experience as it sheds light on how the power of music heals her body after surgery.

An exploratory study demonstrated the positive impact of live music as a holistic patient intervention directed toward reducing pain, anxiety, and muscle tension levels of patients admitted to a tertiary care center for an emergent medical condition. Music can be combined with other holistic interventions to positively impact patient outcomes.[21]

## Dementia/Alzheimer's

Some of the benefits of these non-invasive and non-pharmacological interventions include diminished symptoms, improved relationships, and increased quality of life. Music therapists, who are professionally trained to design, implement, and evaluate music-based interventions, have spearheaded significant advances in the applications of music as treatment in dementia, and these approaches may be successfully used by persons who are not professionally trained music therapists.[22]

A study by Hulme, Wright, Crocker, Oluboyede, and House[23] reviewed "non-drug treatments for dementia in order to provide a source of evidence for informal caretakers who want ideas about non-drug approaches for dementia, that they might try or that they could try to access. Three interventions were found to be effective for use with particular symptoms of dementia: music or *music therapy*, hand massage or gentle touch and physical activity/exercise."

## Preoperative Anxiety

As an archived article at Sciencedirect.com explains,[24] "perioperative patient anxiety is a pervasive problem that can have far-reaching effects. Among these effects are increased postoperative pain, risk for infection, and longer healing times. According to this systematic review of current research literature, perioperative education and music therapy can be used to successfully reduce surgical patients' anxiety."

## Infants

The design of a study by Hodges and Wilson[25] was a one-group repeated-measures crossover design in which infants served as their own controls. Because *music therapy* was already a standard of care in the hospital in which the study was conducted, it was not possible to use an experimental design in which infants were assigned randomly to an experimental group or to a control group.

## Bereavement

Qualitative investigations have indicated that *music therapy* groups may be beneficial for bereaved teenagers. The existing relationship between young people and music serves as a platform for connectedness and emotional expression that is utilized within a therapeutic, support group format. This investigation confirms this suggestion through grounded theory analysis of focus group interviews.

A study by Lindenfelser, Grocke, and McFerran[26] investigated bereaved parents' experiences of music therapy with their terminally ill child. Five global themes emerged from the analysis. These included (a) music therapy was valued as a means of altering the child's and family's perception of their situation in the midst of adversity, (b) music therapy was a significant component of remembrance, (c) music therapy was a multifaceted experience for the child and family, (d) music therapy enhanced communication and expression, and (e) parents shared perceptions of and recommendations for improving music therapy services.

## Pain

Researchers at the Tabriz Hematology and Oncology Center in Iran conducted a study to "quantify and evaluate the effectiveness of *music therapy* interventions on pain and anxiety control for 100 patients undergoing bone marrow biopsy and aspiration. Participants in the study were randomly assigned to one of two groups: one group listened to music during the procedure, and the other did not. Patients completed the Spielberger State-Trait Anxiety Inventory both before and after the procedure and reported pain severity by using a visual analog scale. Results showed that participants who listened to music had lower state anxiety and pain levels than those who did not listen to music."[27]

## Neurological Disorders

Thaut[28] argued that "neurologic music therapy last came into research and clinical focus via cognitive rehabilitation. New imaging techniques studying higher cognitive functions in the human brain 'in vivo' and theoretical advancements in music and brain function have facilitated this development. The emerging clinical literature shows substantial support for these effects in rehabilitative retraining of the injured brain."

Kim and Tomaino[29] reported that "though the notion of the language specificity of neural correlates has been widely accepted in the past (e.g., left-hemispheric dominance including Broca's and Wernike's area, N400 ERP component of semantic processing, and the P600 ERP component of syntactic processing, etc.), recent studies have shown that music and language share some important neurological aspects in their processing, both involving bilateral hemispheric activities." Their article presented a music therapy treatment protocol study of seven non-fluent patients with aphasia. The data and findings are discussed with regard to some of the recent focuses and issues addressed in the experimental studies using cognitive-behavioral, electrophysiological, and brain-imaging techniques, and cited here: http://www.ncbi.nlm.nih.gov/pubmed/19158063.

## Critical Illness/Cancer

As shown by Magill, Levin, and Spodek,[30] "a common challenge of psychotherapy with critically ill patients is that they are often too sick to engage in conventional cognitive-behavioral therapy (CBT), with regular 45-minute sessions and behavioral activation." They piloted a 20-minute, one-session intervention conducted jointly by a music therapist and a cognitive therapist that combined music therapy with CBT to improve coping for distressed, critically ill cancer patients.

They found that music therapy offers a supportive framework that can facilitate communication, enhance comfort via familiar music and lyrics, improve mood, inspire reflection, and strengthen faith. Hendon and Bohon[31] showed that "pediatric hospitals are concerned with both the physical and social well-being of their young patients. These institutions often provide play and music therapy to enhance the child's sense of normality. The purpose of this study was to test whether children in a hospital were happier during music rather than play therapy. Sixty children were observed either during play or music therapy. Happiness was operationally defined as the frequency of smiles during a 3 minute period. The results showed that music therapy led to significantly more smiles than did play therapy. Increasing the amount of time hospitals provide music therapy for child patients may be a way to increase positive effect and ultimately to increase mental and physical well-being in hospitalized children."

And from a study by Robb, Clair, Watanabe, Monahan, Azzouz, and Stouffer,[32] considered how "coping theorists argue that environmental factors affect how children perceive and respond to stressful events such as cancer. Few studies have investigated how particular interventions can change coping behaviors, though. The active music engagement (AME) intervention spotlighted at the CU site was designed to counter stressful qualities of the in-patient hospital environment by introducing three forms of environmental support. Positive facial affect and active engagement were significantly higher during AME compared with ML and ASB ($p < 0.0001$). Initiation was significantly higher during AME than ASB ($p < 0.05$). This study supported the use of the AME intervention to encourage coping-related behaviors in hospitalized children aged 4–7 receiving cancer treatment."

### Performance Anxiety

The purpose of a study by Kim[33] was to "investigate the effects of two music therapy approaches, improvisation-assisted desensitization, and music-assisted progressive muscle relaxation (PMR) and imagery on ameliorating the symptoms of music performance anxiety (MPA) among student pianists. When results of the music-assisted PMR and imagery condition were compared from pretest to posttest, statistically significant differences occurred in 6 out of the 7 measures-MPA, tension, comfort, STAI, MPAQ, and finger temperature, indicating that the music-assisted PMR and imagery treatment was very successful in reducing MPA."

What can one conclude from this admittedly small sample of studies about the effectiveness of music therapy? Apparently, it does not change behavior but it does improve the quality of life. Who can argue with that conclusion? I remember that during the two years I spent in Hillsborough, Kansas, when I first arrived in the United States as an exchange student at Tabor College, its good librarian, sensing my feelings, put me in a cubicle where I could listen on records to music by my favorite composer Peter Tchaikovsky, especially Amabile Cantabile. That listening may not have changed my behavior but it did certainly improve my mood.

From the pleasure of passive listening to the pleasure of active expression, Sugarland's Jennifer Nettles[34] confessed, "There was a period when I felt I couldn't let it show if I was angry or scared. . . . Music was a safe place where I could let out my emotions. Having that outlet at a time when I felt powerless was invaluable to my emotional survival. Art can be such as powerful tool for children to express themselves."

Lucanne Magill, D.A., professor of music therapy at the University of Windsor in Ontario, Canada, was quoted in *The Mind Health Report* of October 2010 reporting that not all music, especially new age CDs, relaxes listeners and lowers stress. Some of this music may agitate listeners "because each of us has a unique response to a particular type of sound and music we dislike will increase stress," *especially if it is loud* (italics mine). She advised readers to find music that gives us a sense of peace or comfort. For some people, upbeat country or rock music, or a thunderous symphony may produce this effect. For others, jazz, blues, or soft romantic songs may do the trick.

Furthermore, our individual differences may vary from day to day. Consequently, if we can choose, it would help to choose what is pleasant at a particular moment and avoid tunes that are associated with unpleasant or even painful experiences. Dr. Magill also suggested making music a daily ritual allowing daily stressors to be forgotten, even if for a moment. It might be helpful to become active listeners by tapping our fingers or feet, and memorizing some of the most beautiful tunes or arias. Singing along, as caretakers do for their infants, may help lower the level of stress. I found whistling some known tunes helpful at times.

## CONCLUSION

Music can be a strong source of pleasure provided we like the kind of music we hear. I cannot stand some music, such as bombastic Wagner's or more recent non-melodic, loud screaming singers whose words seem to convey hate and disgust with life. Whether music can change behavior remains to be seen. I have no doubt that it can make life more enjoyable but the leap from enjoyment to personal change is a wide one. We will need more research to link enjoyment with personal change, but in the meantime, let's enjoy music we love. I could not close this chapter without noting the contribution by Levitin[35,] published in the same year that Ballinger published his book (2008), Levitin thought that music is usually composed of six themes, which he called songs: friendship, joy, comfort, knowledge, religion, and love. Take your pick and see what kind of music you like that fits into these six themes.

## EXERCISE NO. 5

From the major headings of this chapter rank-order the type of music you enjoy the most to the one you enjoy the least. Try to rank-order at least six types of music. Please give one or more reasons why you rank-ordered these sources the way you did.

# 6

# Play Is Just as Important as Work

[P]lay is what lifts people out of the mundane (p. 6) . . . play can save your life (p. 11). . . . Play is the vital essence of life. It is what makes life lively (p. 12).[1]

The pleasures of play throughout our life cycle have been covered already in a published volume.[2] Nonetheless, more recent evidence as to its links to health, well-being, and wellness will be included, such as exercise, dancing or expressive movements, board games, on-line games, sports, etc. In comparison to avocations (Chapter 2 in this volume), there is no production here except activity (doing/performance; Chapter 3 this volume) for the sake of activity itself. The activity in and of itself is pleasurable and rewarding without immediate or distant goals for receiving money or recognition or future recompense. The later would be work, not play, as in many professional sports.

The importance of what Romans used to say, *"Menes Sana in corpore sano-"* ("A sound mind in a healthy body"), is now being discovered by large corporations that recognize that physical rehabilitation is just as important as emotional and mental fitness, that is, physical wellness and psychological well-being, as discussed in the Introduction of this volume.[3] With children and youth it may be actual play[4] but with adults play may evolve or transform itself into exercise, as done in Japan during breaks in large companies, and should be done here in the United States before considering more expensive interventions, such as talk therapy.[5]

## WHAT IS PLAY?

Play is any mental or physical activity performed for its own sake as well as for the pleasure of players involved. Play consists of two components, the objects used to perform an activity, toys, and the sequence that directs or governs how the toys should be used, a game played either by oneself or with others.

### Toys

Toys can vary from a simple stick, a ball, or a cord, requiring simple arm-leg movements to complex electronic equipment requiring fine eye-hand coordination, such as those available on the Internet, among others. A deck of cards is all that is necessary to play with a mental activity underlying how one lays down those cards on a table.

With Barbie and her 1950s heroines and heroes (are you old enough to remember GI Joe? Our 50-year-old son still keep his in my office), with children flocking to digital products (our 10-year-old granddaughter worships American Girl), toy giants such as Mattel are searching for new hits.[6]

### Games

Games can consist of very simple activities requiring practically no rules, such as jumping or running, to very complex, sophisticated games with rather difficult rules, such as chess or bridge.

## WHAT DO WE NEED TO PLAY?

Unfortunately, not everybody *can* play even though everybody *should* play. How can we distinguish who can and wants to play from those who cannot or do not want to play?

### Priorities

The most important aspect of playing is how it fits in our personal and relational priorities (as touched on in Chapter 3 of this volume). Is playing as important as work? What role does play play (awful pun) in our lives? Is it part of our leisure time? Is it consistently included in our daily activities after work, after survival activities, and placed as third in our hierarchy of priorities? Unless we can answer all these questions, we won't be able to introduce play in our list of enjoyable activities.

## Age

Developmentally, toys and games change with age, starting with passively observing moving objects and toys on to touching and moving them in infants, learning simple hand games such as patty-cake in which hand movements, clapping, and sing-song words accompany the movement. As we age, toys and games become more complicated, more interactive, and more cooperative and competitive. Eventually, as we age, as mentioned repeatedly in this chapter, play becomes exercise. I used to play tennis until my 50s but when my arthritic neck started to hurt I had to quit and I moved into tai-chi for four years, but finding it repetitively and increasingly boring I gave it up for strength practice on a foam mattress with weights at legs and arms. When I found that those exercises provoked repeated low back pain in my arthritic spine, requiring acupuncture, I gave that exercise up in favor of swimming, where I have not experienced any pain and, sometimes, if I did have some pain beforehand, it disappeared when and after I went swimming.

Many of my retired buddies found pleasure in going to gamble in casinos within hours of driving from Atlanta. One couple, both professionals, work three weeks straight and then go to gamble in Biloxi, Mississippi, where as regular costumers they receive free board and room. At our age, what can one ask for more? Too bad that I do not like casinos.

## Gender

Until middle school, there may be gender differences with boys playing more and sometimes more aggressive games. However, during puberty, there is a change because girls learn to play more competitive and body-contact games, such as soccer. By high school gender differences give away to group-competition gender-specific sports, such as basketball or baseball.

## Culture

One does not need to be a rocket scientist to be aware of cultural differences in toys and games. However, the Olympic Games have shown us how many similar games unite us with other countries and other cultures. There are sports that are specific to one culture. Bicycle racing and soccer are part of many cultures and ethnic groups; see what happens during the World Soccer Games every four years. In Europe bicycle racing is much more popular than it is in the United States, in spite of American Lance Armstrong being the champion many times in the Tour de France.

## Relational Competence

Relational competence[7, 8] means how effective we are in dealing within ourselves and with intimate and non-intimate others. It takes a certain level of competence to play,[9] as included in multiplicative, additive, and positively static interactions (as in the Introduction of this volume). The chances of being able to play diminish as we go down the ladder to negatively static, subtractive, and divisive interactions. There is no sufficient energy to focus and to be involved in a pleasant activity, as seen in troubled children needing play therapy and adults needing rehabilitation. A summary of relational competence theory is found in L'Abate.[10]

## THE FUNCTIONS OF PLAY

There are at least five functions of play that need little if any elaboration:

- To add flavor and spice to life
- To increase pleasure in life
- To decrease inevitable stresses by relaxation
- To cement and enjoy relationships with selected others
- To educate and to learn

## TYPES OF PLAY

There are many classifications of play. However, most of the dichotomies included below cover the majority of games and toys played in our present society.

### Dangerous versus Safe

Many contact sports, such as boxing and free-wrestling, just as mountain climbing, are inherently dangerous. However, playing cards in our living room, den, or family room is safe. In between these two extremes there are various shades of dangerousness and safety.

### Fantasy versus Reality

While she was around four years old, our granddaughter Alessandra started to *pretend* being a cook and serving us, her grandparents, elaborate three-course imaginary meals. This necessary stage of development became a reality when five years later she began to cook and prepare pancakes for breakfast, not to speak about desserts composed of ingredients she found in our kitchen. Fantasy, therefore, is an important aspect of play. Who does not daydream of becoming a famous basketball player, a well-known movie actress, or a great chef? In the words of a woman who does not want her name cited: "Reality is greatly overvalued." By the same token, fantasy without reality may be just as dangerous as too much fantasy without the correction of reality.

### Indoor versus Outdoor

Playing cards occurs indoors' football occurs outdoors. There is no need here to list which games are played indoors and which games are played outdoors. Readers can figure it themselves.

### Mental versus Physical

Playing cards is mental. Playing football and similar games, such as ice hockey or basketball, is physical because it requires body-to-body contact. On the other hand, there are physical games, such as tennis or volleyball, that do not involve physical contact.

### SOLITARY

Not all types of solitary play can be included in this section. Only some selected examples will be included because playing by oneself is just as important as playing with others. Solitary indoor games would include, for instance, blocks, dolls, Internet games, and Nintendo, among many others.[11]

## Dance

Another example of solitary play is dance, which can be obviously social as well as solitary.[12] However, to study movements that make men more attractive to women during courtship, Nave and McCarty[13] used motion-capture technology to make films like *Avatar*. They recruited 30 student volunteers who did not dance professionally. They were covered with reflective markers that would allow cameras to capture their dancing moves while a constant drum beat was present while the students were told to dance in any way they liked. From an analysis by women participants of films obtained in this fashion, the two most attractive movements were found to be variability and amplitude of the head, neck, and trunk. We humans move on three planes, nodding our heads backward and forward, side to side, or twisting our necks to look over our shoulders.

## Exercise

A personal example of solitary "play" at my old age is exercise and swimming half a mile four or five times a week; this is all I can do in addition to a few minutes of light strength exercises for arms and legs when I remember. I swim in one of those large health clubs that, in addition to a large pool with five lanes, is replete with all sorts of weight-bearing machines to improve completely different arm and leg muscles, including running, climbing, pulling, and shoving. I just started at a piece of equipment that supposedly should strengthen the muscles of my stomach and reduce the pouch I have developed lately. If you do not have muscles, apparently those machines will give them to you. There are also racquetball courts and one basketball court.

Smith, Devine, and Gourgott[14] felt that a health club, like the one I just described, can reach its potential by making its members feel welcome and creating a convivial atmosphere of occasional camaraderie. This kind of club succeeds all over the United States by providing its members a combination of physical health, physique enhancement, and personal development, as well as *enjoyment*.

Many aspects of vigorous exercising in a gym facilitate its members' forming friendships there. Indeed, I have made quite a few friends at the pool and at the spa attached to it. The members have many shared characteristics and exercising in its many forms tends to bring out and develop common reactions and desirable qualities. These characteristics make it easy for members to talk to, understand, care about, enjoy, and like each other. This natural but selective process of developing and sustaining friendships takes place chiefly with members who exercise regularly in relatively close proximity. Good humor and humorous exchanges even among casual members add to the feeling of being at home where warmth and enjoyment occur amid exercising. Therefore, at least at my age and in my experience, this "poor-man's country-club" has become a pleasant setting to go to and enjoy.

According to a pamphlet about exercise and age, a prescription for mature adults, from Harvard Medical School:

> People who say that exercise keeps them young may be more correct than skeptics think. Research now suggests that much of the decline once attributed to aging is actually due to long-term inactivity. Obviously, age and certain medical conditions can affect one's ability to particular kinds of strenuous exercise. But if you can walk and move your arms, you can reap the benefits of regular physical activity, from blood pressure control to increased longevity. These are strong arguments for people of *all* ages to keep moving.

The Cleveland Clinic's Heart Advisor[15] recommends that we should write down the specific goal we have chosen to start exercising in earnest. Let's place whatever goal we have written down somewhere where we can see it readily, such as on the door of the refrigerator or on the mirror of our bathroom. Then tell a family member or a friend about what goal we want to reach, asking them to follow through by asking how we are working toward that goal. Additionally, it would help a great deal if we were to write in our calendar, computer, or cell phone dates and times about when we make an appointment with ourselves to practice what we preach.

The good Cleveland Clinic doctors acknowledge the real, human possibility of backsliding. Therefore, to get back on track, they recommend that we try to answer the following questions: "What was I doing before I 'slipped'? What was I thinking or feeling? Am I following a diet and/or an exercise program that I really like? If not, what can I do to change it? Would it help to give myself a scheduled break now and then?"

Duke Medicine Health News[16] suggests that exercise may be a key to low back pain provided we strengthen our core muscles to enhance physical functions. The issue of motivation to diet, play, and exercise will be expanded further in Chapter 8 of this volume.

## Mind Games

An example of solitary play for adults is given by *Mind Games: A Box of Psychological Play* that includes (1) a three card series that supposedly answer critical questions, such as "What are you like?" "What kind of friend are you?" "What's really going on in your most important relationship?"; (2) the Abstract Image Game where pictures may say a lot about you; (3) card tests that reveal your innermost fears and phobias; (4) Adam Dant's House of Personalities; (5) Questionnaires about your personality, your social life, your anxieties, and much more. Please be advised that this a game is given admittedly as entertainment and that nothing in this game has been scientifically verified.[17]

## Surfing

Surfing, with its risk-taking expanses of tout flesh and sun-bleached hair, has been the coolest sport for more than half a century.[18] I selected surfing because it is more similar to fly-fishing or bird-watching than to parachute jumping or alligator wrestling. All these three sports involve a great deal of patience and waiting for the large wave to occur, the right fish to hook, or the most rare bird to appear. It is, however, much more dangerous than the other two sedentary sports, and in its risks is more similar to parachute jumping or alligator wrestling, as well as mountain climbing.

## Solitary Outdoors

> *Appreciative* includes skiing and canoeing.
> *Consumptive* includes fishing and hunting.
> *Mechanized* includes motor boating and trail biking.

## SOCIAL

Social play involves a minimum of two interacting players, such as in gambling or playing cards, among many other examples.

## Gambling

While in the past gambling implied either face-to-face contact and presence with other gamblers or other players, as in watching wrestling, horse races, etc., the Internet has radically changed the business of gambling. To the extent that gambling requires an exchange of money and is a passive recreation without active intervention, it is not considered a game anymore. It may be entertaining but like any other passive, solitary watching involving payment, it is no longer considered a sport or play.[19] What used to require face-to-face contact now requires an ability to play with money, without personal presence necessary. To that extent this form of entertainment is not a sport. It is strictly entertainment.

## Playing Cards

I consider this kind of play as described in my book especially in old age.[20] I have been playing cards with one group of friends since 1965 and another group since 1975. We play dealer-choice within the umbrella of poker, requiring more chance than skill, even though some of my buddies seem to win more consistently than others. In one group we play with chips and in the second with actual change. In both groups we bet 5, 10, and up to 25 cents but no more than three raises. I consider this play not a sport but as an active, face-to-face entertainment that is not only pleasurable but also very social, especially when we group-members have been playing for decades and we enjoy each other's company. In the second group, we lost two players, and since we like to play with a minimum of five players, it is doubtful that this group will survive.

## Structured versus Unstructured

Most games and plays are usually structured, that is, there is a clear framework, directions, guidelines, or rules that determine beforehand how a game must be played. Unstructured play implies any pleasurable, spontaneous play without any rules or guidelines, such as building a block fort or a sandcastle.

## Collaborative/Competitive

When two or more players are in a team playing one particular game for the purpose of beating another team, here is where collaboration among team players is necessary to compete against another team.

## Violent versus Nonviolent

We now live in a virtual world that has become the daily playground of children, youth, and even adults. However, what does it take to become a player in a virtual community? We need to embed violent videogames within a larger cultural context where weapons, handguns, and rifles are glorified in fantasy, as in movies, as well as in reality, where laws allow free possession and even their permissible public and occasional prideful display of the same.

Within a nonaggressive context but as background to an overall culture of aggression and violence, Kauai,[21] for instance, focused on the virtual world called Why Ville which, at the time of this study, attracted more than 1.2 million players, ages 8 to 16 years, for an average of 12.3 years and girls representing over 68 percent of all players. A guided tour of various places in this virtual site provided information about the kind of games and the range of activities provide insights into what players talk about, with whom they socialize, what they like to play, and how they engage in investigations to find reasons for practically anything. Kauai and other collaborators set out to study Whitwell by recruiting hundreds of participants online and offline in classrooms and after-school clubs by conducting interviews, observations, and surveys about their online activities. Additionally, they reproduced log files that captured their entire online movements and their interactions during a six-month period. All these materials allowed the researchers to share information about forthcoming articles that cover avatar designs, racial representations, cheating practices, including learning how to throw mud balls, and participating in what amounts a virtual epidemic.

Kauai, Fields, and Cook[22] viewed avatars in online games and worlds as key representations of how players see themselves in interactions with each other. These researchers investigated the role of how avatar design and identity within a large scale teen virtual world, the Whitwell net reviewed above. One unique feature of this net is the ability of customize their avatars with various face parts and accessories, all designed and sold by other players participating in the same world. The researchers reviewed their findings concerning expressive resources available for avatar construction, individual teen players' choices and rationales for creating their unique avatars, and online postings about avatar design in the community at large. These online words represent a Teen Second Life and with it the creation of a second identity and self-representation that might determine future behavior, including cheating.[23] Additionally, Kauai, Cook, and Fields[24] investigated racial diversity in avatar design and public discussions about race within the large scale Why Ville described above.

What happens to such identity and self-representation when a young, still susceptible-to-influence player enters into the virtual world of aggression and violence? Are violent videogames harmless for most children? Violent videogames can increase aggression and hostility in some players but they can also benefit others by honing their visual/spatial skills and improving social networking ability, scientists said. Experts, however, are split about the potential harm of violent video games in young children. Much of the research on those games relies on indirect measures to evaluate aggression that do not seem related to real-life aggression. Nonetheless, federal crime statistics suggest that serious violent crimes among youths have decreased since 1996, even as video-game sales have increased tremendously. Parents can protect children from potential harm by limiting use of video games and taking other commonsense precautions. One of these commonsense precautions it to model calm kindness, a minimum of verbal or nonverbal abuse among parents as partners, and partners as parents. To direct children and youth toward less aggressive but more informative and sometime humorous video games, parents could access www.bogost.com.

"Violent video games are like peanut butter," explained Christopher J. Ferguson[25] of Texas A&M International University. "They are harmless for the vast majority of kids but are harmful to a small minority with pre-existing personality or mental health problems." He added that studies have revealed that violent games have not created a generation of problem youngsters. "Recent research has shown that as video games have become more popular, children in the United States and Europe are having fewer behavior problems, are less violent and score better on standardized tests."

Patrick Markey[26] of Villanova University in Pennsylvania found in a study of 118 teenagers that certain personality traits can predict which children will be negatively influenced by videogames. If someone is easily upset, depressed, and emotional or is indifferent to the feelings of other people, breaks rules and fails to keep promises, he or she may be more likely to be hostile after playing violent videogames. "These results suggest that it is the simultaneous combination of these personality traits which yield a more powerful predictor of violent video games," Markey said. Olson[27] found a more normative use of videogames as an important component of adolescent development. For a more detailed review of aggression as a developmental stage, especially in kindergarten, interested readers may consult what I wrote in 2009.[28]

## CONCLUSION

If play is just as important as work and perhaps even more enjoyable than work, then it deserves its place as one of the major sources of pleasure in our lives. It needs to be included in our calendars, either in our daily routines or in a major part of our lives. We may work in a routine, repetitive job, but in play we can forget the unpleasant aspects of our lives and find enjoyment that many of us cannot find anywhere else.

## EXERCISE NO. 6

From the major headings of this chapter rank-order what type of play you enjoy the most to the one you enjoy the least. Rank-order as many types of play as you like. Please give one or more reasons why you rank-ordered these resources the way you did.

# The Body: Sensuality, Sensibility, Sexuality, and Sex

The body is *our* body. It belongs to us and no one can take it away from us. It is the most treasured possession we can and are allowed to have. The body is the ultimate source of our pleasures: the ability to give and receive pleasure through our bodies, as seen through the six previous sources of pleasure in preceding chapters of this volume. However, there are four resources in how and how much our body can experience for good or for bad: sensuality, sensibility, sexuality, and sex must be distinguished according to gender differences in tastes and preferences among all the pleasures obtained from them.

*Sensuality* refers to how and how much we gratify ourselves through the senses, such as aesthetic, auditory, bodily/kinesthetic, cerebral, dermatological, gustatory, olfactory, physiological, spiritual, and visual. Sensuous describes the sensory aspect of any experience that is capable of arousing all those senses, possibly but not always related to sexual arousal.[1]

*Sensibility* deals with how delicate and difficult-to-experience feelings, such as appreciation, gratitude, recognition, as well as hurts, annoyance, grief, bereavement, joy, and surprise, are experienced and received and processed through reason and thinking. These feelings are difficult to define because we are dealing with extremely delicate, almost indefinable, fine-grained experiences that need to be deeply felt for us to express them properly. Here is where feelings of competence and pride are located, just as important as all the other three resources.[2]

*Sexuality* deals with how our senses arouse, elicit, and stimulate our physiological reactions to erotic stimuli (fantasy, person, object, thought, vision) that lead to a physical arousal, such as smelling, touching, caressing, kissing, cuddling, hugging, holding, leaking, stroking, and sucking.[3,4]

*Sex* as a physical act leading to orgasm must be differentiated by gender, the condition of being man or woman. Sex can be *communal* as *being present together* to share one's body, spirit, and soul reciprocally, so to speak, as in pick experiences. Sex as *agency* is based mainly on action, as in sex as performance or sex as production (see Chapter 3 of this volume), according to whether sex is a lifelong-lasting sharing of intimate details, including sharing fears and anxieties about possibly traumatic past sex experiences, versus sex as agency as seen in one-night-stand performances, as entertainment, as a profession, or as production: the sex industry makes billions by selling pornography films, magazines, sexual fantasies, fetishes, and objects, etc.[5]

## SENSES

We receive information through our physical organs: our eyes, ears, nose, mouth, movement, and skin. We send out information verbally through our mouth and physically and nonverbally through our facial and body movements, including writing.[6] This reference[7] is cited for those readers who might want to learn more about the senses than can be covered here. Sight has been covered in Chapter 1, activity and kinesthetic movement have been covered in Chapters 2 and 6, smell and taste have been covered in Chapter 4, and hearing has been covered in Chapter 5 of this volume.

All the senses, including touch, are covered in this chapter because they are all contained at the base of sensitivities, sexualities, and sexes. What can be added that directly and indirectly has not already considered in previous chapters of this volume? For instance, an overlooked sense that has not yet received a great deal of attention in this volume is olfaction.

## SENSIBILITIES

Sensibility consists of the ability to perceive and to receive subtle sensations that may include a particular susceptibility to experience pleasurable or painful events denoting an exquisite acuteness of feelings. This resource includes being receptive and able to discern delicate and sensitive awareness of sometimes difficult contextual and internal sensations. If one does not have words to indicate what experience one is feeling, it will be difficult for that individual to discriminate among subtle feelings elicited from complex situations from strong feelings such as anger, hurt, or fear.

Sensibility includes being aware of our own needs, wants, and likes within a realistic context of our own abilities. One may need, want, and like to receive a million dollars but without a realistic plan on how to work to receive even one tenth of that amount, the want is a hopeless fantasy and an unreachable goal.[8]

## Affection

Non-erotic kissing and touching as well as endearing words and acts require a sensibility and delicate sense of caring for self and intimates that is often difficult to cultivate and learn.[9] Affection may be missing in many families, especially if they are not functioning very well. Indeed, to improve and increase the use of this resource, I have developed an easy exercise and prescription for couples and families to teach them how to *be* together nonverbally with a minimum of demands for performance or production[10] based on hugging, holding, huddling, and cuddling (3HC). Try it with your partner or with family members for 10 to 15 minutes a day, by lying down on a sofa, bed, or carpet, if you can, without talking and see what happens. However, do not try it if you are under medical or psychological treatment unless you do it under medical or psychological knowledge and supervision. OK?

## Appreciation

This term applies to our giving value and importance to whoever or whatever is said, done, or given sometimes in a reciprocal fashion and sometimes in a one-way-street, that is, unilaterally. See also *gratitude* below.

## Compassion

Darwin, the discoverer of evolution,[11] observed and reported many acts of compassion among primates and other animals that were based on empathy, the ability to put oneself in someone else's shoes. Compassion should be used and expressed with people we know and who are close to us. There is a limit to how much compassion we can bestow on strangers, keeping in mind cultural differences about how and how much compassion we can express and share with others. Don't expect compassion to come up spontaneously. We all need to see it in action before we can implement it on ourselves and loved ones.

## Gratitude

According to a major researcher in this area[12] gratitude is one of the most experienced feelings, the tendency to see life as a gift and prolonged appreciation for a helpful act and a generous bestowal of affection and caring. This gratitude may be related to the sharing of painful experiences, forgiveness for one's transgressions, "the positive recognition of benefits received."[13] Emmons[14] thinks that gratitude serves as a moral (1) *barometer* that allows individuals to perceive the importance of a kind gesture or a unexpected gift; (2) *motive* stimulating us to behave more properly and more prosocially than we have done heretofore; and (3) *reinforcer* encouraging us to improve on previous, perhaps still incomplete behaviors.

Gratitude can be expressed verbally, directly and face-to-face, in writing, and nonverbally by reciprocating in different ways. If one feels really grateful, there is no doubt that that feeling can be expressed in one positive way or another. An example of gratitude can be found in an old deacon[15] who found only one room in a hostel with three single beds, two of which were already occupied. Soon after lights were out, one of the other two occupants started to snore so loudly that it was impossible for the deacon to go to sleep. After three or four hours after midnight, the snorer turned around himself in bed, gave a hideous groan, and became silent. The third gentleman, who the deacon thought was asleep, cried out: "He is dead! Thank God! He is dead!"

As Algoe, Gable, and Maisel[16] started and stated in their research that found "gratitude from interactions predicted increases in relationship connection and satisfaction the following day, for both recipient and benefactor":

> A defining feature of close adult relationships is that each member performs actions that benefit the other. Events such as planning a celebratory meal when the other partner gets a promotion, taking the children to the zoo so that the other partner can have some quiet time, or stopping to pick up the other

partner's favorite coffee drink from Starbuck's are each benefits to the recipient. Within ongoing romantic relationships, some of these benefits may become routine and others may seem trivial: many may go unnoticed.

## Peak Experiences

Among the various sensibilities that may become sources of pleasure may be appreciation, gratitude, peak experiences, recognition, as well as mystical and spiritual experiences. For instance, peak experiences may arise from loving or sexual involvement. For instance,[17] themes of peak experiences may include the following:

1. Mystical sex, as in the melding of two bodies into one body during sexual intercourse
2. Mystical love, as in intense, overwhelming feelings of bliss surging through one's body
3. Sexual sense of oneness and unity, ecstasy, and joy when climaxing together
4. Passion as the extreme feelings and behaviors that surround prolonged and extensive foreplay
5. Special sexual when something new has happened, as losing one's virginity during pleasant and pleasurable contextual circumstances
6. Closeness and belonging as in confiding painful past experiences with a trusted partner or friend that promote feeling comfortable enough to be together for a long time
7. Positive feelings about loving and being loved from someone important to our lives
8. Special event or time as in acknowledging a loss or breakdown in an important relationship, such as divorce or death

To this list I would add the experience of sharing joys and hurt feelings and fears of being hurt with a loved one that would promote a sense of intimacy as well as forgiveness of one's errors and transgressions, as discussed in Chapter 3 of this volume.[18, 19]

## Recognition

Sometimes just having our name called out for special recognition is all most of us want, like, and need, especially publically, when there are others present. It means that our contribution, in whatever ways or means may have happened, is considered important to others rather than just to ourselves.

## Serving Others

Volunteering adds years to our lives.[20] When we use our surplus time and energy to dedicate ourselves to others, be they loved ones or strangers, we are becoming all together in how we feel and act. No wonder we live longer when we give ourselves to others in need of us.

## Spirituality

This is not an easy term to define.[21] There are at least two different currents of thought about its definition. One accepts whatever individuals subjectively call spirituality, whatever this word means to the individual. The other definition seeks a reductionist, biological cause for whatever one chooses to call spirituality. This latter position, for instance, is illustrated in an important, three-volume set about how brain and evolutionary studies have altered our understanding of the deity and of religion.[22] For some others, spirituality is based strictly on feelings. For others, spirituality may be a personality trait or a transcendental experience that goes above and beyond words. Who are we to judge?

Whatever its meaning and interpretation, there is no question that such a resource is very important to the process of change and self-help.[23] It is also linked to health and well-being. Supposedly, spirituality also implies a possible transformation in world- and self-views, purposes, goals, and beliefs as shown in religious conversions.[24] This transformation can occur gradually or suddenly, in a one-time dramatic experience. Prayer may be one way through which this transformation may occur. If readers are really interested in practicing spirituality, some of them may like to join the Network of Spiritual Progressives (NSP).

## GENDER DIFFERENCES IN SENSES, SENSIBILITIES, SEXUALITIES, AND SEXES

In the last decade, thanks to unexpected but incredibly progressive advances in technology in psychology, psychiatry, and neurology,[25] a great deal of information has been gathered around gender differences.

For instance, it seems that the intake of alcohol, drugs, and cigarettes may ebb and flow with a woman's monthly cycle, because estrogen may stimulate the brain's pathways, perhaps increasing women's "high" responses to drugs.[26, 27] Gender differences may be small, however, socialization practices in games that are gender-oriented may tend to make them larger.[28, 29] Even male and female monkeys seem to prefer gender-stereotyped toys. One cannot help wonder whether hormonal gender differences, such as testosterone, may be responsible for these preferences. For instance, competition may highly valued in boys. However, girls are becoming more and more aware of the importance to compete not only among themselves but also with boys. While gender may account for almost 3 percent of the variability in toddlers' verbal ability, by comparison, about 50 percent of this ability is determined by the child's immediate environment and exposure to models about how to speak. [30, 31, 32, 33, 34]

Even more interesting, while women may tend to be anxious and depressed, men may tend to get angry and act out their anger. Apparently, starting in the womb and continuing throughout adolescence, sex hormones may play a leading role in differential brain development and mood between men and women. Men are still conforming to the macho's fantasy of invincibility and toughness while women may be following the stereotype of the weak, needy person. These differences may explain why there are differential reactions to some antidepressant medications that may interact with estrogen in women rather than men. Men may deny their dependencies while women may accept them.[35, 36, 37, 38, 39, 40, 41, 42] Men may be more belligerently dangerous. However, women may be just as dangerous in what has been called "relational aggression," that is, indirect ways to retaliate and attack presumed enemies as observable in glaring forcefully at someone, critical eye rolling, gossiping, spreading rumors, and putting someone on Coventry, refusing to talk and to respond verbally to a target.[43, 44, 45]

Moreover, men and women may have different roles when it comes to comedy and jokes. However, laughter may be crucial when it comes to flirtation and long-term commitments. When seeking a mate, for instance, stereotypically, men like women who laugh at their jokes while women may prefer men who can make them laugh. Whether the force of evolutionary sexual selection may be working here remains to be seen. In long commitments, however, the role of humor and laughter may change, because these factors may make a difference on whether the relationship will last or not.[46, 47, 48]

Gender differences may operate on how men and women deal with their own children. For instance, fathers may tend to challenge their children, while mothers may tend to coddle them. Nonetheless, fatherhood in and of itself has undergone a profound change in the last 50 years, mainly because it has been recognized how crucial and important this role is in nurturing and encouraging their children. Children who have stable and involved fathers may be functioning at higher levels emotionally, cognitively, and socially. For instance, mothers may spend about 22 percent of their time with children in interactive activities such as reading, playing, or drawing. Fathers, on the other hand, may spend up to 40 percent of their time doing the same things with their children. Antes[49] summarized the different functions and overlapping roles that parents may play: mothers may act as "Lifeguards," fathers may act as "Cheer-leaders."[50, 51, 52]

In language development, linguist Deborah Tannen[53] argued that even though women and men may speak their own languages, conversationally, gender differences are not as great as some writers make them out to be. Men apparently may talk in terms of relative power, stressing hierarchies and rank-orders in competition, while women may tend to stress emotional and social connections among human beings. These two different but fundamental factors, power and presence, are basic to human relationships.[54, 55] In the family, both factors need to be present in both parents, in their relationship and in their relationships with their children.

We need to be mindful that gender differences may be also influenced by culturally defined roles, especially when considering post-traumatic stress. For instance, Norris, Perilla, Ibanez, and Murphy[56] found that Mexican culture with traditional views of masculinity and femininity tended to amplify these differences, whereas the African American culture with less rigid roles tended to attenuate them. These cultural and gender differences come into play in regard to all the four resources considered in this chapter, along the lines of conservative versus liberal views.

## SEXUALITY

This term has many meanings because sexuality, in my thinking, is much more than foreplay, that is, just the physical preparation and stimulation for the final act of penetration and orgasm. For instance, long before reaching foreplay, sexuality could refer to the overall atmosphere surrounding and preceding foreplay. This context refers to the general nature of the relationship, where the relationship is characterized by love, trust, reciprocity, compassion, and empathy, including intimacy, as defined in Chapter 3 of this volume. In a long-term, what is important is a committed emotional and spiritual involvement with mutual goals to be shared within a past, present, and future temporal perspective. On the other hand, sexuality could be defined as pure entertainment or opportunistic arrangement with short-term goals except the immediacy of the act itself with no future perspective for continuing the relationship except its immediacy. In financial arrangements, sex is all that counts and its context is either denied or devalued, what counts is money and immediate physical release.[57, 58]

## SEX

The laws of which I sing does not trespass on the laws. I shall not lead you into shame or treachery. Listen attentively, you are novices at this game, and it shall go well with you.[59]

Woody Allen[60] was being interviewed for a job and the interviewer was attempting to probe his psychic ability by asking him: "Do you think sex is dirty?" to which Allen nodded his lugubriously face animatedly and answered earnestly: "Yes, I do—if you do it right."

Mr. Jones,[61] having determined to have it out with his older son Johnny, now a pronounced teenager, spent several hours painstakingly explaining sexual physiology to him. At the conclusion, feelings utterly wrung-out, and knowing that he did not want to go through it again with his younger son, said to his son: Now that I have explained it to you, can I count on you passing it on to Jimmy?" "Ok, Dad, not to worry, " said the son to his father reassuringly. Therefore, he went to see his younger brother immediately and when he found him, asked: "Jimmy, I just had a long lecture from Dad, and he wants me to pass on to you what he told me." "Go ahead," said Jimmy. "Well, you know what you and I were doing with those girls behind the barn last month? Dad wants me to tell you that the birds and the bees do it too."

According to a review of the medical literature, sex produces 10 surprising health benefits. According to Doheny,[62] sex relieves stress, boosts immunity, burns calories, improves cardiovascular health, boosts self-esteem, improves intimacy, reduces pain and prostate cancer risk, strengthens pelvic floor muscles, and helps you sleep better. All the research summarized in the 10 benefits of sex listed above fails to distinguish among three different meanings and uses of sex and sexuality. Sex as an act of genital, dermatological, kinesthetic, manual, and oral contact and penetration can be distinguished according to the three modalities of life discussed in Chapter 3 of this volume. The distinction made about the three modalities of life as applicable to food (Chapter 4 of this volume) applies to sex just as well, as already introduced at the beginning of this chapter,[63, 64] but worth repeating, and that is as follows:

**Sex as *Presence***: *Being together,* sharing one's desires and wishes as well as one's anxieties and fears from past pleasurable or painful experiences, as in peak experiences listed above and in intimacy defined as the sharing of joys as well as well as hurts and fears of being hurt.[65] This meaning implies that sex is part of an intimate relationship between two loving people who have shared their own inner anxieties, fears, and even past painful experiences with sex as performance or as production. Being together skin-to-skin, body-to-body, caressing, cuddling, embracing, hugging, licking, touching, stroking, and sucking, may be much more important activities of themselves as processes than just the final act of penetration and relief obtained from the resulting orgasm. The slow, careful, delicate process of getting there is much more important than the final outcome. Here is where sensibilities reviewed above come into being. There has to be appreciation, empathy, and even gratitude to assure that each partner is completely comfortable in doing whatever brings reciprocal pleasure to both and no harm.

**Sex as *Performance***: *Doing it* without any previous contextual preparation, such as a romantic and affectionate atmosphere, music and candle-light, as would be the case of *being together.* Sex as performance would be the case of casual one-night stands, counting how many times it has "been done," how often and with how many partners, frequency, and rate have occurred. And if you want to experience pictorially "The Garden of Love and its delights" consult the discovery of a lost book from the age of the Baroque.[66]

**Sex as *Production***: having to do with exchange of money, as in prostitution, or buying of sexually oriented goods, as in pornography or of objects designed to increase sexual performance, dildos, fetishes, etc.[67]

## THE MERCHANTS OF SEX

It gives me great pleasure to expose scammers who sell sex-enhancing products without any evidence as to their effectiveness. When commonly prescribed medications (Lavitra, Cialis, Testosterone, and Viagra) fail for sexual arousal and hard penal erection, there is a whole world of corrupt, dishonest hucksters who will sell whatever it takes to make a buck at the expense of naive and needy readers, usually older men who do not want to "lose it" or "want to keep it." Consequently, a whole host of expensive, colorful, and often quite explicit brochures, some with clear pictures depicting the male organ at three levels of erection, are mailed to older men who may not have been able to "get it up." For instance, an advertisement by Dr. Edward Robson, described as sexologist, scientist, and professor of medicine, offered the Silver Bullet [*sic*!] for "Fast Response Male Performance Booster" based on the sex secret of the Sultans! Supposedly, this magic power is a 100 percent natural treatment with no undesirable side effects.

Here are the claimed results based on so-called clinical trials, where the number of participants, however, was not given: (1) 97 percent of all men who took Silver Bullet experienced an average 1.2 inch increase in penis size! (exclamation point mine!); (2) 99.3 percent of all men who took Silver Bullet experienced stiffer erections, lasting an average of two hours! (3) 96.2 percent of all men who took Silver Bullet ejaculated a greater volume of semen! (4) 100 percent of all men who took Silver Bullet remained stimulated, even after making love three times in a row! You can try it risk-free for 30 days, what have you got to lose? If the reader answers and buys this product within 48 hours, he will receive a free gift that will boost his sexual power even further. Wow! What older, needy, and naive man could resist such a proposition? The more pills you order the cheaper the prize. And there are so many from whom one can order (Table 7.1).

If you are still "bankrupt in bed" after you have tried the Silver Bullet, do not despair, there is still good news for you, there is now the all-new, all-natural, revolutionary, and "proven" Castrol four-step program that is the first and only treatment that will give you a libido, erection, orgasm, and growth (thickness, wideness, and length) stimulator and prostate rejuvenator. One month supply will cost you only $59.97 (plus S&H $7.95). Two-month supply for only $99.97 plus shipping is the BETTER DEAL. But the BEST DEAL is a three-month supply for only $129.97 plus shipping. Do not worry if this product

**Table 7.1. Companies That Sell Erection-Enhancing or Penis-Enlarging Products**

| Name | Location | Product's Name | Price perUnit[a] in Dollars + S&H |
|---|---|---|---|
| American Innovations and Solutions | Green Cove Springs, FL | ViaSteel | 25.99 + 9.99 |
| A&M Technologies | Oak Park, IL | Natural V + Boost + Blast | 59.95 + not given |
| Anthony Carrera | Fontana, CA | Lyonex | 59.95 + 4.95 |
| Aromalab Institute | Patchogue, NY | EroStick | 39.95 + 6.95 |
| Best Life Herbals | Boise, ID | TestoForce | 23.75 + 4.95 |
| | | Prosterin | 16.96 + 9.95 |
| | | Mandro-RX | 23.46 + 9.95 |
| | | 15 Dragons | 33.96 + 9.95 |
| | | Prosta-Rye | 39.95 + 9.95 |
| Biocentric Health | Centreville, MD | Androx | 39.95 + 6.95 |
| BiCentrics, Inc. | Manteno, IL | Ciatrol | 59.95 + 6.95 |
| BioNutrigenics/Dr. William Judy | Manteno, IL | Ubiquinone | Free trial offer |
| Botanic Choice | Hobart, IN | Black Stallion | 15.00 + not given |
| | | Prostate 9 Complex | 15.00 + not given |
| | | Horny Goat Weed Extract | 10.00 + not given |
| | | Passionate Men's Complex | 5.00 + not given |
| | | Maca | 7.00 + not given |
| | | Pumpkin Seed Oil | 8.00 + not given |
| | | Manatone Power | 10.00 + not given |
| | | Tribulus Terrestris Extract | 7.00 + not given |
| | | Yohimbe Extract (with Saw Palmetto Extract, Lyconpene, Pygeum Extract, Damiana Leaves, & Baron Complex) | 7.00 + not given |

**Table 7.1. (Continued)**

| Name | Location | Product's Name | Price perUnit[a] in Dollars + S&H |
|---|---|---|---|
| Brook's London Clinic for Men | St. Petersburg, FL | Sex Patch | 39.45 + 6.95 |
| Chesapeake Nutritionals | Centreville, MD | Testo24 | 39.95 + 4.95 |
| Dr. David Brownstein | Not available | Prostate Revive | Free trial + 4.95 |
| Dr. Philuppe Moser | Manten, IL | Polycernol | 69.95 + not given |
| Dr. Victor Marchione | Boynton Beach, FL | Healthy Prostate | 49.95 + 8.95 |
| Essential Supplements | Encino, CA | Essential Erection | 49.95 + 5.00 |
| Everest Nutrition | Wilmington, DE | Zenerx | 39.95 + 6.95 |
| Gelactia 200 | New Brunswick, NJ | Galactia 200 | 39.95 + 6.95 |
| Global International Research Labs | Merrick, NY | Bio-Load | 89.95 + 8.95 |
| Goldshield Direct | West Palm Beach, FL | AndroBOOST | 29.95 + 4.95 |
| | | Prostate Health Complex | 27.95 + 4.50 |
| Hampshire Laboratories | Minneapolis, MN | TosterAll | 39.95 + 5.95 |
| | | Testo Rise | 39.95 + 7.95 |
| | | Antiiva | 39.95 + 5.95 |
| | | Prost-10 | 39.95 + 5.95 |
| | | PrepareX | 39.95 + 4.95 |
| | | Acai Berry | 39.95 + included |
| Health Research Laboratories | Carson City, NV | Prostavia | 69.95 + 6.95 |
| Health Research Laboratories | South Portland, ME | TriVasis | 69.95 + 9.95 |
| Hormone Health News | Hueytown, AL | DIM | 29.95 + 6.95 |
| Institute for Vibrant Health | Camp Verde, AZ | ProstaEZ | 39.95 + 7.95 |
| | | Potenex | 49.95 + 7.95 |
| Ironwood Labs | Milford, CT | RigiDerm | 39.90 + 5.95 |

(continued)

**Table 7.1. (Continued)**

| Name | Location | Product's Name | Price perUnit[a] in Dollars + S&H |
|---|---|---|---|
| Jenasol Original | Linden, UT | eXtranol | 49.95 + 4.20 |
| JLPI Avenue of Americas | New York, NY | PrestaPlus | 5.99 + 3.00 |
| Libid Enhancement Products | Hudson, NH | DualFuel | 46.99 + 8.99 |
| Lincoln-Bancroft Group | Sherman Oaks, CA | Libido Crystals | 51.95 + 7.95 |
| Life Extension | Fort Lauderdale, FL | Various objects | Various prices |
| LifeTex, Inc | Glenwood Landing, NY | Prelox | 33.75 + not given |
| MagnaSex Virility Innovations | Scarborough, ME | NuLibido | 9.95 + not given |
| Male Performance Center | Minneapolis, MN | Magnetic Chip | 49.95 + free |
| Mark Rosenberg, MD | Bridgeport, CT | Sniff & STIFF | 39.95 + 6.95 |
| | | Prostanol | 46.95 + 6.95 |
| | | Testomax | 39.95 + 5.95 |
| Maximus 300 | Detroit, MI | Maximus 300 | 59.99 + 9.99 |
| | | EXplode Gel | 29.00 + 9.99 |
| MediQuest | Simi Valley, CA | Marathon 21 | 39.95 + free |
| Miracle Breakthrough Labs | Coral Gables, FL | EDTA Mega Plus | 39.00 + free |
| | | Mega Change Rejuvenation Formula | Free trial |
| Noble Health Products | Spotswood, NJ | Ziprin | 49.95 + 6.00 |
| NorStar Nutritionals | Frederick, MD | Magnum Drive | 49.95 + 6.95 |
| Orexis | Hoboken, NJ | Orexis | Free trial |
| Perpharma | Valendia, CA | Andronol | 49.95 + 7.95 |
| | | Nitric Oxide Gel | 24.95 + 7.95 |
| | | Testosterone Cream | 39.95 + 7.95 |
| | | Penis Enlarge Pump | 29.95 + 7.95 |
| Perform OTC Labs | Selden, NY | Performance-Fusion Chewing Gum | 54.95 + 7.95 |

| Company | Location | Product | Price |
| --- | --- | --- | --- |
| Phero-Game | Marina del Rey, CA | Phero Game | 49.99 + 8.99 |
| PMB | New Hall, CA | RD9 | 39.90 + 6.95 |
| P.R.C. | Marina del Rey, CA | Magnum FX | 56.00 + 9.99 |
| | | Semenex Turbo Charger | 24.00 + 9.99 |
| Proper Health Systems | Newbury Park, CA | Avegria | 39.97 + 6.95 |
| Prost-patch Health | New Lenox, IL | Prost-Patch | 29.95 + 7.94 |
| PureVive | Irvine, CA | Extendium | 39.95 + not given |
| Purity Products | Plainview, NY | Prelox | 39.95 + free |
| Real Advantage Nutrients | Frederick, MD | UltraTurbo HG | 19.95 + 6.95 |
| | | Pro-Support | 19.95 + 6.95 |
| Renaissance Health | Boca Raton, FL | T-Boost | 29.95 + 4.95 |
| Ryvalis | Marina del Rey, CA | Ryvalis | 38.00 + 9.99 |
| SBM | Champlain, NY | Silver Bullet | 49.95 + 9.95 |
| Schweitz Health | Manteno, IL | Virilen | 49.95 + 9.95 |
| Scientific Solutions | Mission Hills, CA | Hardon | 59.95 + free |
| Strong Products for Men | Cadillac, MI | Strong | 39.95 + 7.95 |
| The Silver Edge | Phoenix, AZ | Maca Root | 29.95 +7.95 |
| UniScience Group | Bridgeport, CT | Prost-Xtra Plus | 39.95 + 6.95 |
| | | Masculon-Forte | 39.95 + 6.95 |
| | | Pro-Sterol | 71.95 + 6.95 |
| Vaquerax Laboratories | Sayville, NY | Erection | 39.95 + 6.95 |
| Viarex Labs | Newhall, CA | Viarex | 39.90 + 6.95 |
| VigorAXPure Power | Marina del Rey, CA | VigorAXPure Power | 28.00 + 8.99 |

(continued)

**Table 7.1.** (Continued)

| Name | Location | Product's Name | Price perUnit[a] in Dollars + S&H |
|---|---|---|---|
| Vinboost | Chatsworth, CA | Vinboost | 34.05 + 6.95 |
| Wellspring | Boise, ID | ProstaRye | 19.95 + 4.95 |
| Westhaven Labs | Minneapolis, MI | Zencore Plus | 29.95 + 5.95 |
| | | TosterMax | 29.95 + 5.95 |
| | | Maximum-Me | 29.95 + 5.95 |

[a]Base price for one month trials.

is "proven." You will get your full money-back risk-free guarantee, like all the other similar products, at least so we are told.

Castrol four-step program does not work? You are in luck! Magnum FX and Serene should "literally" give you a full erection in 60 seconds or less and a huge size increase (3.8 inches in length and 2.6 inches in girth!) where and when you need it. You can get a 365-day supply, risk-free, that is five times less expensive than its competitors by giving you a unique targeted delivery system that will help you maximize sensations and intensify your pleasure. A "confidential" clinical study report directed to a Nikolas Stool, Director of a Phoenicia Research Center from Carl H. Patterson, Lucy Allenby, and Samuel Washington, apparently members of a Research & Training Committee, gives you full, detailed results from using the Platinum versus the Gold treatment. What do you have to lose except your money?

Aren't we older and likely vulnerable and hopeful men lucky? There are so many products available to us in our senior years. If the products listed in Table 7.1 do not work, how about the dietary supplement Test Force, claimed to be a better alternative to testosterone injections. If you order a minimum of a one-month supply just to begin, or two- or four- or six-month supply, you will receive three bonus reports as free gifts. All of this comes with an "iron-clad, risk-free money-back guarantee." Do all these promises sound familiar? Don't delay, order Test Force today!

I could go on and on with similar advertisements and promotions of a variety of nostrums designed to make you hope that a particular product will do the trick for us. The products reviewed are an exemplary drop in a bucket, the tip of the iceberg among many other products I have received in the mail but reviewing them all would take much more space that I have allotted for this chapter. What is crucial to know about these products, as well as some advertised products reviewed in Chapter 4 of this volume, is the chemical composition of these nostrums. What kind of chemicals, herbs, vitamins, and minerals are included in these pills? Unfortunately, there is no regulatory agency such as the FDA that can safeguard the public from swindlers. There is no federal or state agency that can control and require accounting for all these products and claims.

Fear of losing it or actual loss is only increased by *The Ugly Truth about Low Testosterone* (Natural Health News Report, Issue No. 128):

- Weak or failed erections
- Damaged penises

- Blindness
- Amputations
- Excruciating nerve pain
- Hearth attacks
- Fat belly
- Low libido
- Early death
- High blood pressure
- No energy
- High cholesterol
- Broken bones
- Loss of muscle

And more!

I initially thought that there may be an exception to the foregoing conclusions in a publication about *The Prostate Answer Book* by the editors of FC&A medical publishers from Peachtree City, Georgia. But I was wrong. In this very readable book, these editors do review "Remedies and cures for every man, and what your doctor never tells you about surgery." This book is full of technical information about the prostate written in an easily understandable fashion, including also professional and scientific references, a rarity in most of the publicly available information.

If I were interested in knowing more about my prostate, I might start with reading this book, provided I question its claims of (1) improving chances of staying healthy and cancer-free; (2) giving five simple strategies for "super-savings on prescriptions drugs for the prostate," and (3) how to get the most out of our medical coverage *now*! Apparently, I would reduce my risk of developing prostate cancer by 45 percent if I were to follow what this book tells me. Additionally, I may have been misdiagnosed about my prostate cancer if I have been prescribed antibiotics and instead I could use natural remedies to help my urinary problems without drugs and surgery. All of this with an additional note about Jesus Christ as a "gift more precious than diamonds and gold." What else can I say?

I do not know whether this information will redeem good Dr. Jonathan V. Wright; remember him from Chapter 4? However, in all fairness, in Issue No. 8 of the 17th Volume, October 2010, of his *Nutrition & Healing* newsletter, he does review a great deal of the research to "Bring the fire back to the bedroom ... without even touching one of those little blue pills." You know which blue pills he is referring to. In the same issue, another article by his coworker Kerry Bone (yes, that's his name) supports the use of Ashwaganda as "an anti-aging tonic that boosts testosterone and relieves anxiety." Fortunately, both writers do not sell any product, at least in this newsletter. Unfortunately, both failed to give bibliographical references about the research they reported. Hence, the reader cannot establish the validity of results reported in their articles.

Consequently, in spite of this possible but questionable exception, all I can say is "caveat emptor": Buyer beware, be careful. Avoid false and deceiving claims with absolutely no proof and no evidence except what we are told by people who could prey on us, needy, naive, and, likely, older men (as I am). Nowhere in their advertisements is the reader given information about how many men were given this formula, prescription, or product. Whether there was a control group that received a placebo. Whether evaluation was performed over time, and how tests were performed under controlled conditions. To begin with, one should start at least measuring the testosterone level of men who are willing to serve as subjects. That level would serve as the baseline for any claimed improvement in sexual performance. Without this basic information, any claimed results are essentially baseless and useless.

In case you believe risk-free claims for all these products, before I could write what I wrote above, I want you to know that I used myself as a willing and conscious guinea pig for some of these products for a month. In one case where I used the nostrum for a couple of months in a three-month supply without any tangible (forgive the pun!) results, I sent back empty jars for full refund since absolutely nothing had happened to me. No such refund was ever received. I chuck my experiences and costs to research for humanity! I hope the IRS will believe me when I charge these costs to research! I shall continue to use and sacrifice myself as a guinea pig in the name of science to make sure I am not misleading and letting my readers down. If you want to receive responsible and accurate information about the prostate, then get the Prostate Bulletin from Johns Hopkins Medicine.

I want to report at least two exceptions to my failure to report not receiving refunds for not-working supplements. One refunded back the price of my original purchase. Hurrah for them? After I received a letter from Sophia, Costumer Service Team Member, requesting delayed payment for their pills, which I tried for one month without visible or even tangible (another pun!) results. Here is her reply to my refusal to pay on two counts: (1) I had returned all the full jars after one month trial; and (2) I received no indication that this product produced results it claimed to produce.

Dear Luciano L'Abate:

Thank you for writing that you have already returned the following merchandise Extension Order Number 1162686, product 811-60. We have applied this return to your account and credited accordingly. What happened is your return simply crossed in the mail with the bill that we sent you. We apologize for any inconvenience this may have caused you, and want you to know how deeply we appreciate your business.

P.S. We have found that it takes varying amounts of time (anywhere from one to 90 days) for our customers to notice results with our products. It may be possible that you returned your (*sic!*) product to us BEFORE it had a chance to work properly. If so, and you would like to try it further, simply place this letter in the envelope provided. Mail it to me. I'll send you another fresh 30-day supply on the same FREE TRIAL basis, again. Remember, use it for a full 30 days, then make your decision.

Please notice that there is no evidence given to report how the company "found" that it takes varying amounts of time to produce results. How many costumers did report results? What was the nature of those customers in regard to age, education, income, and state of health? More importantly and specifically, what was the testosterone level before administration of the product? These are the kind of questions that any responsible manufacturer of these products should be able to answer, not to count what evidence was used before selling a product to the market and to us gullible old men.

Nonetheless, on a letter dated September 23 and received October 9, 2010, this is what the same Costumer Service Team Member wrote:

RE: Request for Refund

Dear Luciano L'Abate

We are deeply grateful for having you as a costumer, however, in order to be eligible for a refund, it IS REQUIRED [capital letters hers] for you to return the empty container(s) or unused portion of the paid product(s) within 40 days of the ship date.

Your order was shipped on 5/26/2010, so the container(s) should have been returned before 7/05/2010. However, your product was actually returned on 08/24/2010 and is therefore ineligible for a refund.

Sincerely,

Sophia

Draw your own conclusions. None of these requirements were included in the original "risk-free" advertisement.

## CONCLUSION

If the FDA cannot police all these people with grand claims, perhaps a not-for-profit, consumer-lead Center for the Evaluation of Health and Sexuality Products may be necessary to protect the public. One way to divide shoddy producers from bona-fide manufacturers would consist of asking them to support and sustain such a center. Sustaining members of this center would need to develop their own code of ethics about the integrity of their products, clinical trials, controlled conditions, nature of experimental sample, nature of control sample, etc. I doubt whether this will ever happen or that manufacturers of these products would ever be willing and able to police themselves. It might happen if manufacturers spent their money to evaluate their products rather than spend money for expensive advertisements and mailing.

# Conclusion

# Moderation, Self-Control, and Self-Monitoring

No matter what we call it, moderation by any other word means continuous control and careful regulation over self. Self-monitoring means constant awareness of who and what is pleasurable and who and what is not, such as weighing ourselves every morning when we get up, being aware of how and how much we drink and eat, how we spend our time and energy every day with or without someone or something. As far as I know, we Americans use the largest number of agendas in the world *per capite*, by how Americans use those planners. If you do not have it, get one. Here is where *corrective reflection* is crucial to self-control, that is, awareness and knowledge of one's self-abilities, strengths and limits, including when to say no to ourselves and to others. Saying yes is easy. Saying no is much harder and many of us do not say it often enough or strongly enough.

In this chapter, various ways will be made available to whoever wants or needs to use them to learn self-control and self-monitoring: mostly to help us become aware of what we like and dislike. This process includes how to avoid making an obsession or an addiction out of a source or resource of pleasure. For instance, a simple **Extra Exercise**

**A** would consist of asking ourselves to rank-order, following personal preferences, the seven sources of pleasures according to how much pleasure each gave to us with an explanation about why that rank-order was performed.

An **Extra Exercise B** could consist of a form asking ourselves to complete all the possible questions about origins, development, growth, progress, personal and relational outcomes of one particular source or resource of pleasure on a specific topic (i.e., photography, food, music). In this final chapter, I plan to include additional ways to increase awareness and sensitivity to particular sources and resources of pleasure.

If we want to live a long, healthy life we may follow, among many other suggestions, besides diet and exercise, one may follow the recommendations of Dr. Robert Butler,[1] one of the pioneers in geriatric medicine, who passed away recently:

- Maintain mental vitality by active pursuit of interests and activities of an intellectual nature
- Nurture your relationships with loved ones and friends[*]
- Seek essential sleep[*]
- Set stress aside by managing and performing pleasant and pleasurable activities, such as playing cards and exercising[*]
- Connect with your community, whether attending church, joining a club of people with similar interests, and especially volunteering.[2]
- Live the active, purposeful life, don't spend most of your time watching TV mindlessly, develop a plan on how you want to live, set realistic goals, and try to achieve them one at a time, not all of them at the same time.[*]
- Eat your way to health by being careful with what and how much you eat
- Practice prevention by approaching and promoting healthy routine and avoiding negative thoughts, self-defeating practices, and unhealthy habits, such as smoking, overeating, or overdrinking

This chapter will be outlined according to the acronym STOP to see whether we can learn to appreciate whatever source and resource of pleasure is available to us in this life. I am using the pronouns "we" and "us" decidedly. If readers think that I am writing this chapter for

---

[*]This asterisk indicates which of these recommendations are more important than others. This list can be used as **Extra Exercise C** by rank-ordering these recommendations according to how important, urgent, and needed they are to each particular reader.

them, they are wrong. I am sorry to correct and disappoint them, but I am writing this chapter for my benefit first as well as for their benefit, if it helps. I do not want to fall into the trap of preaching from the pulpit and thinking for one minute or a second that I am exempt from any correction or improvement. Very likely I need it the most.

Remember what I wrote at the beginning of Chapter 4 of this volume? I am still a chocaholic and I am still struggling every day to check on my weight, promising myself to do better in how and how much I eat, but to no avail. I am still addicted to chocolate as well as to food. I am continuously struggling to avoid eating too much chocolate and limiting my food intake to a minimum. I am a sinner, no matter how charitable and forgiving I may try to be with myself.

Hence, I am sorry, but whatever I write in this chapter is written primarily for my sake and secondarily for readers. I do not want this chapter to be *me* versus *you*, with me preaching from the pulpit down to other poor sinners. We are in it together. I need to pay attention to what I am writing ahead of whoever you are who will read what I wrote. Nevertheless, I hope readers will profit by what I am writing. I shall try to make it as painless as I can. If I cannot avoid including also some pain, as in the old saying: "No pain no gain," I am sorry. Additions and obsessions may be pleasurable in the short but painful in the long run. Giving up addictions and obsessions for the short run may be unpleasant and painful, but once they are under control, they will become pleasurable. I promise.


## PREPARING TO FIGHT TEMPTATIONS

It's a continuous fight to ward off daily temptations. After my lunch of salad and two or three pieces of fruit, I just need a piece of chocolate. I got rid of the nuggets to make sure I would not have them in the house. However, my beloved granddaughter Alessandra loves Nutella and keeps a jar in our kitchen. Once I finish lunch, that Nutella calls me desperately and I cannot help it. It's so delicious and, furthermore, it's made in Italy! It has a wonderful taste and an added emotional value to me.

As much as I try to minimize my evening meal with medium-sized plates and similar size portions, occasionally my wife, who has been a great cook since we got married, cooks a dish of linguini with red clam source, and how can I not eat such a dish? How in the world is anybody going to be able to limit portions with that dish? I have to eat it also because I do not want to offend or even hurt my wife's feelings. Right?

If and when we plan to go out, a couple of our friends are smart enough to order just a single order to split between them. We are not smart enough. My wife demands that if we go out and she is not cooking, she has the right to an entire order. How can I follow my friends since I do not have an order to split in half with anybody else? When we go out to eat, with the best of my initial intentions, and you know what the road of best intensions leads to, I have tried to order two appetizers instead of a main entree but once a fish soup is on the menu (bouillabaisse), I love fish soup, I will have to order it and forget about the two appetizers!

Can you see how I am fighting a battle I cannot win? The only solution is to stick to a plan and follow it religiously, but I do not have a plan as yet and I do not follow any diet available on the market except trying to use a small plate and small portions.[3] At this point, I am in a no-win situation. Let's see whether writing this chapter will give me a win-win plan to follow.

## PREPARING TO STOP

Before we even start to consider STOPping, we need to learn how we decide on who or what to be with or without, do something with or without, and have something with or without. There are four separate, sure-fire, but overlapping questions we need to ask ourselves before we select someone or something to be, do, or have with or without:

Question No. 1. Do I *Like* her, him, or it?
Question No. 2. Do I *Want* him, her, or it?
Question No. 3. Do I *Need* either one or it?
Question No. 4. Do I *Love* her, him, or it?

We may like a lot of people, family members, friends, and even acquaintances. However, liking in and of itself may not be enough to justify being, doing, or having something with them. There is not enough time to be together with all the people we like to do activities or things to approach to have. This means that whether we like it or not, we must be selective in how many people, how many activities, chores, sources, and resources of pleasure we will be, do, have with. This selectivity means that we must continuously consider and rank-order who we like or not, what we do or not like, and how much we like somebody or something. Life is too short to like everybody and everything. We like someone or something more than other people and things.

Consequently, these are the four questions that need to be asked before we start and plan to start anything with anybody, including just ourselves. For instance, I *like* to drink decaffeinated espresso coffee almost every morning for breakfast. However, do I *want* it all the time? No, I do not. Sometimes I like to drink tea (decaf as well). Sometimes I make it myself at home. Sometimes I go to the nearest Starbucks store during a mid-morning or early afternoon break. Do I *need* to drink decaffeinated espresso? I used to look at my espresso as a unnecessary but pleasurable habit acquired decades ago without any attached health advantage. However, now that new research attests to its health advantages, I am drinking it is an even greater pleasure (with less guilt!). Must I have it? Of course not. I can do without it, maybe for a day or two. . . .

Loving someone or something (see Chapter 3 this volume) includes all four previous answers to the point that that someone or something is so important that we cannot do without her or him or it. Of all possible choices, that particular person, activity, or object win over and are unique over other persons, activities, and objects. That means that we want to be, do, and have with that person, activity, or object most of the time if not all the time.

However, here is where danger lies: loving someone or something to the exclusion of self-importance, becoming so dependent on that person or something that it becomes an obsession or worse an addiction. When that extreme is reached that's when we need to set the breaks and introduce STOP!

The Italian language has an interesting word for addictions: *tossico-dependenza*, which translated literally means, "being dependent on something that is toxic or lethal to us." How do we know when we are obsessed with someone or to something that is dangerous? The answer is not an easy one but we know we are obsessed when we ruminate about that person, activity, or object all or most of the time to the point of excluding thinking realistically about other persons, activities, or objects. When that rumination turns into action that's when addictions begin and starts to destroy our relationships with loved ones, or our work and leisure performance, and how we spend our money. We have become so addicted to that person, activity, or object to the exclusion of other people who love us. They love us enough to want to be with us, want to do something fun with us, and want to have a good time with us. When that happens and we forget about them to concentrate on our obsession, we are in trouble. That's when we need to be strong enough to ask for help from friends, family, and, if that does not work, professional helpers, as I have done from time to time in periods of crisis in my life. One must be strong to admit being weak, to the point of asking for professional help. Many troubled individuals do not feel strong enough to do it.

Unfortunately, many people who are addicted are not strong enough to ask for help. As discussed in Chapter 6 of this volume, part of this weakness is denial of being addicted and no awareness of our being sick and needing help. If I cannot control my addiction to chocolate and overeating by myself at the end of this chapter, I will have to follow the strict diet followed by my wife and our two children. All three are able to keep in good shape in their weight while I still have a pouch I do not like. I would like to lose it. If that does not work I will again ask for professional help.

## A Matter of Priorities

Liking, wanting, needing, and loving, however, are not enough. To be selective and to rank-order according to how important (remember Chapter 3?) that person or that activity or object is to us, we must decide whether we *want* to *be* with someone or something, *do* something with or without someone, or *have* something really bad that we cannot live without that someone or something.

Wanting means liking someone or something more than just liking. Can we survive without someone or something? Can we enjoy that much being, doing, or having with that someone or that something? Some of us, for instance, like to go shopping with a friend, either for just the sheer company of that person or to use that person's judgment and taste to help us what to do or what to buy and to have. My wife, for instance, during our courtship (but not after we were married), more than half a century ago, wanted me to go with her to shop and buy something she needed and wanted. However, her meaning for shopping was and still is completely different from mine. For her shopping is a highly selective, painful process of carefully analyzing and comparing prices, colors, shapes, labels, and stores, going from one store to another, painstakingly considering the cost, context, and nature of the object to buy. All these factors are usually secondary to me. That does not mean that I do not worry about cost. Of course I do, but if and when I go shopping, I want to go by myself and select something I really want because I *need* it. Unless I love something and I need it, I do want it and if I do not want it I do not like it.

Really loving and wanting someone or something is a higher degree of liking, because it represents a *necessity:* Do we love and need that someone or something to survive and to enjoy? Family, friends, and food, for instance, are necessary for our survival. However, how necessary are they for our enjoyment and pleasure? There may be many people we love, need, want, and like to be with. However, among all those many people we have to decide which ones we love the most, want, and need to be with.

How much food we like and what kind of food we want depends on how much food is necessary for us to survive and to enjoy. The answer to that issue is: Not very much; we do not need as much food as we like to eat. Do we need a certain family member or a friend? Do we need that many calories? Can we survive without that person, that chore, or that object? We all may like and want money, but how much money do we need beyond taking care of our basic needs for shelter, warmth, clothes, water, or food? For some people taking care of basic needs is all they can afford. There is nothing left after taking care of those needs. However, there are people who want more friends, more activities, and more money that they can possibly like or want. Hoarders and tycoons, for instance, need more objects and more money to enjoy. However, the drive to accumulate more objects and more money is such that no enjoyment is present or if enjoyment is present it is only temporary.

On the other hand, as already discussed in different ways in different chapters of this volume, there are people who do not need 30 suits of clothing, 25 pairs of clothes, 100 ties, etc. There are people who are perfectly satisfied with all they have. However, there are people who no matter how much money, clothes, friends, objects, and "things" they have, they are never satisfied. Where is the balance?

## A Matter of Abilities

There are four other related questions that we need to ask ourselves in deciding who and what to select in our lives, and they are:

*Question No. 1. Can I?* This is a question of ability and affordability. Do we have sufficient moral, physical, time, and energy to devote and spend time and/or money with that someone or with that something? If our answer is that we can, that we do have the ability to carry out whatever we feel and think we would like to be with, do, and have, then we can go to the next question.

*Question No. 2. Should I?* This is a question of duty or responsibility. Is this person, activity, or object worthy of my presence to be with, do, or have, as one of my valued friend, relevant and useful activity, or important possession?

*Question No. 3. Must I?* This is a question of necessity that goes back on the third question asked earlier. Do I really *need* this (person, activity, object) or can I be, do, and have without her or him or it? How much do I love her or him or it to the point that I cannot live with either one or it? I love my espresso, but can I live without it? Of course. During my first 30 years in the United States there was no espresso to be had (except in New York City) in the Middlewest where I lived without it extremely well. However, once it was available practically everywhere in the United States, and I got used to it, I must have it.

*Question No. 4. Ought I?* This is a question of obligation in the sense that perhaps you must return a favor or reciprocate a deed or favor given to you. I ought to lose weight and decrease my eating chocolate and my food intake. This is an obligation to myself if I want to live a long life, sometimes pleasurable and sometimes not so pleasurable. We were never promised a rose garden, were we?

The process of selecting people, activities, or possessions is based on important resources that must be used if we ever want to make sound decisions. This is a resource that although available, oftentimes we do not or forget to use it. It is called *thinking*. Many of us go directly and immediately from liking to being, doing, or having without thinking about what repercussions or consequences will be in the near or distant future. If you happen to belong to this kind of people, join the club! More about "thinking" below.

There is at least one major way to learn before being, doing, or having with someone or something, and here it is:

## STARTING TO STOP

Each of the letters in STOP means something important as in successive steps we must (get it? Must?) take to learn how to enjoy life: one step at the time. It's a must when we cannot think (get it? Think?) of any other way to solve a problem. Are we ready?

## Savoring

*Savoring* the moment means a process that should have happened earlier throughout this book[4] as the capacity to cultivate, attend, appreciate, and enhance the positive experiences of our lives (p. xi):

> With that capacity, people can better enjoy love, truth, beauty, community, God, sexuality, spirituality, and whatever preferred values and individual goals they deem important. (p. xi)

In writing a whole book about the process of savoring, Bryant and Veroff (B&V)

> reasoned . . . that there had to be a yet-unmeasured dimension of psychological well-being having to do with controlling one's one positive experiences, not really "happiness" or "satisfaction," but the sense that one can actively engage life with enjoyment. (p. xii)

Therefore, the whole process of savoring takes us back to the beginning of this book, where in the introductory chapter of this volume, we indeed reviewed happiness, well-being, and positivity. However, perhaps in that chapter, I might have failed to indicate how we can enjoy life *if* we care to learn how to do it, rather than expect enjoying it freely within what the Founding Fathers of our country called "the pursuit of happiness." Happiness is by no means a given automatically granted to us without any effort on our part. On the contrary, we *must* (remember what was written above about can, should, must, and ought?) put time and energy in learning how to enjoy sources and resources of pleasure, and the first step in this process is *savoring*. Whether we *ought* to do it remains to be seen. Somewhere I have read that "By their fruits, thou shall know them." I do not remember where it was written but words are not enough to learn how to savor. Actions here count more than words.

Let's see whether with the help of the wisdom and hard research performed by B&V we can learn how to savor. First of all, I found it interesting in regard to what was written in the introductory chapter, to quote these authors and researchers again because I do not want to misquote or misinterpret them at all, especially when they are making some important points:

> Indeed, among psychologists studying positive psychology, there has been relatively little analysis of the processes underlying positive psychology. It is as if positive emotions are assumed to flow naturally as consequences arising from positive events or from positive personality styles. What the fledging field of positive psychology lacks are cogent ideas about the dynamics of positive experience, ideas about the processes that link positive events or positive personality styles with positive emotions.

Without formal models of such processes, psychology lacks an understanding of the dynamics of positive psychology. (p. xiii)

Wow! I would not have had the courage to write such a criticism but I am glad that B&V had the courage to proffer it. As long as we are beating up on positive psychology and what was written in the Introduction, I would not want to kick a horse when it's riding high on its popular and professional appeal. However, I believe that psychology in general, as a science and as a profession, has suffered by occasional fads and fashions that I have called "theoretical orphans." These are notions that have appeared almost suddenly, out of the work of a creative individual or group of like-minded individuals, spreading out quickly in the popular, professional, and scientific literature, reaching a peak of scientific and professional popularity and success without any link or connection to any theory or conceptual scheme.[5] After reaching that peak, they have disappeared from the psychological literature never to reappear again. That is usually the nature and destiny of fads and fashions. They come and go, without leaving a lasting effect on their particular brand, particularly in the arts (see Chapter 1 in this volume), performances and productions of artists, and in music (see Chapter 5 of this volume).

Among the orphans you are already familiar with (see Chapter 3 in this volume), for example, one of the most popular has been "self-esteem." I am sorry to say, and my esteemed colleagues won't like my pronouncing such an anathema, but I do believe that positive psychology with its happiness, well-being, and positivity allies, no matter how popularly successful they might have been, are all theoretical orphans. They have failed, as far as I know, to connect with and link to any larger theoretical framework. Furthermore, calling a glass of water half full denies that that glass can be also called half empty. Calling both views that a glass is half empty and half full is a matter of finding a theory that considers both views of the glass. There may be an exception perhaps in attachment theory, the view that our development and personality are the products of who we have been attached to throughout our lives,[6] and very likely, relational competence theory.[7, 8]

In short, I believe that positive psychology and its friends purposely failed to consider properly the other side of our everyday reality, the empty one, the downside, the troubled, the down-trodden, the poor, the sick, and the handicapped. Wearing rose-colored glasses as positive psychology would like us to wear is like wearing blinders. They do not allow us to see the whole, actual picture, slanting reality in a direction that negates an important side of what we see every day, whether we like it or not: the negative side. That fragmentary focus denies and negates the inevitable negativity of our lives[9] to the point that Prof. Fredrickson, if you remember her in the Introduction of this volume, gave it a restrictive value of one, as if in that one number one could encapsulate all ills of humankind.

All right, finally I got this criticism out of my chest, but I needed the help of B&V to break the ice. I just hope that my esteemed colleagues will understand that my criticisms are directed *ad ideam* and not *ad hominem*, not toward them but toward some, not all, of their ideas. I just hope that my readers won't mind this diversion from the topic of savoring, but I needed to set the record straight.

Having said all this, forgive me for that digression, but I thought it was necessary to understand where savoring stands within a larger professional and scientific background. Let's go back to review savoring. However, from the outset I have to correct those worthy writers B&V's use or type of a Latin word for *taste*, which they called "sapere," which means "knowledge" in Italian (p. 3). The correct Italian word for taste is *sapore*, likely a typo rather than an error on their part. Nonetheless, savoring is different from pleasure because we may taste something we do not like, which might not give us any pleasure, but which we need to savor before reaching a judgment of unpleasantness.

Both pleasure and savoring have an infinite number of possible expressions. B&V cite their own research to document such a tremendous variability about the sources of pleasure (p. 6): "Individuals are highly idiosyncratic about what they find pleasurable" (p. 7).

One aspect of savoring is mindfulness, remaining and staying in the here and now, concentrating on the moment and avoiding distracting influences.[10] Part of savoring is anticipation of near and distant pleasures: "We suggest that people can *choose* [italics theirs] to bring savoring processes into their future lives when they feel bereft of them in the present" (p. 9). When we assume a state of non-judgmental mindfulness it is crucial to avoid personal concerns and social responsibilities that might interfere and at times derail the whole process of savoring.

Essentially, we must concentrate and focus on the nature of the object we are experiencing, be it auditory, visual, or kinesthetic. A close process that perhaps may help us increase our savoring is meditation, relaxing and focusing on what is going on inside ourselves, and in some types of meditation, completely avoiding what is going on inside and outside ourselves by repeating a mantra.[11]

Savoring, however, is different from daydreaming to the extent that the former is concerned with real experiences, while more often than not, daydreaming may relate to wishful thinking. If we remember what was said in Chapters 1, 5, and 7 of this volume, savoring is close that what has been called an aesthetic pleasure, so evanescent, light, and delicate that some people might not be able to experience it. One must possess certain sensibilities to enjoy it, as discussed in Chapter 7 of this volume

B&V explore also various conceptual issues about favoring that I will quote verbatim to avoid possible errors of interpretation:

"**Issue No. 1**: Are savoring experiences limited to simple sensory events or can an awareness of complex thoughts also be savored (p. 26)? The answer to this question is *yes* especially in the process of discovering new relationships and insights, as will be expanded under the O of STOP.

**Issue No. 2**: Does savoring necessarily reflect conscious awareness (p. 28)? Yes and no, depending on which kind of awareness one depends on. A more satisfactory answer will be given when we reach O.

**Issue No. 3**: What forces are at work that impel a savoring experience or call it to a halt (p. 29)? Clearly, here one must enter the brain to answer this question[12] and how we feel and think while we are savoring something.

**Issue No. 4**: What is the role of intentionality in the savoring process (p. 31)? Our intentions may not be necessary. Once we establish the importance of savoring and we STOP to do it, it may become a habit that must be repeated often lest we forget.

**Issue No. 5**: Does one's time perspective on the past and on the future bear on the topic of savoring? Even though savoring occurs best in the here and now, we cannot forget past events and experiences that relate to the moment we taste something. As you can see throughout this volume, writing about anything specific brought about pleasant and unpleasant remembrances from my past. Unfortunately, I cannot predict the future, but as discussed under the T in STOP, I can only think about possible or most likely occurrences in my life.

**Issue No. 6**: In what ways do our relationships with other people enter in our savoring experiences? Savoring is not limited just to arts, avocations, drink, food, music, sports, and sexuality (note that I used this term rather than just 'sex'). Relationships can be savored and enjoyed in and of themselves. We can savor companionship with our partner. We can savor correspondence with friends and colleagues. We can savor a sunset and a sunrise with someone we love, even better."

Eventually, B&V reached an interesting model of perceived control[13] avoiding "bad" things, the ability to cope with "bad" feelings and things, obtaining a certain degree of personal control over "good" things, and savoring itself, which includes the ability to enjoy "good" things frequently. As excellent psychologists, B&V constructed a questionnaire[14] to evaluate savoring through anticipation, savoring the moment, and savoring through reminiscences. Not satisfied with the results from administering this questionnaire, they also constructed an even more detailed Ways of Savoring Checklist.[15]

What are the conditions that give rise to savoring? The answer to that question is this: "One powerful force for savoring comes from modeling others who are savoring an ongoing experience and hence alerting us to it."[16] Another factor that influences the process of savoring is the intensity and frequency of the enjoyment experienced,[17] how much those experience(s) reduce our stress level, the complexity of the experience being savored, how much we focus and pay attention to pleasurable experiences, including, of course, self-monitoring as well as our connections with relevant others.

What does savoring consist of? The most pleasurable savoring experience is going on a vacation, going out with someone we care about, sharing pleasant and pleasurable experiences with loved ones, remembrances of pleasurable moments, self-congratulations, and many other factors too many to include here.

What are the basic functions of savoring?

- Prolonging the moment and extending it over time, the longer the better
- Reminiscing and recalling pleasurable and pleasant events and experiences, as I have attempted to do throughout the course of writing this book
- Sharing after the moment of savoring is passed but the pleasure could still linger on
- Intensifying the moment by amplifying the savoring by writing it down, and sharing with a confidant or a friend

B&V made another important distinction between self- versus world-focused types of savoring, especially in regard to internal emotional experience versus external focus on the immediate as well as distant context, whatever human, animal, physical, and nonphysical entities are surrounding the savoring. Furthermore, these writers distinguished between emotional and cognitive (thinking) experiences and their different processing of savoring related to the past, present, and future. Additionally, B&V covered savoring in children, preadolescents, adolescents, and adults. Predictably, and I can attest to this finding: "compared to college students, older adults reported a higher capacity to savor positive experience in relation to the past, present, and future."[18]

Now every day is a blessing that I savor fully in a variety of ways. Now I linger longer in my bed than I used to when I wake up. I spend more time having a leisurely breakfast and drinking my espresso or tea. I allow myself to take long breaks if and when I am working, and if I do not feel like working it's OK. No one is going to put a gun to my head to work immediately, except those nasty copywriter's deadlines with proofs of manuscripts to correct (copywriters, nothing personal, I am aware you are doing your job and this book would not see the light of day without your work).

All of the above begs the question of how we can enhance savoring. As discussed already in the introductory chapter, we can indeed improve our level of happiness if and when we like, want, and need to try, not expecting to improve our happiness level without any effort. After reviewing past research, B&V listed six general factors that enhance both coping and savoring:[19] (1) social support from family and friends; (2) writing especially about traumatic life experiences, as suggested by the work of my friend Jamie Pennebaker[20] and my written, interactive practice exercises,[21] which I do not advise using except with the help of a qualified professional helper;[22] (3) think of the present situation in comparison to past similar situations and see whether you can find the good in it; (4) humor, including reading comic strips, and watching comedies rather than violence-filled war or aggressive movies; (5) spirituality and religion "not only provide a source of strength, comfort, hope, and meaning in facing and overcoming adversity, but are also linked to higher level of happiness;"[23] and (6) awareness of the fleeting nature of our experiences.

According to B&V, there are three essential preconditions for savoring:[24] (1) becoming relatively free from social and esteem concerns, our savoring may have nothing to do with what other people may think or with our self-regard and importance; (2) focusing strictly on the present rather than on the past or the future; and (3) enhancing our attentional focus on our positive rather than on our negative experiences. To achieve these preconditions and enhance the context of savoring, B&V suggest three exercises[25] about taking a daily vacation by participating in something pleasurable, identifying activities and experiences that you are experiencing in the present or have experienced in the past, and using a camera to "immortalize" the moment of your pleasurable experience.

As we can readily see, B&V did not leave any stone unturned about savoring. From this short summary of their important work readers have received only a glimpse of their research-based conclusions.

## Thinking

What is thinking and how do we think about immediate and long-term consequences of our actions? What is the difference between *bad* and *good* thinking? Thinking consists of "series of ideas directed, however vaguely, toward the solution of a problem."[26] If you really want to learn how to think in a more detailed and concrete fashion than can be done here, I would recommend Beardley's 1966 (already outdated) book or any updates you can find of it. Thinking can be *creative* in the sense of including new ideas, but the ideas in and of themselves may be banal or irrelevant.

Therefore, to be creative we need to go back to Chapter 1 of this volume to understand creative thinking as the rise of original and unique ideas. What is more relevant to this topic in this chapter is the nature of *critical* thinking, the ability to evaluate our as well as others' ideas, weighing their pros and cons and, on the basis of this process, accept or reject those ideas. For instance, think about all the advertising we are subjected to every day about an infinite number of products. Even more specifically think about the products listed in Tables 4.3 and 7.1. Think about any product sold on the market in line with what we can identify a huckster, a scammer, and a cheat, as described in Chapter 4. That is the kind of critical thinking necessary before we start or embark on almost anything. Remember the process I described about how my wife went about shopping? That is a prime example of critical thinking at its best and I usually regret not using it more often in my life. As Beardsley suggested: "To judge the worth of any kind of claim—whether to knowledge or to an estate—we must have some standards, some principles of legitimacy that can be applied to the case at hand" (p. 3).

### Step 1. Break Down Your Plan to Achieve Your Goal

We do not reach the Himalaya in one single, straight climb. We must have way-stations to reach the summit. Consequently, before we think about any person, activity, object, or problem, we must be sure we have as much information about the issue at hand as we can. I have had many individuals in my life who wanted to know from me how to write a book. In this case, for one instance among many, an extremely successful, young and mature newspaper editor wanted to write a book about his sister who had a chronic disease and was recovered in an institution. He even took me out to lunch to receive my advice! I told him that if he wanted to write such a book, he would have to read all the literature about his sister's disease before attempting such a chore, springing from his love for his sister, I am sure. But, as you know well by now, good ideas and good intentions are not enough. That was five years ago and I am not aware that he wrote such a book. We must gather relevant information before we attempt to think. Not only that, but we must be open to critical comments and feedback from people we know and trust. The best example readily available here to us lies in the writing of this book.

As stated earlier, I arrived to think about this kind of book while I was writing a book about hurt feelings.[27] Once I realized that I had a great deal of information about the nature of sources of pleasure, I formulated a proposal, which went directly to an editor, who immediately suggested a subtitle, revised the proposal, suggested I seek definitions of sources of pleasure, and commented about my proposed outline and Table of Contents, after which she produced a book contract, then left me alone "to do my own thing."

The same process has been followed throughout my publishing career, where some acquisition editors either ignored a proposal completely, not even answering my submission, some explained to me the reason(s) for rejecting the proposal, and in many cases, accepting and considering critically the proposal, as did several editors acknowledged at the front of this book.

### Step 2. What Are Our Goals?

The next step in thinking is formulation of a mission statement; what do we want to accomplish? What is our goal in *thinking* what to do next? If we want to reach the top of Mount Everest, we will never reach it with a straight route. To reach it, we must have small steps, way-stations to stop, rest, and take care of ourselves. Not only that but we must prepare ourselves physically, mentally, and emotionally for an extremely hard undertaking. Gathering information, as suggested above, is the first step in reaching the goal of writing a book or formulating a plan. For instance, in wanting to write this book, I had to have a proposal where I wrote about its purpose and submitted a tentative Table of Contents (TOC). Chapters in that TOC were my way-stations to complete this book. If I want to lose weight, I will have to think about what I should do to reach such an objective: (1) limit my intake of food; (2) eat a salad and fruits for lunch; (3) exercise almost every day; (4) limit supper to only one dish, preferably meat and fish. No seconds or refills, and no deserts.

If you really want to *think*, go back to the questions asked on pages 189–190 about reasons for doing something. Why and what do you want to do it? (1) Do you like, want, need, and love to do it? And (2) could, should, must, and ought to do it? It would be important at this junction to start writing answers to those questions in light of your goal. No goal, no answers, no change.

### Step 3. Pros and Cons of Plan

Once we have completed this step, the next step is to start thinking about the pros and cons of whatever you plan to do, likely in answering each of the eight points in the two sets of question. Why should you do it in writing? I can tell you with many years of experience why it is important to start writing. Once it's in writing, then we can move from there by starting to ruminate on what we write, so than when we are working or even sleeping, we will come up with new points to add those already written.

Thus far, we do not need to worry about our English, grammar, punctuation, syntax, and all the other niceties of language. If you really want to answer the eight questions, you can take a sheet of paper, draw a vertical line in the middle of the paper, and on top of the page write down Pros on the left and Cons on the right.

### Putting It All Together Critically

Now that you have completed all three exercises prescribed at the outset of this chapter, perhaps you may be ready to exercise another phase of learning how to think, and that is *criticality*, the ability to go over, correct, change, and criticize what one has said or written to find errors in grammar, style, and especially content. Were the exercises completed correctly or incorrectly? Was there a correct sequence of arguments followed by consistent progression of ideas and answers? In addition to a progressive sequence of ideas and arguments, what was the consistency or inconsistency among them? Did one answer followed logically from a previous one? What kind of conclusion were you able to extract from everything we wrote? For instance, as I just finished writing this paragraph I had to go back to the beginning of this chapter to see whether I had followed a consistent outline, used proper headings and subheadings, whether my grammar was correct, and whether exercises and questions presented to readers were given in consistent and logical sequence. Corrections can be made when writing is present. It is practically impossible to correct and change talk unless we register it.

Now that that we reviewed what has been written thus far, we may be ready to progress to the next component of STOP.

## Observing

Observing here is different from the previous two components of STOP, because in addition to looking critically to what we have written thus far, we must look inside ourselves as well as outside of ourselves to the close and distant context of what we have done and written. Rather than thinking, at this juncture we need to ask ourselves how we feel about what has been going on inside and outside ourselves throughout the process of reading this book. Are we happy and satisfied about reading this book and just reading this chapter? Are we completely or somewhat completely satisfied about its progression? Should a different progression have been used? How about those awful puns that were used at times? Should they have been eliminated?

The process of answering these and many other questions is called *awareness*, the corrective feedback or critical *awareness of personal error* above and beyond the role of critical thinking already done earlier. While thinking is oriented toward the present and the future, awareness of personal error is oriented toward the present and the past. What have I said and done that I could correct and improve in myself as well as in my relationships with others? Was I too self-obsessed in writing? In my previous books I avoided using the personal pronoun

"I" like the plague and wrote without personal reminiscences, jokes, or, worst, puns. Should have I not used personal reminiscences? What about jokes and awful puns? Should I have eliminated them from the text? While thinking was restricted to exercises and questions in this chapter, awareness expanded to the whole enterprise of writing this book. Have I written it too technically, not too technically, or not technically at all? What possible errors may I have committed in writing this book, above and beyond an inconsistent use of past and present verbs?

Why is observing through our own awareness of personal error and individual responsibility so important? Because this process, also known in the psychological literature as *corrective* or *negative feedback* or *insight*, is present in normal and absent in abnormal functioning.[28, 29] We are functioning normally, just like most other people, because we are able to see the errors of our ways and correct them as we go or thereafter. Without this so-called negative feedback loop we would be unable to correct ourselves and keep ourselves functioning like most everybody else. Unfortunately, sometimes even so-called normal persons commit unforgivable errors that cannot be corrected and changed.

## Planning, Preparing, and Procrastinating

Once we have completed satisfactorily the three previous components of STOPping, we may be ready to plan whatever we want to *be*, *do*, and *have* in our lives. This last component brings to mind two fellow Florentines close to my heart and both connected to planning. Galileo Galilei was first responsible for creating (through planning) the scientific method with controlled observations: "Which is heavier, a pound of lead or a pound of feathers?" He found out the answer because he was careful in controlling the experiments he planned to conduct. Can we? I have been trying to apply this method to clinical psychology and psychotherapy through distance writing rather than through talking, but it will take some time before my esteemed colleagues will catch up with being in this century rather than remaining in the past one.[30, 31, 32] We can control what we write but is it difficult to control what and how we and others talk. Writing can be controlled and, therefore, it can be replicated. Replicability is the earmark of the scientific method. Therefore, if clinical psychology and psychotherapy will ever become "scientific," they will have to use replicable operations, such as writing, not just talk.

A second fellow Florentine, Nicolo' Machiavelli, got a bum rap from American psychologists. He wrote a small book about *The Prince*, which he described as a conductor, that is, the one who has a plan before attacking or starting a fight or a war. Anybody come to mind? Adolf Hitler and Benito Mussolini, for instance, started World War II without the advice and even knowledge and consent of their generals. Can you think of anybody in recent times who did the same? The conductor wrote a plan to battle, he created a detailed score, just as a conductor of an orchestra follows in music. In nature a conductor does not allow heat to go through, like in wood. I have used the analogy of a conductor in human relationships, as someone who keeps cool, does not get upset during a critical moment, and follows a problem-solving score.

Unfortunately, my American psychological colleagues chose to call this process "Machiavellism" and gave it a completely negative connotation, as an individual being manipulative, shrewd, underhanded, and calculatingly evil, as the Grey Eminence Cardinal Richeleu in France and Rasputin in Russia. Can you think of many politicians who did not and would not hesitate to say and do whatever is necessary to win for their cause, regardless of the consequences to enemies and without regard to reality or truth? The most important thing in the pursuit of power is winning at the expense of the adversary, courtesy or civility be dammed, as in war, no compromise or hostages.

Psychologists even constructed tests to measure this characteristic. I, for one, chose to give this characteristic a positive connotation or spin, as, for instance, the conductor of an orchestra and, even more close to home, a leader in intimate relationships[33, 34] including contributing what I called "relational creativity."[35] It occurs if and when we are able to go above and beyond reacting repetitively to inevitable relational challenges or threats. We respond instead with a creative-conductive style found in multiplicative and additive interactions already explained in the Introduction.

As in Machiavelli's *The Prince*, the creative-conductive individual is in charge of self and keeps cool by having or developing a plan before responding to inevitable challenges. That's when procrastinating is necessary. We must wait to respond until we are ready. While waiting, a conductor considers all the various possibilities available, that is, priorities (already considered in Chapter 3 of this volume) and pros and cons in a situation, and chooses to respond in ways that will modify the situation for the better: acknowledging the importance of whoever is involved where "Everybody wins. Nobody loses."

The issue here is: How do we choose to behave? Should we just allow things to go on without a plan? Should we keep a stiff upper lip and let things take care of themselves? As you see, the conductor is the one who keeps control of oneself and does not leave things to occur without a plan. I got rid of chocolate nuggets in the house. I limit myself to one spoon of Nutella after lunch. I am avoiding carbohydrates like the plague, not eating bread, pastas, potatoes, and rice, and eating five to eight pieces of fruit a day. To diminish my pouch I exercise my stomach muscles at the gym and at home before and after I swim. Whether I will follow faithfully this plan depends strictly on me and not on anyone else. If I fail, I will not have anyone else to blame but myself.

We have the choice to behave as conductors and keep control of ourselves to avoid letting things go without control and thus having those things control us. The outcome of no control is chaos. The outcome of control is enjoyment of life. We make our choices and we pay the price. Make your choice. If you are looking for a source on *Fitness for Seniors* (or mature adults for that matter), you may look up the book by the editors of FC&A Medical Publishing of Peachtree City, Georgia, that give us a fairly reliable plan for "super health" replete with recipes for cooking with healthy foods, and a complete list of calorie counting at a glance. Take this as a suggestion, not a recommendation, if you do not know or can find better sources of information about health. OK?

## CONCLUSION

After all of what has been written in this volume and especially in this final chapter, this conclusion is inevitable. If we want to *enjoy* the sources and resources of pleasure available to us during our lifetime, we *must*, no ifs, no buts, no cans, no shoulds, or no oughts, be in control of ourselves. The other choice is not pleasant and unbearable to even think about.

## FINAL EXERCISE NO. 8

Go back to the list you made at the beginning of this book. If you kept it in your computer, so much the better. Look at the way you rank-ordered sources of pleasure then. After you have ranked those sources now compare your present rank-order and see whether there is any difference in your rank-orders. Please give one or more reasons about why you rank-ordered these resources the way you did now that is different or the same from the rank-order you made at the beginning of this book.

# Notes

## Foreword

1. Bierce, A. (1958). *The devil's dictionary*. New York: Dover.

2. Augarde, T. (Ed.). (1991). *The Oxford dictionary of modern quotations*. Oxford: Oxford University, p. 109.

3. Rycroft, C. (1968). *A critical dictionary of psychoanalysis*. New York: Basic Books, p. 121

## Preface

1. Kazantzis, N., & L'Abate, L. (Eds.). (2007). *Handbook of homework assignments in psychotherapy: Research, practice, and prevention*. New York: Springer-Science.

2. L'Abate, L. (Ed.). (2007). *Low-cost approaches to promote physical and mental health*. New York: Springer-Science.

3. Harwood, T. M., & L'Abate, L. (2010). *Self-help in mental health: A critical evaluation*. New York: Springer-Science.

4. L'Abate, L. (2009). Paradigms, theories, and models: Two hierarchical frameworks. In L. L'Abate, P. De Giacomo, M. Capitelli, & S. Longo (Eds.), *Mind, science, and creativity: The Bari symposium* (pp. 107–56). New York: Nova Science Publishers.

5. L'Abate, L. (2011). *Hurt feelings: Theory, research, and applications in intimate relationships*. New York: Cambridge University Press.

6. Ibid.

7. Pinsky. R. (2009). *Essential pleasures*. New York: W. W. Norton.

8. L'Abate. *Mind, science, and creativity*.

## Introduction

1. Asimov, I. (1979). *Treasury of humor*. New York: Houghton Mifflin.

2. Fuller, E. (Ed.). (1970). *2500 anecdotes for all occasions*. New York: Avenel Books.

3. L'Abate, L. (2011). *Hurt feelings: Research and applications in intimate relationships*. New York: Cambridge University Press.

4. McGowan, K. (2009). Seven deadly sins. *Discovery Magazine*, September 2009, pp. 4–7.

5. Seligman, M. E. P. (2002). *Authentic happiness: Using the new positive psychology to realize our potential for lasting fulfillment*. New York: The Free Press.

6. L'Abate, L. (2009). Paradigms, theories, and models: Two hierarchical frameworks. In L. L'Abate, P. De Giacomo, M. Capitelli, & S. Longo (Eds.), *Mind, science, and creativity: The Bari symposium* (pp. 107–56). New York: Nova Science Publishers.

7. Bok, D. (2010). *The politics of happiness: What government can learn from the new research on well-being*. Princeton, NJ: Princeton University Press.

8. Graham, C. (2010). *Happiness around the world: The paradox of happy peasant and miserable millionaires*. New York: Oxford.

9. Haidt, J. (2006). *The happiness hypothesis*. New York: Basic Books.

10. Seligman. (2002). *Authentic happiness*.

11. Lyubomirsky, S. (2008). *The how of happiness: A new approach to getting the life you want*. New York: Penguin Books.

12. Mininni, D. (2005). *The emotional toolkit: Seven power-skills to nail very bad feelings*. New York: St. Martin Griffin.

13. Franks, D. D., & Heffernan, S. M. (1998). The pursuit of happiness: Contributions from a social psychology of emotions. In W. F. Flack Jr. & J. D. Laird (Eds.), *Emotions in psychopathology: Theory and research* (pp. 145–57). New York: Oxford University Press.

14. Kolbert, E. (2010, March 22). Everybody have fun: What can policy makers learn from happiness research? *The New Yorker*, pp. 72–74.

15. L'Abate, L. (2011). *Sourcebook of interactive practice exercises in mental health*. New York: Springer-Science.

16. Lyubomirsky, S., Sheldon, K. M., & Schkade, D. (2005). Pursuing happiness: The architecture of sustainable change. *Review of General Psychology, 9*, 111–31.

17. Sheldon, K. M., & Lyubomirsky, S. (2007). Is it possible to become happier? (And if so, how?). *Social and Personality Psychology Compass, 1*, 129–45.

18. Lyubomirsky et al., Pursuing happiness.

19. Fordyce, M. W. (1977). Development of a program to increase personal happiness. *Journal of Counseling Psychology, 24*, 511–21.

20. Fordyce, M. W. (1983). Development of a program to increase personal happiness: Further studies. *Journal of Counseling Psychology, 30*, 483–98.

21. Fordyce, Development of a program.

22. Fordyce, *Journal of Counseling Psychology.*

23. Lyubomirsky et al., Pursuing happiness.

24. Sheldon & Lyubomirsky, Is it possible to become happier.

25. Gilbert, D. (2005). *Stumbling on happiness.* New York: Vintage.

26. Ibid.

27. Gilbert, D. T., & Gill, M. J. (2000). The momentary realist. *Psychological Science, 11,* 394–98.

28. Gilbert, D. T., & Wilson, T. D. (2000). Miswanting: Some problems in the forecasting of future affective states. In J. P. Forgas (Ed.), *Feeling and thinking: The role of affect in social cognition* (pp. 178–97). New York: Cambridge University Press.

29. Wilson, T. D., Wheatley, T., Meyers, J. M., Gilbert, D. T., & Axsom, D. (2000). Focalism: A source of durability bias in affective forecasting. *Journal of Personality and Social Psychology, 78,* 821–36.

30. Wilson, T. D., Meyers, J., & Gilbert, D. T. (2001). Lessons from the past: Do people learn from experience that emotional reactions are short-lived? *Personality and Social Psychology Bulletin, 27,* 1648–61.

31. Gilbert, D. T., and Ebert, E. J. (2002). Decisions and revisions: The affective forecasting of changeable outcomes. *Journal of Personality and Social Psychology, 82,* 503–14.

32. Gilbert, D. T., Driver-Linn, E., & Wilson, T. D. (2002). The trouble with Vronsky: Impact bias in the forecasting of future affective states. In L. F. Barrett & P. Salovey (Eds.), *The wisdom in feeling: Psychological processes in emotional intelligence* (pp. 114–43). New York: Guilford Press.

33. Dunn, E. W., Wilson, T. D., & Gilbert, D. T. (2003). Location, location, location: The misprediction of satisfaction in housing lotteries. *Personality and Social Psychology Bulletin, 29,* 1421–32.

34. Wilson, T. D., Meyers, J., & Gilbert, D. T. (2003). "How happy was I anyway?" A retrospective impact bias. *Social Cognition, 21,* 421–46.

35. Morewedge, C. K., Gilbert, D. T., Keysar, B., Berkovits, M. H., & Wilson, T. D. (2007). Mispredicting the hedonic benefits of segregated gains. *Journal of Experimental Psychology, 136,* 700–709.

36. Gilbert, *Stumbling on happiness.*

37. Haybron, D. M. (2008). Philosophy and the science of subjective well-being. In M. Eid & R. J. Larsen (Eds.), *The science of subjective well-being* (pp. 17–43). New York: Guilford.

38. Diener, E., & Biswas-Diener, R. (2008). *Happiness: Unlocking the mysteries of psychological wealth.* Malden, MA: Blackwell.

39. Eid, M., & Larsen, R. J. (Eds.). (2008). *The science of subjective well-being.* New York: Guilford.

40. Larsen, R. J., & Eid, M. (2008). Ed Diener and the science of subjective well-being. In M. Eid & R. J. Larsen (Eds.), *The science of subjective well-being* (pp. 1–13). New York: Guilford.

41. Ibid.

42. Oishi, S., & Koo, M. (2008). Two new questions about happiness: *"Is happiness good?"* and *"Is happier better?"* In M. Eid & R. J. Larsen (Eds.), *The science of subjective well-being* (pp. 290–306). New York: Guilford.

43. King, L. A. (2008). Interventions for enhancing subjective well-being: *Can we make people happier, and should we?* In M. Eid & R. J. Larsen (Eds.), *The science of subjective well-being* (pp. 431–48). New York: Guilford.

44. Larsen & Eid, *The science of well-being.*

45. Haybron, *The science of well-being.*

46. L'Abate, *Hurt feelings.*

47. Diener & Biswas-Diener, *Happiness.*

48. L'Abate, L. (1975). A positive approach to marital and familial intervention. In L. R. Wolberg & M. L. Aronson (Eds.), *Group therapy 1975: An overview* (pp. 53–75). NewYork: Stratton Intercontinental Medical Book Corporation.

49. Diener & Biswas-Diener, *Happiness.*

50. L'Abate, *Hurt feelings.*

51. Fredrickson, B. L. (2009). *Positivity.* New York: Crown Publishers.

52. L'Abate, *Hurt feelings.*

53. Ibid.

54. L'Abate, *Group therapy 1975.*

55. Weeks, G. R., & L'Abate, L. (1982). *Paradoxical psychotherapy: Theory and practice with individuals, couples, and families.* New York: Brunner/Mazel.

56. L'Abate, L., Hewitt, D., & McMahan, O. (2007). An overview of paradoxical counseling and its congruence with biblical writings. *The Journal of Pastoral Care & Counseling, 61,* 231–42.

57. L'Abate, *Sourcebook of interactive practice exercises.*

58. L'Abate, *Hurt feelings.*

59. Ibid.

60. L'Abate, L. (2007). A completely preposterous proposal: The dictionary as an initial vehicle of behavior change in the family. *The Family Psychologist, 23,* 39–43.

61. L'Abate, *Sourcebook of interactive practice exercises.*

62. Gottman, J. M. (1994). *What predicts divorce? The relationship between marital processes and marital outcomes.* Hillsdale, NJ: Erlbaum.

63. L'Abate, *Hurt feelings.*

64. L'Abate, L., Cusinato, M., Maino, E., Colesso, W., & Scilletta, C. (2010). *Relational competence theory: Research and mental health applications.* New York: Springer-Science.

65. L'Abate, *Hurt feelings.*

66. Gottman, *What predicts divorce?.*

67. Cusinato, M., & L'Abate, L. (Eds.). (in press). *Relational competence theory: With special attention to alexithymia.* New York: Nova Science Publishers.

## Chapter 1: Arts and Creativity

1. J. Z. Torre (personal communication, 7/22/10; 10/14/10). I owe a note of gratitude to artist, art teacher, and blog writer J. Z. Torre in "J. Z. Torre—Fine Art & Portraits" (http://www.jztorre.com/) and to Binders Art Supplies of Atlanta for allowing me to use portions of their materials in this chapter.

2. Amy Dacyczyn.

3. Brenda Ueland.

4. Carl Jung, 1875–1961.

5. George Lois.

6. Joseph Chilton Pearce.

7. Norman Podhoretz.

8. Scott Adams, 1957, *The Dilbert Principle*.

9. Stephen Nachmanovitch.

10. Asimov, I. (1979). *Treasury of humor*. New York: Houghton Mifflin.

11. American Psychological Association (APA). *Dictionary of Psychology* (2007).

12. Haufman, J. C. (2009). *Creativity 101*. New York: Springer Publishing Company.

13. Simonton, D. K. (2008). Creativity and genius. In O. P. John, R. W. Robins, & L. A. Pervin (Eds.), *Handbook of personality: Theory and research* (pp. 679–701). New York: Guilford; Simonton, D. K. (2009). *Genius 101*. New York: Springer Publishing Company.

14. Grey, A. (2001). *The mission of art*. Boston, MA: Shambhala.

15. Ibid.

16. Gill, J. F. (2010). Ghosts of New York. *The Atlantic*, June, pp. 66–70.

17. Temmer, R. (2010). *The Economist*, July, 2010.

18. *The Atlantic*, July/August, 2010, p. 23.

19. Fuller, E. (Ed.). (1970). *2500 anecdotes for all occasions*. New York: Avenel Books.

20. Ibid.

21. Vecchio, W., & Riley, R. (1968). *The fashion makers*. New York: Crown Publishers.

22. Grey, *The mission of art*.

23. Vecchio & Riley, *The fashion makers*.

24. Dingfelder, S. F. (2010, February). *Monitor on psychology, 40*, pp. 34–38.

25. Gilbert, Daniel T. (2007). *Stumbling on happiness*. New York: Vintage Books, p. 59.

26. Dingfelder, *Monitor on psychology*.

27. Gilbert, D. T., Gill, M. J., & Wilson, T. D. (2002). The future is now: Temporal correction in affective forecasting. *Organizational Behavior and Human Decision Processes*, 88, 430–44.

28. Byrne, A., & Hilbert, D. R. (Eds.). (1997). *Readings on color*. Cambridge, MA: MIT Press.

29. Asimov, *Treasury of humor*.

30. Fuller, *2500 anecdotes*.

31. Ibid.

32. Asimov, *Treasury of humor*.

33. Ibid.

34. Graham-Dixon, A. (2010). *Caravaggio: A life sacred and profane*. London, UK: Allen Lane.

35. Bryant, F. B., & Veroff, J. (2007). *Savoring: A new model of positive experience*. Mahwah, NJ: Erlbaum.

36. L'Abate, L. (2009). *The Praeger handbook of play across the life cycle: Fun from infancy to old age*. Westport, CT: Praeger.

37. Johnson, V., & Stanley, J. (2007). Capturing the contribution of community arts to health and well-being. *The International Journal of Mental Health Promotion, 9*, 28–35.

38. VicHealth, 2005.

39. Gussak, D., & Ploumis-Devick, E. (2004). Creating wellness in correctional populations through the arts: An interdisciplinary model. *Visual Arts Research, 29*, 35–43.

40. Pendleton, P. (1999). Painting a path of well-being: Art therapy as a link to mental health treatment. *Art Therapy, 16*, 31–36.

41. Reynolds, F. (2004). Textile art promoting well-being in long-term illness: Some general and specific influences. *Journal of Occupational Science, 11*, 58–67.

42. Reynolds, F., Vivat, B., & Prior, S. (2008). Women's experiences of increasing subjective well-being in CFS/ME through leisure-based arts and crafts activities: A qualitative study. *Disability and Rehabilitation: An International, Multidisciplinary Journal, 30*, 1279–88.

43. Soden, L. (1999, July). Insight imagery: Towards personal wellness through spontaneous art-making and empathic co-reflection. *Dissertation Abstracts International Section A, 60*, 0047.

## Chapter 2: Avocations

1. Post, S. G. (Ed.). (2007). *Altruism & health: Perspectives from empirical research*. New York: Oxford University Press.

2. Anderson, J. S. (2007). Pleasant, pleasurable, and positive activities. In L. L'Abate (Ed.), *Low-cost approaches to physical and mental health: Theory, research, and practice* (pp. 201–17). New York: Springer-Science.

3. Asimov, I. (1979). *Treasury of humor*. New York: Houghton Mifflin.

4. Fuller, E. (Ed.). (1978). *2500 anecdotes for all occasions*. New York: Avenel Books.

5. Anderson, *Low-cost approaches*.

6. Ibid.

7. Post, *Altruism & health*.

8. Booher, B. (2010, July–August). *Duke Magazine*, pp. 36–41.

9. Ibid.

10. Beiser, M. (1974). Components and correlates of mental well-being. *Journal of Health and Social Behavior, 15,* 320–27.

11. Dik, B., & Hansen, J. (2008). Following passionate interests to well-being. *Journal of Career Assessment, 16,* 86–100.

12. Meir, E., Melamed, S., & Abu-Freha, A. (1990). Vocational, avocational, and skill utilization congruencies and their relationship with well-being in two cultures. *Journal of Vocational Behavior, 36*(2), 153–65.

13. Coster, J., & Schwebel, M. (1997). Well-functioning in professional psychologists. *Professional Psychology: Research and Practice, 28,* 5–13.

14. Heintzman, P. (2000). Leisure and spiritual well-being: A social scientific exploration. *Dissertation Abstracts International Section A, 60,* 2674.

## Chapter 3: Being, Doing, and Having

1. Foa, U., & Foa, E. (1974). *Societal structures of the mind.* Springfield, IL: C. C. Thomas.

2. L'Abate, L. (2007). Animal companions. In L. L'Abate (Ed.), *Low-cost approaches to physical and mental health: Theory, research, and practice* (pp. 473–83). New York: Springer-Science.

3. Baumeister, R. F. (Ed.). (1993). *Self-esteem: The puzzle of low self-regard.* New York: Plenum.

4. Bednar, R. L., Wells, M. G., & Peterson, S. R. (1989). *Self-esteem: Paradoxes and innovations in clinical theory and practice.* Washington, DC: American Psychological Association.

5. Mruk, C. (1995). *Self-esteem: Research, theory, and practice.* New York: Springer Publishing Company.

6. McKay, M., Fanning, P., Honeychurch, C., & Sutker, C. (1999). *The self-esteem companion: Challenge your inner critic, celebrate your personal strength.* New York: MJF Books.

7. Baumeister, *Self-esteem.*

8. L'Abate, L. (1986). *Systematic family therapy.* New York: Brunner/Mazel.

9. L'Abate, L. (1994). *A theory of personality development.* New York: Wiley. L'Abate (1997). *The self in the family: Toward a classification of personality, and psychopathology.* New York: Wiley.

10. L'Abate, L. (2005). *Personality in intimate relationships: Socialization and psychopathology.* New York: Springer-Science; L'Abate, L. (2011). *Sourcebook of interactive practice exercises in mental health.* New York: Springer-Science; L'Abate, L., & DeGiacomo, P. (2003). *Intimate relationships and how to improve them: Integrating theoretical models with preventive and psychotherapeutic approaches.*Westport, CT: Praeger.

11. Milulincer, M., & Shaver, P. (2007). *Adult attachment.* New York: Guildford.

12. Cusinato, M., & L'Abate, L. (Eds.) (in press). *Advances in relational competence theory: With special attention to alexithymia.* New York: Nova Science Publishers.

13. L'Abate, L. (2009). Paradigms, theories, and models: Two hierarchical frameworks. In L. L'Abate, P. DeGiacomo, M. Capitelli, & S. Longo (Eds.), *Science, mind and creativity: The Bari symposium* (pp.107–53). New York: Nova Science Publishers; L'Abate, L. (in press). Essentialism. In L. L'Abate (Ed.), *The role of paradigms in theory constructions.* New York: Springer-Science.

14. L'Abate, *Personality in intimate relationships.*

15. *Atlanta Journal-Constitution* (August 25, 2010).

16. L'Abate, *Personality in intimate relationships.*

17. Ibid.

18. Calogero, R., & Pedrotty, K. (2007). Daily practices for mindful exercise. In L. L'Abate (Ed.), *Low-cost approaches to physical and mental health: Theory, research, and practice* (pp. 141–217). New York: Springer-Science; Harwood, T. M., & L'Abate, L. (2010). *Self-help in mental health: A critical review.* New York: Springer-Science; L'Abate, L. (2011). *Sourcebook of interactive practice exercises in mental health.* New York: Springer-Science; McGrady, A. (2007). Relaxation and meditation. In L. L'Abate (Ed.), *Low-cost approaches to physical and mental health: Theory, research, and practice* (pp. 161–75). New York: Springer-Science; Sias, P. M., & Bartoo, H. (2007). Friendship, social support, and health. In L. L'Abate (Ed.), *Low-cost approaches to physical and mental health: Theory, research, and practice* (pp. 455–72). New York: Springer-Science.

19. Sternberg, R. J. (1998). *Cupid's arrow: The course of love through time.* New York: Cambridge University Press.

20. L'Abate, *Personality in intimate relationships.*

21. Hegi, K. E., & Bergner, R. M. (2010). What is love? An empirically-based essentialist account. *Personal Relationships, 27*, 620–36.

22. Singer, I. (1984). *The nature of love. Volume I: From Plato to Luther* (2nd ed.). Chicago, IL: University of Chicago Press.

23. Ibid.

24. Hillix, W. A., & L'Abate, L. (2011). The role of paradigms in science and theory construction. In L. L'Abate (Ed.), *The role of paradigms in theory construction* (pp. 0-00). New York: Springer-Science.

25. Ibid.

26. L'Abate, L. (2011). *Hurt feelings in intimate relationships: Theory, research, and applications.* New York: Cambridge University Press.

27. Ibid.

28. L'Abate, L., & Cusinato, M. (1994). A spiral model of intimacy. In S. M. Johnson & L. S. Greenberg, (Eds.), *The heart of the matter: Perspectives on emotion in marital therapy* (pp. 122–38). New York: Brunner/Mazel.

29. L'Abate, *Hurt feelings in intimate relationships.*

30. Sternberg, *Cupid's arrow.*

31. Stevens, F. E., & L'Abate, L. (1989). Validity and reliability of a theory-derived measure of intimacy. *American Journal of Family Therapy, 17,* 359–68.

32. Mashek, D. J., & A. Aron (Eds.). (2004). *Handbook of closeness and intimacy.* Mahwah, NJ: Erlbaum.

33. Prager, K. J. (1995). *The psychology of intimacy.* New York: Guilford.

34. L'Abate, L. (1977). Intimacy is sharing hurt feelings: A reply to David Mace. *Journal of Marriage and Family Counseling, 3,* 13–16.

35. L'Abate, *Personality in intimate relationships.*

36. Firestone, R. W., & Catlett, J. (1999). *Fear of intimacy.* Washington, DC: American Psychological Association.

37. L'Abate, *Hurt feelings in intimate relationships.*

38. L'Abate, *Systematic family therapy.*

39. L'Abate, *Hurt feelings in intimate relationships.*

40. Vangelisti, A. L., & Beck, G. (2007). Intimacy and fear of intimacy. In L. L'Abate (Ed.), *Low-cost approaches to promote physical and mental health: Theory, research, and practice* (pp. 395–414). New York: Springer-Science.

41. Bloom, P. (2010). *How pleasure works: The new science of why we like what we like.* New York: W. W. Norton & Company.

42. Joshua Bell (p. 117).

43. Mesquita, B., Barrett, L. F., & Smith, E. R. (Eds.). (2010). *The mind in context.* New York: Guilford.

44. Walter Isaacson (2010).

45. L'Abate, L. (1986). *Systematic family therapy.* New York: Brunner/ Mazel.

46. Walter Krin (2010).

47. Anderson, C. (2007). *Pleasant, pleasure, and positive activities.* In L. L'Abate. (Ed.), *Low-cost approaches to physical and mental health: Theory, research, and practice* (pp. 201–17). New York: Springer-Science

48. Walter Krin (2010).

49. L'Abate, L. (1992). *Programmed writing: A self-administered approach for interventions with individuals, couples and families.* Pacific Grove, CA: Brooks/ Cole; L'Abate, L. (1997a). Distance writing and computer-assisted training. In S. R. Sauber (Ed.), *Managed mental health care: Major diagnostic and treatment approaches* (pp. 133–63). Bristol, PA: Brunner/Mazel; L'Abate, L. (Ed.). (2001a). *Distance writing and computer-assisted interventions in psychiatry and mental health.* Westport, CT: Ablex; L'Abate, L. (2001b). Hugging, holding, huddling, and cuddling (3HC): A task prescription in couples and family therapy. *The Journal of Clinical Activities, Assignments, & Handouts in Psychotherapy Practice, 1,* 5–18; L'Abate, L. (2004a). *A guide to self-help workbooks for clinicians and researchers.* Binghamton, NY: Haworth; L'Abate, L. (2004b). Systematically written homework assignment: The case for homework-based treatment. In L. L'Abate, *Using workbooks in mental health: Resources in prevention, psychotherapy, and rehabilitation for clinicians and researchers* (pp. 65–102). Binghamton, NY: Haworth; L'Abate, L. Boyce, J., Fraizer, I., & Russ, D. A. (1992). Programmed

writing: Research in progress. *Comprehensive Mental Health Care, 2,* 45–62; L'Abate, L., & De Giacomo, P. (2003). *Intimate relationships and how to improve them: Integrating theoretical models with preventive and psychotherapeutic approaches.* Westport, CT: Praeger; L'Abate, L., & Goldstein D. (2007). Protocols to promote mental health and life-long learning. In L. L'Abate (Ed.), *Low-cost approaches to promote physical and mental health: Theory, research, and practice* (pp. 285–302). New York: Springer-Science; L'Abate, L., & Kern, R. (2002). Workbooks: Tools for the expressive writing paradigm. In S. J. Lepore & J. M. Smyth (Eds.), *The writing cure: How expressive writing promotes health and emotional well-being* (pp. 239–55). Washington, DC: American Psychological Association.

50. Shermer, M. (1997). *Why people believe weird things: Pseudo-science, super-stition, and other confusions of our time.* New York: MJF Books.

51. L'Abate, *Personality in intimate relationships.*

52. Keating, P. (2010). *The Economist,* July 11.

53. Walter Krin (2010).

54. *The Wall Street Journal* (2010, September). pp. 38–49.

55. The Economist (2010). Editorial, pp. 11–12, 25–28.

56. L'Abate, *Programmed writing.*

57. Ibid.

58. Crawford, M. (2010). *The case for working with your hands: Or why office work is bad for us and fixing things feels good.* New York: Viking.

59. Ibid.

60. Biswas-Diener, R. (2008). *Happiness: Unlocking the mysteries of psychological wealth.* Malden, MA: Blackwell.

61. L'Abate, L. (2010). *Sourcebook of practice exercises in mental health.* New York: Springer-Science; L'Abate, L. (1999). Taking the bull by the horns: Beyond talk in psychological interventions.*The Family Journal: Counseling and Therapy for Couples and Families, 7,* 206–20; L'Abate, L. (2002). *Beyond psychotherapy: Programmed writing and structured computer-assisted interventions.* Westport, CT: Ablex; L'Abate, L. (2007a). A completely preposterous proposal: The dictionary as an initial vehicle of change in the family. *The Family Psychologist, 23,* 39–42; L'Abate, L. (2007c). Introduction: Section IV. Writing. In L. L'Abate (Ed.), *Low-cost approaches to promote physical and mental health: Theory, research, and practice* (pp. 219–66). New York: Springer-Science; L'Abate, L. (Ed.). (2007d). *Low-cost approaches to promote physical and mental health: Theory, research, and practice.* New York: Springer-Science; L'Abate, L. (2008a). A proposal for including distance writing in couple therapy. *Journal of Couple & Relationship Therapy, 7,* 337–62; L'Abate, L. (Ed.). (2008b). *Toward a science of clinical psychology: Laboratory evaluations and interventions.* New York: Nova Science Publishers; L'Abate, L. (2008c). Working at a distance from participants: Writing and nonverbal media. In L. L'Abate (Ed.), *Toward a science of clinical psychology: Laboratory evaluations and interventions* (pp. 355–83). Hauppauge, NY: Nova Science Publishers; L'Abate, L. (2010a). Beyond reliability and validity: Specificity in clinical psychology. Manuscript submitted

for publication; L'Abate, L. (in press-a). Psychotherapy consists of homework assignments: A radical iconoclastic conviction. In H. Rosenthal (Ed.), *Favorite Counseling and Therapy Homework Techniques: Classic Anniversary Edition* (pp. 219–29). New York: Routledge; L'Abate, L., & Cusinato, M. (2007). Linking theory with practice: Theory-derived interventions in prevention and family therapy. *The Family Journal: Counseling and Psychotherapy with Couples and Families, 15*, 318–27; L'Abate, L., L'Abate, B. L., & Maino, E. (2005). A review of 25 years of part-time professional practice: Workbooks and length of psychotherapy. *American Journal of Family Therapy, 33*, 19–31.

62. Bloom, P. (2010). *How pleasure works: The new science of why we like what we like.* New York: W.W. Norton & Company.

63. L'Abate, L. (in press-c). *The role of paradigms in theory construction.* New York: Springer-Science.

64. L'Abate, L. (in press-b). *Hurt feelings: Theory, research, and applications in intimate relationships.* New York: Cambridge University Press.

65. L'Abate, *The role of paradigms.*

66. Ibid.

67. Ibid.

68. L'Abate, L. (1997b). *The self in the family: Toward a classification of personality, criminality, and psychopathology.* New York: Wiley.

69. Guinote, A., & Vescio, T. K. (Eds.). (2010). *The social psychology of power.* New York: Guilford.

70. L'Abate, *Personality in intimate relationships.*

71. Firestone, R. W., & Catlett, J. (1999). *Fear of intimacy.* Washington, DC: American Psychological Association.

72. Ibid.

73. Shermer, *Why people believe weird things.*

74. Vangelisti, A. L., & Beck, G. (2007). *Intimacy and fear.* In. L. L'Abate (Ed.), *Low-cost approaches to promote physical and mental health: Theory, research, and practice* (pp. 395–414). New York: Springer-Science.

75. Frost, R. O., & Steketee, G. (2010). *Stuff: Compulsive hoarding and the meaning of things.* New York: Houghton Mifflin Harcourt.

76. Hefferman, V. (2010, May/June). Hoard mentality: Why are we so obsessed with people who are obsessed with stuff? *Mother Jones*, pp. 67–68.

77. Garzia, O. (2010, August 29). Body buried in home clutter: Month-long search for missing Vegas hoarder ends at her own house. *Atlanta Journal-Constitution*, A4.

78. *Atlanta Journal Constitution* (Sunday, August 28).

79. *The Economist* (2010, September), p. 72.

## Chapter 4: Food

1. C. Trillin. (2010, March 1) Where is Chang? The chef that cannot shake his followers. *The New Yorker*, pp. 24–29.

2. Foer, J. S. (2009). *Eating animal*. New York: Little & Brown; Masson, J. M. (2009). *The face on your plate: The truth about food*. New York: W. W. Norton.

3. Asimov, I. (1979). *Treasury of humor*. New York: Houghton Mifflin.

4. Gopnik, A. (2010, April 5). No rules! Is Le Fooding, the French culinary movement more than a feeling? *The New Yorker*, pp. 36–41.

5. Lisa Abed. (2010, June 21). Celebrity Cooking TV shows. *Time*, pp. 63–65; Joel Stein. (2010, August 23). Proteins and diets: Less meats and more vegetables. *Time*, pp. 51–53.

6. Lisa, *Time*.

7. Josh Ozersky. (2010, August 30). Natural and organic foods compared. *Time*, pp. 30–36.

8. Anonymous. (2010, July 26). Medical research and Big Pharma. *Time*, p. 21; Massimo Calabresi. (2010, August 23). FDA and Big Pharma. *Time*, p. 27.

9. Dog, T. L. (2010). The role of nutrition in mental health. *Alternative Therapies in Health and Medicine, 16*, 42–46.

10. Perlmutter, D., & Coleman, C. (2004). *The better brain book*. New York: Riverhead Books.

11. Feinstein, A. (Ed.). (2009). *Nutri-cures: Food and supplements that work with your body to relieve symptoms & speed healing*. New York: Rodale Inc.

12. *Life Extension* (2010). P.O. Box 407198, Fort Lauderdale, FL 33340-7198.

13. Rodale Books. (2008). *Healing with vitamins: The best nutrients to slow, stop, and reverse disease: Straight from nature, backed by science*. New York: Rodale Inc.

14. Ibid.

15. Life Extension Media. (2004). *Disease prevention and treatment: Scientific protocols and integrate mainstream and alternative medicine* (extended 4th ed.). Hollywood, FL: Life Extension Foundation.

16. Trillin, Where is Chang?.

17. L'Abate, L. (2007). Primary interventions: Nutritional approaches. In L. L'Abate (Ed.), *Low-cost approaches to promote physical and mental health: Theory, research, and practice* (pp. 41–45). New York: Springer-Science.

18. Katz, D. L., Yeh, M-C., O'Connell, M., & Faridi, Z. (2007). Diets, health, and weight control: What do we know? In L. L'Abate (Ed.), *Low-cost approaches to promote physical and mental health: Theory, research, and practice* (pp. 47–72). New York: Springer-Science.

19. Finke, M. S., & Huston, S. J. (2007). Low-cost obesity interventions: The market for foods. In L. L'Abate (Ed.), *Low-cost approaches to promote physical and mental health: Theory, research, and practice* (pp. 73–85). New York: Springer-Science.

20. Akhondzadeh, S. (2007). Herbal medicines in the treatment of psychiatric and neurological disorders. In L. L'Abate (Ed.), *Low-cost approaches to promote physical and mental health: Theory, research, and practice* (pp. 119–38). New York: Springer-Science.

21. Giovannucci, E. (2007). Vitamins, minerals and health. In L. L'Abate (Ed.), *Low-cost approaches to promote physical and mental health: Theory, research, and practice* (pp. 103–18). New York: Springer-Science.

22. Umhau, J. C., & Dauphinais, K. M. (2007). Omega-3 polyunsaturated fatty acids and health. In L. L'Abate (Ed.), *Low-cost approaches to promote physical and mental health: Theory, research, and practice* (pp. 87–101). New York: Springer-Science.

23. Calabresi, M., Park, A., & Weill, S. Foraging behavior. (2010, August 23). *Time*, p. 34.

24. Elliott, C. (2010, September/October). Making a killing: Clinical trials have become marketing exercises for Big Pharma—and cash-strapped universities are helping make the sale. *Mother Jones*, pp. 55–65; Mayer, J. (2010, August 30). A reporter at large: Covert operations. *The New Yorker*, pp. 44–55.

25. Blumenthal, K., & Volpp, K. G. (2010). Enhancing the effectiveness of food labeling in restaurants. *Journal of the American Medical Association, 103*, 553–54.

26. Harwood, T. M., & L'Abate, L. (2010). *Self-help in mental health: A critical review*. New York: Springer-Science; Ladner, J. D., & Wilson, G. T. (Eds.). (2007). *Self-help approaches for obesity and eating disorders: Research and practice*. New York: Guilford.

27. Curtis, W. (2010, June). Who invented the cocktail? *The Atlantic Monthly*, p. 24.

## Chapter 5: Music Does Not Need to Be Loud to Be Enjoyable

1. Asimov, I. (1979). *Treasury of humor*. New York: Houghton Mifflin.

2. Blanning, T. (2008). *The triumph of music: The rise of composers, musicians and their art*. Cambridge, MA: Belknap Press of Harvard University Press.

3. Anderson, C. (2009). *Free: The future of a radical price*. New York: Hyperion.

4. Jeans, J. (1937, 1968). *Science and music*. New York: Dover Publications.

5. Leeds, J. (1999). *Sonic alchemy: Conversations with leading sound practitioners*. Sausalito, CA: InnerSong Press.

6. Drury, N. (1985). *Music for inner space: Techniques for meditation & visualization*. San Leandro, CA: Prism Press.

7. Halperin, S., & Savary, L. (1985). *Sound health: The music and sounds that make us whole*. San Francisco, CA: Harper & Row.

8. Bonny, H. L., & Savary, L. M. (1990). *Music & your mind: Listening with a new consciousness*. Barrytown, NY: Station Hill Press.

9. Beaulieu, J. (1987). *Music and the sound in the healing arts*. Barrytown, NY: Station Hill Press.

10. Gardner, K. (1990). *Sounding the inner landscape: Music as medicine*. Stonington, ME: Caduceus Publications.

11. Goldman, J. (1992). *Healing sounds: The power of harmonics*. Rockport, MA: Element.

12. Miles, E. (1997). *Tune your brain: Using music to manage your mind, body, and mood*. New York: Berkley Press.

13. Kahn, H. I. (1983). *The music of life*. New Lebanon, NY: Omega Publications.

14. Maddock, O. D. (1993). *The book of sound therapy: Heal yourself with music and voice*. New York: Simon & Schuster.

15. Bulfone, T., Regattin, L., Quattrin, R., Brusaferro, B. & Zanotti, R. (2009). Effectiveness of music therapy for anxiety reduction in women with breast cancer in chemotherapy treatment. *Holistic Nursing Practice, 23*, 238.

16. Matzo, M. (2009). Music and stress reduction. *The American Journal of Nursing, 109*, 40.

17. Silverman, M. (2008). Quantitative comparison of cognitive behavioral therapy and music therapy research: A methodological best-practices analysis to guide future investigation for adult psychiatric patients. *Journal of Music Therapy, 45*, 457–506.

18. Grocke, D., Bloch, S., & Castle, D. (2009). The effect of group music therapy on quality of life for participants living with a severe and enduring mental illness. *Journal of Music Therapy, 46*, 90–104.

19. Silverman, M. (2009). The effect of single-session psycho-educational music therapy on verbalizations and perceptions in psychiatric patients. *Journal of Music Therapy, 46*, 105–31.

20. Lee, K. (2010). An autoethnography: Music therapy after laser eye surgery. *Qualitative Inquiry, 16*, 244.

21. Sand-Jecklin, K., & Emerson, H. (2010). The impact of a live therapeutic music intervention on patients' experience of pain, anxiety, and muscle tension. *Holistic Nursing Practice, 24*, 7.

22. Mills, W., Maier, J., & Salerno, J. (2008). Music-based interventions and the resilience of persons with dementia: Practical applications, outcomes, and future directions. *The Gerontologist: 61st Annual Scientific Meeting, 48*, 251–52.

23. Hulme, C., Wright, J., Crocker, T., Oluboyede, Y., & House, A. (2010). Non- pharmacological approaches for dementia that informal carers might try or access: A systematic review. *International Journal of Geriatric Psychiatry, 25*, 756.

24. Bailey, L. (2010). Strategies for decreasing patient anxiety in the perioperative setting. *Association of Operating Room Nurses Journal, 92*, 445–60.

25. Hodges, A., & Wilson, L. (2010). Effects of music therapy on preterm infants in the neonatal intensive care unit. *Alternative Therapies in Health and Medicine, 16*, 72–77.

26. Lindenfelser, K., Grocke, D., & McFerran, K. (2008). Bereaved parents' experiences of music therapy with their terminally ill child. *Journal of Music Therapy, 45,* 330–48.

27. Shabanloei, R., Golchin, M., Esfahani, A., Dolatkhah, R., & Rasoulian, M. (2010). Effects of music therapy on pain and anxiety in patients undergoing bone marrow biopsy and aspiration. *Association of Operating Room Nurses Journal, 91,* 746–51.

28. Thaut, M. (2010). Neurologic music therapy in cognitive rehabilitation. *Music Perception, 27,* 281–85.

29. Kim, M., & Tomaino, C. (2008). Protocol evaluation for effective music therapy for persons with non-fluent aphasia. *Topics in Stroke Rehabilitation, 15,* 555.

30. Magill, L., Levin, T., & Spodek, L. (2008). One-session music therapy and CBT for critically ill cancer patients. *Psychiatric Services, 59,* 1216.

31. Hendon, C., & Bohon, L. (2008). Hospitalized children's mood differences during play and music therapy. *Child Care, Health and Development, 34,* 141.

32. Robb, S., Clair, A., Watanabe, M., et al. (2008). Randomized controlled trial of the active music engagement (AME) intervention on children with cancer. *PsychoOncology, 17,* 699.

33. Kim, Y. (2008). The effect of improvisation-assisted desensitization, and music-assisted progressive muscle relaxation and imagery on reducing pianists' music performance anxiety. *Journal of Music Therapy, 45,* 165–91.

34. *Atlanta Journal and Constitution,* October 10, 2010.

35. Levitin, D. J. (2008). *The world in six songs: How the musical brain created human nature.* New York: Dutton.

## Chapter 6: Play Is Just as Important as Work

1. Brown, S., with Vaughan, C. (2009). *Play: How it opens the brain, opens the imagination, and invigorates the soul.* New York: Avery.

2. L'Abate, L. (2009). *The Praeger handbook of play across the life cycle: Fun from infancy to old age.* Westport, CT: Praeger.

3. Schumpeter. (2010, July 10). Menes Sana in corporation sane. *The Economist,* pp. 23–24.

4. L'Abate, *The Praeger handbook.*

5. L'Abate, L. (2005). *Personality in intimate relationships: Socialization and psycho-pathology.* New York: Springer-Science.

6. Fonda, D. (2010, September). Toying with Mattel's future. *Smart Money: From the Wall Street Journal,* pp. 20–21).

7. Cusinato, M., & L'Abate, L. (Eds.). (in press). *Advances in relational competence theory: With special attention to alexithymia.* New York: Nova Science Publishers.

8. L'Abate, L. (2011). *Sourcebook of interactive practice exercises in mental health*. New York: Springer-Science

9. L'Abate, *The Praeger handbook*.

10. Ibid.

11. Ibid.

12. Dulicai, D., & Hill, E. S. (2007). Dulicai, D., & Hill, E. S. (2007). Expressive movement. In L. L'Abate (Ed.), *Low-cost approaches to physical and mental health: Theory, research, and practice* (pp. 177–200). New York: Springer-Science.

13. Nave & McCarthy. (2010, September 11). Lord of the dance. *The Economist*.

14. Smith, J., Gourgott, C., Devine, P. (2001). The great good gym. In R. Oldenburg (Ed.), *Celebrating the third place: Inspiring stories about the "Great Good Places" at the heart of our communities* (pp. 130–40). New York, NY: Marlowe & Company.

15. Cleveland Clinic's Heart Advisor. (2010, October). Volume 13.

16. Duke Medicine Health News, Volume 7H.

17. Gooding, M., & Rothenstein, S. (Eds.). (Undated). *Mind games: A box of psychological play*. Boston, MA: Tambala Publications.

18. Scott-Moore, M. (2010). *Sweetness and blood: How surfing spread from Hawaii and California to the rest of the world, with some unexpected results*. UK: Rodale. Reviewed in *The Economist*, July 10, 2010. *"Great Good Places" at the heart of our communities* (pp. 131–40). New York: Marlowe & Company.

19. *The Economist* (2010, July 10). pp. 3–16.

20. L'Abate, *The Praeger handbook*.

21. Kauai, J. B. (2010). World of Why Ville. *Games & Culture, 5*, 3–22.

22. Kauai, Y. B., Fields, D. A., & Cook, M. S. (2010). Your second selves. *Games & Culture, 5*, 23–42.

23. Fields, D. A., & Kauai, Y. B. (2010). "Stealing from Grandma" or generating cultural knowledge? *Games & Culture, 5*, 64–87.

24. Kauai et al., Your second selves.

25. Ferguson, C. I. (2010). Blazing angels or resident evil? Can violent video games be a force for the good? *Review of General Psychology, 14*, 68–81.

26. Markey, P. M. (2010). Vulnerability to violent video games: A review and integration of personality research. *Review of General Psychology, 14*, 82–91.

27. Olson, C. K. (2010). Children's motivation for video game play in the context of normal development. *Review of General Psychology, 14*, 180–87.

28. L'Abate, *The Praeger handbook*.

## Chapter 7: The Body

1. Sprecher, S., & McKinney, K. (1993). *Sexuality*. Newbury Park, CA: Sage.

2. Francoeur, R. T., Koch, P. B., & Weis, D. L. (Eds.). (1998). *Sexuality in America: Understanding our sexual values and behavior*. New York: Continuum.

3. Abramson, P. R., & Pinkerton, S. D. (2002). *With pleasure: Thoughts about the nature of human sexuality*. New York: Oxford University Press.

4. Buss, D. M. (1994). *The evolution of desire: Strategies of human mating*. New York: Basic Books.

5. Macy, M. (1996). *Working sex: An odyssey into our cultural underworld*. New York: Carroll & Graf.

6. Sweeney, M. S. (2007). *Brain: The complete mind*. Washington, DC: National Geographic Society.

7. Ibid.

8. Baumeister, R. F., & Tice, D. M. (2001). *The social dimension of sex*. Boston, MA: Allyn & Bacon.

9. Gulledge, A. K., Hill, M., Lister, Z., & Sallion, C. (2007). Non-erotic physical affection: It's good for you. In L. L'Abate (Ed.), *Low-cost approaches to physical and mental health: Theory, research, and practice* (pp. 371–83). New York: Springer-Science; Jones, N. A., & Mize, K. D. (2007). Touch interventions positively affect development. In L. L'Abate (Ed.), *Low-cost approaches to physical and mental health: Theory, research, and practice* (pp. 353–69). New York: Springer-Science.

10. L'Abate, L. (2001). Hugging, holding, huddling, and cuddling (3HC): A task prescription in couple and family therapy. *Journal of Clinical Activities Assignments, & Handouts in Psychotherapy Practice, 1*, 5–18.

11. Ekman, P. (2010). Darwin's compassionate view of human nature. *Journal of the American Medical Association, 103*, 557–58.

12. Emmons, R. A. (2008). Gratitude, subjective well-being, and the brain. In M. Eid & R. J. Larsen (Eds.), *The science of subjective well-being* (pp. 469–89). New York: Guilford.

13. Ibid.

14. Ibid.

15. Fuller, E. (Ed.). (1970). *2500 anecdotes for all occasions*. New York: Avenel Books.

16. Algoe, S. B., Gable, S. L., & Maisel, N. C. (2010). It's the little things: Everyday gratitude as a booster shot for romantic relationships. *Personal Relationships, 17*, 217–33.

17. Woodward, A. J., Findlay, B. M., & Moore, S. M. (2009). Peak and mystical experiences in intimate relationships. *Journal of Social and Personal Relationships, 26*, 429–42.

18. L'Abate, L. (in press). *Hurt feelings: Theory, research, and practice in intimate relationships*. New York: Cambridge University Press.

19. Wieselquist, J. (2009). Interpersonal forgiveness, trust, and the investment model of commitment. *Journal of Sexual and Personal Relationships, 26*, 531–48; Rhoades, G. K., Stanley, S. M., & Markman, H. J. (2010). Should I stay or should I go? Predicting dating relationships stability from four aspects of commitment. *Journal of Family Psychology, 24*, 543–50.

20. Post, S. G. (Ed.). (2007). *Altruism & health: Perspectives from empirical research*. New York: Oxford University Press.

21. Cross, C. L., & Weeks, G. R. (2007). Sex, sexuality, and sensuality. In L. L'Abate (Ed.), *Low-cost approaches to physical and mental health: Theory, research, and practice* (pp. 385–94). New York: Springer-Science.

22. McNamara, P. (Ed.). (2006). *Where God and science meet: The neurology of religious experience* (Vol. I, II, III). Westport, CT: Praeger.

23. Harwood, T. M., & L'Abate, L. (2010). *Self-help in mental health: A critical evaluation*. New York: Springer-Science.

24. Sperry, L., Hoffman, L., Cox, R. H., & Cox, B. E. (2007). Spirituality in achieving physical and psychological health and well-being: Theory, research, and low-cost interventions. In L. L'Abate (Ed.), *Low-cost approaches to physical and mental health: Theory, research, and practice* (pp. 435–52). New York: Springer-Science.

25. L'Abate, L., & Kaiser, D. L. (Eds.). (in press). *Handbook of technology in psychology, psychiatry, and neurology: Theory, research, and practice*. New York: Nova Science Publishers.

26. *Women under the influence.* (2005). National Center on Addiction and Substance Abuse of Columbia University. Baltimore, MD: Johns Hopkins University Press.

27. Women and Sex/Gender Differences Research Program. National Institute on Drug Abuse. Retrieved from www.drugabuse.gov/WHGD/WHGDHome.html

28. L'Abate, L. (2009). Paradigms, theories, and models: Two hierarchical frameworks. In L. L'Abate, P. De Giacomo, M. Capitelli, & S. Longo (Eds.), *Science, mind, and creativity: The Bari symposium* (pp. 107–53). New York: Nova Science Publishers.

29. Shaver, P., & Hendrick, C. (Eds.). (1987). *Sex and gender.* Newbury Park, CA: Sage.

30. Owen-Blakemore, J. E., Berenbaum, S. A., & Liben, L. S. (2008). *Gender development.* New York: Psychology Press.

31. Halpern, D. (2000). *Sex differences in cognitive abilities.* Mahwah, NJ: Erlbaum.

32. Hines, M. (2005). *Brain gender.* New York: Oxford University Press.

33. Hyde, J. S. (2005). The gender similarities hypothesis. *American Psychologist, 60*, 581–92.

34. Lippa, R. A. (2002). *Gender, nature, and nurture.* Mahwah, NJ: Erlbaum.

35. Baron-Cohen, D. F., Knickmeyer, R. C., & Belmonte, M. K. (2005). Sex differences in the brain: Implications for explaining autism. *Science, 310*, 819–22.

36. Cochran, S. V., & Rabinowitz, F. E. (1999). *Men and depression: Clinical and empirical perspectives.* San Diego, CA: Academic Press.

37. Goel, N., & Bale, T. L. (2009). Examining the intersection of sex and stress in modeling neuropsychiatric disorders. *Journal of Neuroendocrinology, 21*, 415–20.

38. Goldstein, J. M., Jerram, M., Abbs, B., Whitfield-Gabrieli, R. W., & Makris, N. (2010). Sex differences in stress response circuitry activation-dependent on female hormonal cycle. *Journal of Neuroscience, 30*, 431–38.

39. Manson, J. E. (2008). Prenatal exposure to sex steroid hormones and behavioral cognitive outcomes. *Metabolism: Clinical and Experimental, 57, Supplement 2*, 516–21.

40. National Institute of Mental Health. (no date). Real men, real depression. Retrieved from www.nimh.nih.gov/health/publications/real-men-real-depression-easy-to-read/index.shtmt.

41. Young, E. A., & Becker, J. B. (2009). Sex matters: Gonadal steroids and the brain. *Neuropsychopharmacology, 34*, 537–38.

42. Zahn-Waxler, C., Shirtcliff, E. A., & Marceau, K. (2008). Disorders of childhood and adolescence: Gender and psychopathology. *Annual Review of Clinical Psychology, 4*, 11–29.

43. Archer, J. (2004). Sex differences in aggression in real-world settings: A meta-analyic review. *Review of General Psychology, 8*, 291–322.

44. Bennett, S., Farrington, D. P., & Huesmann, L. R. (2005). Explaining gender differences in crime and violence: The importance of social cognitive skills. *Aggression and Violent Behavior, 10*, 263–88.

45. Crick, N. R., & Grotpeter, J. K. (1995). Relational aggression, gender, and social psychological adjustment. *Child Development, 66*, 710–22.

46. Bressler, E. R., Martin, R. A., & Balshine, S. (2006). Production and appreciation of humor as sexually selected traits. *Evolution and Human Behavior, 27*, 121–30.

47. Martin, R. A. (2007). *The psychology of humor: An integrative approach.* San Diego, CA: Academic Press.

48. Provine, R. R. (2000). *Laughter: A scientific investigation.* New York: Penguin Books.

49. Antes, E. (2010, June). Family guy. *Scientific American: Mind*, 46–53.

50. Parke, R. (2004). Fathers, families, and the future: A plethora of plausible predictions. *Merrill-Palmer Quarterly, 50*, 456–70.

51. Lamb, M. (Ed.). (2004). *The role of the father in child development.* New York: Wiley.

52. Pruett, K., & Kline-Pruett, M. (2009). *Partnership parenting.* New York: Da Capo Press.

53. Tannen, D. (2010, May–June). He said, she said. *Scientific American; Mind*, 55–59.

54. L'Abate, L. (2005). *Personality in intimate relationships: Socialization and psychopathology.* New York: Springer-Science.

55. L'Abate, Paradigms, theories, and models.

56. Norris, F. H., Perilla, J. L., Ibanez, G. E., & Murphy, A. D. (2001). Sex differences in symptoms of posttraumatic stress: Does culture play a role? *Journal of Traumatic Stress, 14*, 7–28.

57. Baumeister & Tice, *Social dimension of sex.*

58. Kimmel, M. (Ed.). (2007). *The sexual self: The construction of sexual scripts.* Nashville, TN: Vanderbilt University Press.

59. Ovid. (1931). *The art of love.* New York: Liveright Publishing Corporation.

60. Asimov, I. (1979). *Treasury of humor.* New York: Houghton Mifflin.

61. Ibid.

62. Doheny, K. (2008). Retrieved from http://www.webmd.com/sex-relationships/features/10-surprising-health-benefits-of-sex.

63. L'Abate, *Personality in intimate relationships.*

64. L'Abate, L., & Hewitt, D. (1988). Toward a classification of sex and sexual behavior. *Journal of Sex and Marital Therapy, 14,* 29–39.

65. L'Abate, Paradigms, theories, and models.

66. Warncke, C-P. (Ed.). (undated). *Theatre d'amour: A complete reprint of the coloure Emblemata amatoria of 1620.* Koln, GE: Taschen.

67. L'Abate, *Personality in intimate relationships.*

## Conlusion: Moderation, Self-Control, and Self-Monitoring

1. Butler, R. (2010). *The longevity prescription: The 8 proven keys to a long, healthy life.* New York: Avery.

2. Post, S. G. (Ed.). (2007). *Altruism & health: Perspectives from empirical research.* New York: Oxford University Press.

3. Harwood, T. M., & L'Abate, L. (2010). *Self-help in mental health: A critical evaluation.* New York: Springer-Science.

4. Bryant, F. B., & Veroff, J. (2007). *Savoring: A new model of positive experience.* Mahwah, NJ: Erlbaum.

5. L'Abate, L. (2010). Seven psychological orphans in search of a theory: Toward a neo-behaviorism of behavior and relationships. Manuscript in preparation.

6. Mikulincer, M., & Shaver, P. R. (2007). *Attachment in adulthood: Structure, dynamics, and change.* New York: Guilford.

7. Shapiro, S. L., & Carlson, L. E. (2009). *The art and mind of mindfulness: Integrating mindfulness into psychology and the helping professions.* Washington, DC: American Psychological Association.

8. L'Abate, L., Cusinato, M., Maino, E., Colesso, W., & Scilletta, C. (2010). *Relational competence theory: Research and mental health applications.* New York: Springer-Science.

9. L'Abate, L. (2011). *Hurt feelings: Theory and research in intimate relationships.* New York: Cambridge University Press.

10. McGrady, A. (2007). Relaxation and meditation. In L. L'Abate (Ed.), *Low-cost approaches to promote physical and mental health* (pp. 161–76). New York: Springer-Science.

11. Ibid.

12. 11. Lehrer, J. (2008, July 28). The eureka hunt: Why do good ideas come to us when they do? *The New Yorker*, pp. 40–45.

13. Bryant & Veroff, *Savoring*.

14. Ibid.

15. Ibid.

16. Ibid.

17. Ibid.

18. Ibid.

19. Ibid.

20. De Giacomo, P., L'Abate, L., Pennebaker, J. M., & Rumbaugh, D. M. (2010). From A to D: Amplifications and applications of Pennebaker's analogic to digital model in health promotion, prevention, and psychotherapy. *Clinical Psychology & Psychotherapy, 17*, 355–62.

21. L'Abate, L. (2011). *Sourcebook of interactive practice exercises in mental health*. New York: Springer-Science; Colesso, W., & L'Abate, L. (2010). Relational creativity: A redundant construct and teachable competence. Manuscript submitted for publication.

22. L'Abate, L. (in press). Psychotherapy consists of homework assignments: A radical iconoclastic conviction. In H. Rosenthal (Ed.), *Favorite counseling and therapy homework techniques: Classic anniversary edition*. New York: Routledge.

23. Ibid.

24. Bryant & Veroff, *Savoring*.

25. Ibid.

26. Beardsley, M. C. (1966). *Thinking straight* (3rd ed.). Englewood Cliffs, NJ: Prentice-Hall.

27. L'Abate, *Hurt feelings*.

28. L'Abate, L. (2005). *Personality in intimate relationships: Socialization and psychopathology*. New York: Springer-Science.

29. L'Abate, *Sourcebook of interactive practice*.

30. L'Abate, L. (1999). Taking the bull by the horns: Beyond talk in psychological interventions. *The Family Journal: Therapy and Counseling for Couples and Families, 7*, 206–20.

31. L'Abate, L. (2008). *Toward a science of clinical psychology: Laboratory evaluations and interventions*. New York: Nova Science Publishers.

32. L'Abate, *Sourcebook of interactive practice*.

33. L'Abate, *Personality in intimate relationships*

34. L'Abate, *Sourcebook of interactive practice*.

35. L'Abate, L. (2009). Paradigms, theories, and models: Two hierarchical frameworks. In L. L'Abate, P. De Giacomo, M. Capitelli, & S. Longo (Eds.), *Mind, science, and creativity: The Bari symposium* (pp. 107–56). New York: Nova Science Publishers; Colesso, W., & L'Abate, L. (2010). Relational creativity: A redundant construct and a teachable competence. Manuscript submitted for publication.

# Index

*Note*: Page numbers followed by a *t* refer to tables. Page numbers followed by an *f* refer to figures.

Abend, Lisa, 96–97
Abilities, 189–90
Able, 81
Abstract expressionism, 50–52
Abstract Image Game, 156
Abstract painting, 56*f*
Abu-Freha, A., 69
Abuse, 80
Accidie, 6
Acrylic paint, 54–55
Action, 30–31, 85, 162
Active hobbies, 66
Active music engagement
   (AME), 146
Activity, 9, 149, 155, 184. *See also*
   Exercise
Activity participation, 71
Adam Dant's House of Personalities,
   156
Adaptogenics, 106
Addictions, 185, 187–88
Additive interactions, 21
Advanced Bionutritionals,
   105, 107*t*
Advanced ResVPlus formula, 123
Advantages, 1
Adverse Drug Reaction Bulletin, 121
Advertising, 117. *See also* Scams/
   scammers

Affection, 163
Affective forecasts, 13
African American culture, 168
Age, 101, 151
Agency, 162
Aggression, 159–60
Alcohol, 100, 130–31
Alfalfa sprouts, 103
Algoe, S. B., 164
Alighieri, Dante, 6
Alizarin Crimson, 41, 46
Alizarin Crimson Hue, 46
Alizarin Permanent, 46
Allen, Woody, 169
Allenby, Lucy, 177
Alzheimer's disease, 102–3, 143
Ambivalent love-hate dislike,
   125–26
American Innovations and Solutions,
   172*t*
American Psychological Association
   (APA), *Dictionary of Psychology*,
   27–28
Ancient Greece, 41
Anderson, Chris, 83, 85
Andres, Jose, 96
Anger, 6–7, 19, 78
Anorexia, 83
Antes, E., 168

Anthracene, 46
Antidepressants, 167
Antioxidant vitamins, 103
Anxiety, 143–44
Appreciation, 81, 156, 163
Architecture, 30
Arithmetical interactions, 21
Armory Show, 51
Armstrong, Lance, 152
Aromalab Institute, 172*t*
Arsenic, 41
Arthritis, 102–3
Artisan, 98
Art-making, 63–64
Art modalities, 59
Arts: in America, 51; defined, 26–27;
   food as, 34; goods/possessions, 87;
   heroes and heroines, 26, 34–36;
   masterpieces in, 32; observation, 25;
   production, 25; as therapy, 61–63.
   *See also* individual artists and styles
*Arts & Health: An International Journal
   for Research, Policy and Practice*, 61
Arylamide Yellow, 47
Ashwaganda, 179
Asimov, I., 95
Aspirin, 101
AthroZyme, 118
*Atlanta Journal and Constitution*, 31, 76,
   91, 98
Attention/Attentiveness, 16, 81
Audience, 25
Automobile industry, 47
Availability, 78, 81
Avandia, 126
Avant Garde Books, 57
Avarice, 6–7
*Avatar*, 154
Avatars, 158–59
Avocational congruence, 69
Avocations, 65–69
Awareness, 80–81, 194, 196, 200

*Bad Drugs and Big Lies: Big Pharma's
   Secret Assault to Your Health*, 120
Baker, Jerry, 113–14
Balzac, 32
Barbie, 150

Basilcello recipe (Liquore al Basilico),
   131–32
Batali, Mario, 96
Battino, Charlotte and Rubin, 66
Beacon Hill Publishing, 127
Beaulieu, J., 141
Beethoven, 139
Behavior, 10
Being, 73–74, 91, 94, 188: alive, 80;
   attentive, 81; available, 81; aware,
   80–81; present, 80–81; present
   together, 162; together, 170
Beiser, M., 69
Bell, Joshua, 81
Bell's palsy, 101
Bel Marra, 107*t*
Bel Marra Nutritionals, 107*t*
Belonging, 89, 165
Bereavement, 144
Bergner, R. M., 77
Bernays, Martha, 3
Best Life Herbals, 107*t*, 172*t*
Be together, 90, 94
Beverages, 130–31
BiCentrics, Inc., 172*t*
Bicycle racing, 152
Billion-Dollar Secret for Superhuman
   Health, 106
Biocentric Health, 108*t*, 172*t*
Biomolecular, 108*t*, 121
BioNutrax, 108*t*, 123–24
BioNutrigenics, 172*t*
Biowell, 108*t*
Biswas-Diener, R., 85
Blanning, T., 135–36, 139–40
Bloch, S., 142
Blood type, 102
Bloom, Paul, 81, 87, 89
Blue, 43–44, 46–47
Blumenthal, K., 128
Bocce, 89
Boccio, Ian, 36–37, 39–55
Body, 161–62
*Body Movement and Dance in
   Psychotherapy*, 61
Bohon, L., 146
*Bon Appétit*, 94
Bone, Kerry, 179

Bonny, H. L., 141
Booher, Bridget, 68
Boredom, 82
Boric Acid, 44
Botanic Choice, 172*t*
*Bottom Line*, 119
BottomLine Books, 106
Brain-boosting foods, 104*t*
Braques, Georges, 56
Breakfast, 102
Brook's London Clinic for Men, 173*t*
Brownstein, David, 173*t*
Bryant, F. B., 61, 191–97
Bulimia, 83
Burnt Sienna, 38
Burnt Umber, 38–39
Bush, George W., 14
Butler, Robert, 184
Byrne, Blake, 68

Cadmium, 44–45
Cadmium Red, 40, 44
Cadmium Red Light, 41
Cadmium Yellow, 40, 44
Caffeine, 101, 131
Calabresi, Massimo, 126
Calling, 85–86
Calories, 101
Cancer, 145–46
*Canterbury Tales* (Chaucer), 6
Caravaggio, Michelangelo Merisi da, 47–50
Cardiovascular disease, 102
Cards, 157
The Cardsharps, 49
Card tests, 156
Carducci, Bernardo, 4–5
Career, 85–86
Carmine, 41
Carrera, Anthony, 172*t*
Case studies, 18, 22
Cash, 87
Castle, D., 142
Castrol four-step program, 171, 177
*A Catechism of Christian Doctrine for General Use*, 6
Cave paintings, 37
Celebrity chefs, 96–97

The Changing American Diet, 129
Chaptal (France), 43–44
Charlatans, 122–28
Chaucer, *Canterbury Tales*, 6
Chaucer, *The Parson's Tale*, 6
Checks, 87
Chefs, 96–97
Chelation therapy, 101
Chemical components, 128
Chemotherapy, 103
Chesapeake Nutritionals, 173*t*
Chiaroscuro, 49
Chicken, 102
Children, 146, 168
Chocolate, 101, 185
Choices, 203
Cholesterol, 100
Chondroitin, 103
CHO-WA, 121
Chrome Red, 40
Chrome Yellow, 40
Churchill, Dana, 127
Classical Lyceum, 27
Clay, 37
Cleveland Clinic's Heart Advisor, 155
Closeness, 78, 165
Cluster analysis, 71
Cobalt Blue, 43–44
Cobalt Violets, 42
Cochineal, 41, 45
Coffee, 100, 103
Cognitive-behavioral therapy (CBT), 145
Cole, Nat King, 35
Collaboration, 157
Collage, 55–59, 60*f*
Collecting, 68
Collier brothers, 91
Colman, Carol, 103
Colon cancer, 102
Colonization, 83
Colon Medical News, 127
Colors, 36–47, 57–59
Coloxin, 127–28
Columbus, Christopher, 35
Commercial companies, 129
Commercials, 102
Commitment, 78

Communal, 162
Communication, 25–26, 62
Compassion, 163–64
Competence, 161
Competitiveness, 157, 167
*Complete Guide to Digestive Health* (Hampshire Labs), 113
Computers, 83–84
Con artists, 106
Conspiracy, 126–27
Constructive behavior, 62
Constructive hobbies, 66
*Constructivist Vision*, 59, 61
*Consumer Reports*, 121
*Consumer's Reports on Health*, 133
Consumptive, 156
*Cook's Illustrated*, 94
Copper acetoarsenite, 41
Correctional institutions, 62
Corrective feedback, 201
Corrective reflection, 183
Costa, Mary, 5
Coster, J., 70
Covetousness, 6
Cow urine, 42, 45
Crafts, 67
Craftsman, 30
Crafty Kids Playhouses, 32
*Creative Art Therapies Journal*, 61
Creativity: action and, 30–31; creative solution, 28; creative synthesis, 28; creative thinking, 28; defined, 25, 27–28; education and, 29; imagination and, 28–31; invention and, 31; masterpieces in, 32; quantifying, difficulty in, 43; skills and, 29; thinking and, 197; as a work classification, 82
Credit cards, 87
Cremnitz White, 40
Crimson, 41, 46
Critical illness, 145
Criticality, 199–200
Critical thinking, 197
Cubism, 56
Culture, 151–52, 168
Cure, 117
Cure-alls, 127

*The Cure Conspiracy: Medical Myths, Alternative Therapies, and Natural Remedies Even Your Doctor May Not Know* (FC&A Medical Publishing), 125–26
Curtis, W., 131

Dada movement, 56
Dairy products, 103
D'Amico, Robert, 106
Dante, *Devine Comedy,* 7
Dante Alighieri, 6
Darwin, Charles, 163
DASH (Dietary Approach to Stop Hypertension), 129
Da Vinci, Leonardo, 35–36
Daydream, 82
Decaffeinated coffee, 101, 103
Declaration of Independence, 68
Degas, 42
De Kooning, Willem, 51–52
Delaunay, 45
Dementia, 143
Depression Adjective Check Lists and Happiness Measures, 10
Deprivation, 25
*Desserts for Defeating Heart Disease*, 103
Devine, P. J., 154
*Devine Comedy* (Dante), 7
Diabetes, 112
Di Buonarotti, Michelangelo, 48
*Dictionary of Psychology* (APA), 27–28
Diener, Ed, 15, 85
Diets, 129–30
Diet soda, 102
Dik, B., 69
Dioxazine Purple, 42
Direct expression, 64
Direction of pleasure, 6
Disadvantages, 1
Discretionary time, 65
Disease, 63. *See also* Food; Health food
Disney, Walt, 136
Displeasure, 1, 6
Distance, 78
Distant context, 82
Distraction interpretation, 13
Divisive interactions, 21

Doctors Health Press (DHP), 103, 117, 121

*Doctors' Vitamin Cures That Work: A Special Report*, 121

Doheny, K., 169

Doing, 73, 81–82, 90–91, 94, 188

Doing it, 170

Douglass, William Campbell II, 126–27

*The Douglass Report*, 127

Downs, Hugh, 119

*The Downside of High Self-Esteem* (Rosemond), 76

Drawing, 67

Drawing skills, 57

Drury, N., 141

Duke, James A., 116

*Duke Magazine*, 68

Duke Medicine Health News, 155

Dumas, 35

Durability bias, 12–13

Duration of pleasure, 5

Earth Pigments, 37–38

*Eat and Health* (FC&A Medical Publishing), 114

Eating disorders, 83

*Eat to Beat the Top 27 Health Problems*, 113

*The Economist*, 85

Education, 27

Egypt, 41

Eiffel Tower, 30, 32–33

Elliot, C., 126

Emblematic prototypes, 33

Emerald Green, 41

Emmons, R. A., 164

Emotions, 19

Enamel paints, 54

*Encyclopedia Britannica*, 26

*Encyclopedia of Pragmatic Medicine* (West), 120

Endurance of masterpieces, 32–33

Energy drinks, 131

Enjoyment, 2, 93, 154

Entertaining/Entertainment, 66–67, 157

*Environmental Nutrition Newsletter for Food, Nutrition, and Health*, 133

Environmental Working Group, 102

Envy, 6–7

Erection-enhancing products, 172t–76t, 177–79

Errors, 200–201

Essentialism, 88

Essential Supplements, 173t

Estrogen, 167

Everest Nutrition, 173t

Evil geniuses, 34

Exchanges, 2

Exercise, 20–23, 72, 79, 134, 148, 183–84, 203

Exercise (physical), 64–66, 101–2, 141, 143, 149, 151–55. *See also* Activity

Expensive health products, 123

Experience, 43, 161, 163, 196–97

Expressive arts, 62

Eyesight, 61

Facebook, 84

Factor Analysis of the LSP Scale, 71

Fads, 97

Families, 168

*Fantasia*, 136

Fantasy, 153

Fathers, 168

Fear, 19

Federal Consumer Protection Agency, 128

Federal Drug Administration (FDA), 122, 125–26

Feelings, 19, 161, 165

Ferguson, Christopher J., 159

Fiction, 87–88

Film, 61

Flake White, 40

Flora Source, 120

Focalism, 12–13

Food, 93–112; in America, 95; as art, 34; for conviviality, 94; customs, 96; defined, 93; fresh, 96; as fuel, 94; "good," 106–22; and health, 99, 104t, 107t, 112–22, 184; as a hobby, 66–67; labeling, 128; molecular, 96; as an obsession, 94; organic, 96–97; for pleasure, 87, 95; portions, 96–98; slow, 96; for thought, 99; vegetarian, 96

Foraging, 98
Fordyce, Michael W., 10–11
Forgiveness, 79
Fox, Richard M., 121
Frazer, John, 96
Fredrickson, Barbara L., 17–22, 193
*Free Stuff and Bargains for Seniors: How to Save on Groceries, Utilities, Prescriptions, Taxes, Hobbies, and More!*, 89–90
Free verse, 57
French Impressionists, 35
Frequency of pleasure, 5
Fresh food, 96
Freud, Sigmund, 3
Friendships, 154–55
Frugality, 25
Fruits, 102
Fuchs, Nan Kathryn, 105
Fugitive pigments, 39–42
Fuller, DicQie, 117
Functional beverages, 131

Gable, S. L., 164
Galilei, Galileo, 201
Gambling, 151, 156–57
Games, 150, 184
Gardens, 68
Garner, Charlotte, 112
Gelactia 200, 173*t*
Gender, 151, 166–68
Geniuses, 34
Gifts, 89
GI Joe, 150
Gilbert, Daniel T., 12–15
GlaxoSmithKline, 126
Global International Research Labs, 173*t*
Glucosamine, 103
Gluttony, 6–7
Glycemic-index, 100
Goals, 155, 184, 198–99
Goji-Vitality treatment, 124
Golden, 54
Goldshield Direct, 108*t*, 173*t*
Goods, 87–90
Gore, Al, 14
Gottman, John, 21

Gourgott, C. J., 154
Gratitude, 164–65
Greed, 6–7
Green, 41–42
*Green Pharmacy* (Duke), 116
Grocke, D., 142
Grumbacher Red, 47
*Guide to the Complete Digesting Health* (Wood), 112

Halperin, S., 141
Hampshire Labs, 109*t*, 113, 124, 173*t*
Hansa Yellow, 47
Hansen, J., 69
Happiness: activities and practices, 11; circumstantial factors, 11; defined, 5–6, 8; extraneous factors, 12; genetic determination, 11; intervention effects, 11; miswanted, 12; sources of, 9–10; study of, 10; and subjective well-being (SWB), 16
Harmony Company, 109*t*
Harvard Medical School, 100
Hatfield, Quinn, 96
Having, 73, 86–91, 94, 188
*Healing with Vitamins: The Best Nutrients to Slow, Stop and Reverse Disease* (Rodale), 115
Health & Healing, 121–22
*Health & Nutrition Letter*, 133
Health clubs, 154
Health food, 99–103, 104*t*, 105–6
Healthier News LLC, 118
Health News, 131
Health Research Laboratories, 173*t*
Health Resources, 109*t*, 123
Health revelations, 100–101
Health Sciences Institute, 118–19
Heart attack, 101
Heart disease, 104*t*
Hedonic benefits, 14–15
Hegi, K. E., 77
Heintzman, P., 70–71
Hendon, C., 146
Herculaneum, 41
Heroes, 26, 34–36
Heroines, 26, 34–36
Hiccups, 100

Hirshorn, Michael, 83
Hitler, Adolf, 139
Hoarders, 91
Hobbies, 65–69
Hoffman, Hans, 51
Holy Grail of Love, 77
HomeCures, 109*t*
Hormonal gender differences, 167
Hormone Health News, 173*t*
Hucksters, 106, 122, 171, 172*t*–76*t*,
    177–79
Hugging, holding, huddling, and
    cuddling (3HC), 163
Human relationships, 82
Human rights, 16
Humor, 167, 196
Hurt feelings, 20–21
Hurts, 20–21, 79–80
Hypertension, 103

Ibanez, G. E., 168
Ibuprofen, 101
Illness, 63, 143, 145–46. *See also* Food;
    Health food
Illustration, 57
Image-contemplation, 64
Image-making, 64
Imagination, 25, 28–31
Immediate context, 82
Immigrants, 30
Immunocorp, 109*t*
Impact bias, 14
Importance, 74–78, 80, 82
Improvisation-assisted desensitiza-
    tion, 146
Income, 15
Independence Celebration for
    Waldenses, 66–67
Indian Yellow, 42, 45
Indigo, 42, 45
Individualism, 15
Infants, 144
Information, 81–85, 162
Ingraham, Michael, 120–21
Inmates, 62
Insight, 201
Insight Imagery, 64
Institute for Vibrant Health, 173*t*

Institute for Vibrant Living, 109*t*
Integrative Digestive Formula, 105
Intensity of pleasure, 6
Intentional activity, 9–10
Intentionality, 194
Interdisciplinary Wellness Arts
    Education (IWAE), 62
Interest, 69
*International Journal of Art Therapy*:
    *Inscape*, 61
Interpretation, 16
Intimacy, 73, 78–80
Intrinsic nature, 88
Invention, 31
Investment, 77
Iron, 37–38
Ironwood Labs, 173*t*
Isaacson, Walter, 82
Isbell, Paul, 31–32
Italian music, 135–36

Japanese food, 34
Jenasol Original, 174*t*
Jesus Christ, 20, 76
JLPI Avenue of Americas, 174*t*
Job, 85
Johns Hopkins Medicine's Quick
    Reference Prevention Tips, 133
Johnson, V., 62
Jordan, Karin, 5
*Journal of Creativity in Mental
    Therapy*, 61
*Journal of Healing Discoveries*, 117
*Journal of Modern Health*, 117–18
*Journal of Natural Medicine*, 105
*Journal of Poetry Therapy*, 61
Juan, David, 117, 121, 133
Judy, William, 172*t*
Juvenon, 109*t*

Kauai, J. B., 158
Kessler, John, 98
Kim, M., 145
Kincaid, Thomas, 48
Kinesthetic communication, 25–26
Kirn, Walter, 82
Kluger, Jeffrey, 97
Knights of Malta, 50

Knowledge, 193
Koch, Charles and David, 126
Kumato Labs, 121
KurZime, 117

L'Abate, Bess, 66–67
L'Abate, Luciano, 4, 27, 61, 136–38
Labeling, 128
Lascaux caves, 37
La Società Italiana, 89
Laughter, 167
Layout drawing, 57
Lead paints, 40
Lechery, 6
Lectures, 67
Legitimate products, 128–29
Leisure, 65–66, 68, 70–71
Leisure-Spiritual Processes (LSP)
    Scale, 71
Levin, T., 145–46
Levitin, D. J., 148
Libid Enhancement Products, 174*t*
*Library of Traditional Chinese Medicine
    Healing Miracles*, 121
Liebman, Bonnie, 129
Life, pathology of, 91–92
Life cycle stage, 76, 91
*Life Diet Book* (Rosenbaum), 114
Life Extension, 109*t*, 174*t*
*Life Extension* *, 133
Life Extension Foundation, 116
LifeTex, Inc, 174*t*
Like, 186–87
Limitations, 80
Limoncello, 131
Lincoln-Bancroft Group, 174*t*
Liquid food, 130–32
Liquitex, 54–55
Liquor, 130–31
*The Little Book of Big Savings: How to
    Save on Everything from Automobiles
    to Zip-Lock Bags*, 90
Long-term illness, 63
Long-term satisfaction, 69
Louis XIV, 139
Love, 73, 76–78, 165, 186–87
Love-hate dislike, ambivalent, 125–26
Low-carbohydrate foods, 102

Lust, 6–7
Lyceum, 27
Lyubomirsky, S., 9

Machiavelli, Nicolò, 202
Machiavellism, 202
Macular degeneration, 101–2
Madder plant, 45–46
Magill, L., 145–47
Magna Carta, 68
MagnaSex Virility Innovations, 174*t*
Magnum FX, 177
Maisel, N. C., 164
Male Performance Center, 174*t*
Manganese, 42
Marchione, Victor, 105, 108*t*, 121, 173*t*
Markey, Patrick, 159
Mars space program 500, 84
Mass Media Type, 71
Masterpieces, 32–33
Mattel, 150
Maximus 300, 174*t*
Mayer, J., 126
McCarty, K., 154
Mechanized, 156
Media reports, 102
Medici family, 30
Medicine, 125–26
MediQuest, 174*t*
Mediterranean Diet, 99–100
Meir, E., 69
Melamed, S., 69
Memory, 16
Mental illness, 61, 78, 91, 141–42
Merchants, 106, 112–15
Merchants of sex, 171, 177–81
Mercury, 41, 102
Mexican culture, 168
Michelangelo, 48
Micronutrients, 100
Microwave containers, 103
Miles, E., 141
Miller, Glenn, 135–36
Mindell, Earl, 108*t*
Mindful, 81
Mind games, 156
*Mind Games: A Box of Psychological
    Play*, 156

*The Mind Health Report*, 147
Minerals, 100, 115–22
Miracle Breakthrough Labs, 109*t*, 174*t*
Mission, 86
Miswanted, 12
Moderation, 183–85
Modern Art expression, 55
Modern Art movement, 45, 51–53, 56
Modernism, 50
Molecular gastronomy (MG), 98
Mona Lisa, 33, 35–36
Monet, Claude, 41, 45
Money, 86–88, 91
Moral barometer, 164
Moral motive, 164
Moral reinforcer, 164
Morris, William, 32
Moser, Philuppe, 173*t*
Most Significant Change, 62
Mothers, 168
Motivated/Motivation, 17, 30, 81
Movies, 61
Mozart, 139
Multiplicative interactions, 21
Murphy, A. D., 168
Museums, 68
Music: as a hobby, 67; Italian, 135–36;
    as magic, 140–41; and musicians,
    139; as patriotic expression, 140;
    rebellion, as a form of, 140;
    secularization of, 139–40; and stress,
    147; therapy, 141–47; triumph of,
    138–40; types, 135–36, 139–40;
    World War II, 136–38
Music-assisted progressive muscle
    relaxation (PMR), 146
Musicians, 139
Music performance anxiety
    (MPA), 146
Mystical love, 165
Mystical sex, 165

Namuth, Hans, 52
Naphthol Crimson, 41
Naphthol Red, 47
Narrative, 57
Natural Health Report, 124
Nature City, 110*t*

Nature of pleasure, 6
*Nature's Fountain of Youth*
    (Rosenbaum), 114
Natures Wave, 110*t*
Neanderthals, 38
Neave, N., 154
Necessity, 189
Needs, 163, 186–87, 189–90
Negative emotions, 19
Negative feedback, 201
Negativity, 20–21, 69
Negotiation, 78
Netflix, 83
Nettles, Jennifer, 147
Network of Spiritual Progressives
    (NSP), 166
Neurological disorders, 145
Newman, Barnett, 51–52
Niacin, 100
Noble Health Products, 174*t*
Non-reciprocal doing, 73
Nopal Cactus Fruit, 131
*Nordic Journal of Music Therapy*, 61
Norris, F. H., 168
NorStar Nutritionals, 174*t*
North, Max, 55, 56*f*
NorthStar Nutritionals, 110*t*
No-self, 78, 80
Novelty, 4
Nutri-Health Supplements,
    111*t*, 118, 120
*Nutrition Action Health Newsletter*, 129
*Nutrition Action Newsletter*, 133
*Nutrition & Healing*, 118–19, 178
NutritionExpress, 111*t*

Obesity, 93
Observing, 200–201
Obsessions, 185
Ochre, 38
Oil paint, 54
Olive oil, 100
Olson, C. K., 159–60
Olympic Games, 151
Omega-3 fatty acids, 97, 99–100,
    112, 122
Ontario Parks Camper Survey, 70
Orexis, 174*t*

Organic food, 96–97
Organic pigments, 45–47
Original creations, 32
Other Peoples Money, 67
Ought, 191
Overall Active Type, 71

Pain, 144–45
Pain relief, 104*t*
Paint brushes, 53–54
Painting, 36, 59, 67
Painting methods, 52–54
Painting techniques, 49, 53–55
Paints, 54
Paleolithic sites, 37
Pannetier, 44
Paradoxical psychotherapy, 20
Parenting, 168
Paris Green, 41
Park, Alice, 126
Parrish, Maxfield, 44
*The Parson's Tale* (Chaucer), 6
Pascarella, Gabe, 131
Passion, 165
Passive acquisition of information, 66
Path Analysis, 71
Pathology of life, 91–92
Patterson, Carl H., 177
Pauling, Linus, 124
Peak experiences, 165
Peanut butter, 103
Penicillin, 35
Penis-enlarging products, 172*t*–76*t*,
    177–79
Pennebaker, Jamie, 196
Performance, 81–82, 90, 94, 170
Performance anxiety, 146–47
Perform OTC Labs, 174*t*
Perilla, J. L., 168
Perlmutter, David, 103
Peroperative anxiety, 143–44
Perpharma, 174*t*
Personal Development Type, 71
Pesticides, 97, 99
Pharmacological companies, 125–27
Phero-Game, 175*t*
Phoenicia Research Center, 177
Photography, 56

Phthalocyanine Blue, 46–47
Phthalo Green, 41
Physical illness, 143
Phytenol's Extended Life Formula, 121
Picasso, Pablo, 35, 56
Pioneers, 35
PLACE, 71
Placebo effect, 122
Planning, 198–99, 201–3
Planning fallacy, 13
Play: age and, 151; cards, 157;
    collaborative/competitive, 157;
    culture and, 151–52; dance, 154;
    dangerous vs. safe, 152–53; defined,
    150; exercise and, 154–55; fantasy
    vs. reality, 153; functions of, 152;
    gambling, 156–57; games, 150;
    gender and, 151; as a hobby, 66;
    importance of, 149; indoor vs.
    outdoor, 153; instinct, 25; mental vs.
    physical, 153; mind games, 156;
    outdoor, 156; priorities, 150–51;
    relational competence, 152;
    requirements for, 150–51; social, 156;
    solitary, 153, 156; structured vs.
    unstructured, 157; surfing, 156; toys,
    150; types of, 152; violent vs.
    nonviolent, 158–60
Pleasure: active, 4–5, 8, 26; arts, 25;
    availability, 7; creativity, 25; defined,
    2–6, 8; food for, 95–99; giving, 2;
    passive, 4–5, 8, 26; and positivity,
    17–19; receiving, 2; selection criteria,
    7; in sharing, 8; sources of,
    1–2, 7–8, 15
PMB, 175*t*
Poetry, 57, 59, 60*f*
Pollock, Jackson, 51–55
Pompeii, 41
Poor of Lyons, 92
Portions, 97–98
Positive feelings, 165
Positive geniuses, 34
Positive psychology, 9, 191–93
Positive reframing, 19–20
Positivity, 17–21, 69
Possessions, 87–90
Possick, Kare, 131

Postmodernism, 52
Potassium, 101
Potassium Bichromate, 44
Pottery, 61
Pouring Medium by Liquitex, 55
Power, 168
Prayer, 166
P.R.C., 175*t*
Preoperative anxiety, 172*t*
Preparing, 201–3
Presence, 74, 94, 168, 170
*Prevention Magazine*, 112, 116
Pride, 6–7, 161
Primal Force, 111*t*
*The Prince* (Machiavelli), 202
Printing press, 31
Prior, S., 63
Priorities, 188–89
Problem solving, 78
Procrastinating, 201–3
Production, 86–90, 94, 170
Products, 128–29
Proper Health Systems, 127, 175*t*
Pros and cons, 199
Prose poetry, 57
Prostate, 178
*The Prostate Answer Book*, 178
Prostate Bulletin (Johns Hopkins
   Medicine), 179
Prost-patch Health, 175*t*
Proximas, 123
Psycho-educational music therapy, 142
Psychological wealth, 16
Psychology, 9–10
Psychopathology, 61
Puck, Wolfgang, 96
PureVive, 175*t*
Purity Products, 175*t*
Purple, 41–42, 45

Quacks, 122–28
Questionnaires, 79, 156, 195
Quinacridone Red, 47

Radiation, 103
Rate of pleasure, 5–6
Raw Sienna, 38
Raw Umber, 38–39

Reading, 67
Real Advantage Nutrients, 111*t*, 175*t*
*Real Cures* (Shallenberger), 113
Realism, 49
Reality, 153
Recipe books, 94
Recipes: Basilcello recipe (Liquore al
   Basilico), 131–32; L'Abate family,
   98–99
Recognition, 26, 165–66
Recreation, 66
Red, 40–41, 44, 47
Red Ochre, 38
Red Oxide, 38
Red wine, 101
Reflection, 23
Rejuva Naturals, 111*t*
Rejuventation Laboratories, 111*t*
Relational aggression, 167
Relational competence, 152
Relational Competence Theory, 77
Relational creativity, 202
Relationships, 184, 195
Religion, 166, 184, 196
Religious orders, 92
Renaissance artists, 30
Renaissance Health, 175*t*
Renaissance period, 38–39
REPRESSION, 71
Research, 84
Resources, 1, 8, 16, 133
Resveratrol, 123
Resvital, 131
Retrospective impact bias, 14
Reynolds, F., 63
Robson, Edward, 171
Role models, 35
Rosemond, John, 76
Rosenbaum, Michael E., 108*t*, 114
Rosenberg, Mark, 174*t*
Rothko, Mark, 51–52
Rowen, Robert Jay, 105
Rubinstein, David M., 68
Ruskin, John, 42
Ryvalis, 175*t*

SACRALIZATION, 71
Sadness, 19, 78

Sake, 77
Salt, 102
Sanders-Goodwin, Nancy, 68
Sap Green, 42
Savary, L. M., 141
Savoring, 190–97
SBM, 175*t*
Scams/scammers, 106, 115–22, 171, 172*t*–76*t*, 177–79
Scare tactics, 127
Schkade, D, 9, 11
Schwebel, M., 70
Schweiz Health, 111*t*, 175*t*
Sciencedirect.com, 143–44
Scientific Lyceum, 27
Scientific Solutions, 175*t*
Seafood, 102
*Second Opinion*, 105
Secret, 117
*Secret Herbal Cures to Combat Sickness* (Doctors Health Press), 117
Self-aggrandizement, 124
Self-awareness, 62
Self-control, 183–85
Self-directed activity, 9
Self-esteem, 74–76, 84, 192
Self-expression, 62
Selffulness, 76, 80
Selfhood Model, 78
Self-importance, 75
Selfishness, 77, 80
Selflessness, 78, 80
Self-love, 77
Self-monitoring, 183–85
Self-Other Profile, 78
Self-regard, 74
Self-study programs, 10
Self-worth, 74
Senses, 80, 162, 166–67
Sensibilities, 80, 161–63, 166–67
Sensualities, 80, 161
Serene, 177
Sermon on the Mountain, 20
Services, 81, 85–86
Serving others, 166
Seurat, 45
Seven deadly sins, 6–7

*The Seven Greatest Secrets of Beating Diabetes* (Whitaker), 121–22
Sex, 87, 162, 169–70
Sex-enhancing products, 171
Sexes, 166–67
Sexual abuse, 80
Sexualities, 80, 161–62, 166–69
Sexual sense, 165
Shallenberger, Frank, 108*t*, 113
Shapiro, Jeffrey, 121
Sharing, 78–80
Sheldon, K. M., 9, 11
Shopping tips, 102
Sickness, 91, 117
Sienna, 38
Silver Bullet, 171
The Silver Edge, 175*t*
Silverman, M., 141–42
Simons, Matthew, 118
Singer, I., 77
Sistine Chapel, 48
Skill utilization, 69
Slavin, Doug, 3–4
Sleep, 101, 184
Sloth, 6–7
Slow food, 96
Smalt, 44
*Smart Money: From the* Wall Street Journal, 84
*The Smart Shopper's Guide to Organic Foods*, 97
*The Smart Shopper's Guide to Organic Foods, Lifesaving Recipes That Will Blow Your Taste Buds Away*, 103
Smight, Edward W., 3
Smith, Edward, W., 6
Smith, J. F., 154
Soccer, 152
Social support, 196
Societal equality, 16
Society for the Arts in Healthcare, 61
Soda, 102
Soden, L., 64
Software technology, 58
Solid food, 95
Sound therapy, 141
*South Pacific*, 82
Special event, 165

Special sexual, 165

Spielberger State-Trait Anxiety Inventory, 145

Spirituality, 166, 196

Spiritual well-being, 70–71

Spodek, L., 145–46

Spontaneous art-making, 64

Sports/Social/Media Type, 71

Stamp collecting, 68

Stanley, J., 62

Static negative interactions, 21

Static positive interactions, 21

Stengler, Mark, 106

Steroid anti-inflammatory, 101

Stimulus-avoidance motivations, 71

St. John's Wort, 100

Stool, Nikolas, 177

STOP, 187, 190–201

Stop Aging Now, 111*t*

Stopping, 186–88, 190–91

Strengths, 80

Stress, 184

String Gel by Liquitex, 54–55

Stroke, 102

Strong Products for Men, 175*t*

Studies: dance, 154; happiness, 10–15; leisure and spiritual well-being, -70–71; music and bereavement, 144; music and children, 146; music and infants, 144; music and neurological disorders, 145; music and pain, 144–45; music and pediatric hospitals, 146; music and performance anxiety, 146; music as therapy, 142; music's effect on dementia, 143; subjective well-being (SWB), 15, 69; virtual games, 158–59; well-being (WB), 69; well-functioning, 70

Subjective well-being (SWB), 11, 15–16, 69

Subtractive interactions, 21

Successful problem solving, 78

Sun Chlorella, 114

Sunscreen lotion, 101

*Super Foods for Senior* (FC&A Medical Publishing), 114

*SuperHealing Unlimited*, 119

*SuperMarket Super-Remedies*, 113–14

Supplements, 99

Support, 30, 81

Surfing, 156

Surrealistic movement, 56

Survival/Survivors, 2, 35, 93

Sustainable happiness model, 9, 11

Sweeney, Laura G., 56, 58–59, 60*f*, 61, 135

Symbolism, 57

SYNESTHESIA, 59

Synthetic colors, 43–47

Tabak, 111*t*

Tabriz Hematology and Oncology Center, 144

Tannen, Deborah, 168

Tapas, 98

Tar Gel by Golden, 54–55

Targeted Nutrients, 111*t*

Taste, 193

Teas, 101

Technology, 58, 82–84

Teenagers, 144, 158–59, 169

Teen Second Life, 158

Teleplan, Bill, 96

Temptations, 185–86

Tenebrism, 49

Test Force, 177

Testimonials, 124

Testosterone, 167

Textile art, 63

Thaut, M., 145

Theoretical orphans, 192

Thinking, 190, 197–99

Thompson, Jenny, 126

Thought, 99

*Time Magazine*, 127

Time perspective, 194

Titanium White, 40

Titian, 48

Togetherness, 90, 94

Tomaino, C., 145

Torch Project, 62

Toxic pigments, 39–41

Toys, 150

Traditional medicine, 125–26

Trans fats, 101, 103

Travel, 67
Treatment programs, 62
Triangle of life, 73, 91
True Health, 111*t*
*Tufts University Health & Nutrition Letter*, 101–3
Turnan, Sean, 31–32
Turner, 42
Twain, Mark, 39
*24 Hour Pharmacist* (Rodale Books), 112
The Two Most Powerful and Important Health Discoveries of Our Time, 127
2000 Old Ways Preservation and Exchange Trust, 130
*2009 Bottom Line Yearbook*, 119–20
Tyrian Purple, 41, 45
*The Ugly Truth about Low Testosterone* (Natural Health News Report), 177

Ultimate Artery Cleanse, 124–25
*Ultimate Healing*, 119
Umber, 38–39
Unique creations, 32
UniScience, 111*t*
UniScience Group, 175*t*
Unproven personal claims, 124
Urine, 42, 45
Useful gadgets, 31

Van Gogh, Vincent, 41, 44–45
Vaquerax Laboratories, 175*t*
Vegetables, 96, 102
Vegetarian Health Diet, 130*f*
Verbal arts, 57, 59
Verbal communication, 25–26
Verdi, 140
Vermilion, 40–41
Veroff, J., 61, 191–97
Viarex Labs, 175*t*
VicHealth Mental Health Promotion Framework, 62
Videogames, 159
VigorAXPure Power, 175*t*
Vinboost, 176*t*

Violence, 159
Violet, 42
Violet Oxide, 38
Viridian, 41, 44
Virtual Reality food, 83–84
Visual arts, 57–59, 62
Visual communication, 25–26
*Vital Health Secrets*, 118
Vital3, 121
Vitamin B3, 100
Vitamin D, 101–2
Vitamin Doctor, 117, 133
Vitamin K, 116
Vitamins, 99, 115–22
Vitamin Science, 111*t*
Vittorio Emanuale Re D'Italia, 140
Vivat, B., 63
Vocational congruence, 69
Volitional behavior, 10
Volpp, K. G., 128
Volunteer work, 67, 166, 184

Wagner, Richard, 139
Walking, 101
Wants, 12, 163, 186–87
Washington, Samuel, 177
Waterfront Theater, 33
Ways of Savoring Checklist, 195
Weight control, 129–30
Weill, Susan, 126
Weingarten, Gene, 81
Well-being (WB), 69
WellMed, 111*t*
Wellness Research and Consulting, 111*t*
Wellspring, 176*t*
West, Bruce, 120
Westhaven Labs, 176*t*
Wheel, 31
Whistler, James McNeil, 39, 42
Whitaker, Julian, 121
White, 40
Whitwell, 158
Why Ville, 158–59
Willful activity, 9
Wine, 101, 131

Winsor Blue, 47
Wood, Gayle K., 112–13
Work classifications, 85
World Wide Web, 83
Wrath, 7
Wright, Jonathan V., 118–19, 178
Writing, 57–59, 196, 198–99

Xerox 914, 31

Yellow, 40, 42, 44–45, 47
Yellow Ochre, 38

Zampleton, Eugene R., 121
Zimbardo, Philip R., 3

About the Author

LUCIANO L'ABATE, PhD, ABEPP, is professor emeritus of psychology at Georgia State University in Atlanta. He is a Diplomate and former Examiner of the American Board of Professional Psychology, and Fellow and Approved Supervisor of the American Association of Marriage and Family Therapy. Author or coauthor of more than 300 papers, chapters, and book reviews in professional and scientific journals; he is also author, coauthor, editor, or coeditor of over 50 books. His work has been translated in Argentina, China, Denmark, Finland, French-Canada, Germany, Italy, Japan, Korea, and Poland. In 2009 he was the recipient of the American Psychological Association's Award for Distinguished Professional Contribution to Applied Research.